Beyond Capital

The financial/social cataclysm that began in 2007 ended notions of the "Great Moderation" and the view that capitalism had overcome its systemic tendencies to crisis. The subsequent failure of contemporary social formations to address the causes of the crisis gives renewed impetus to better analysis in aid of the search for a better future. This book contributes to this search by reviving a broad discussion of what we humans might want a post-capitalist future to be like. It argues for a comparative anthropological critique of capital notions of value, thereby initiating the search for a new set of values, as well as identifying a number of selected computing practices that might evoke new values. It articulates a suggestive set of institutions that could support these new values, and formulates a group of measurement practices usable for evaluating the proposed institutions. The book is grounded in contemporary social science, political theory, and critical theory. It aims to leverage the possibility of alternative futures implied by some computing practices while avoiding hype and technological determinism, and uses these computing practices to explicate one possible way to think about the future.

David Hakken is Professor of Social Informatics at the School of Informatics and Computing at Indiana University Bloomington, and a Fellow at the University of Trento.

Maurizio Teli is a Research Fellow in the Department of Information Engineering and Computer Science at the University of Trento.

Barbara Andrews is a writer and an independent researcher on arts, education, and technology.

Routledge Advances in Sociology

For a full list of titles in this series, please visit www.routledge.com

Beyond Capital

Values, Commons, Computing, and the Search for a Viable Future

David Hakken, Maurizio Teli, and Barbara Andrews

Routledge
Taylor & Francis Group

LONDON AND NEW YORK

First published 2016
by Routledge

2 Park Square, Milton Park, Abingdon, Oxfordshire OX14 4RN
52 Vanderbilt Avenue, New York, NY 10017

Routledge is an imprint of the Taylor & Francis Group, an informa business

First issued in paperback 2020

Library of Congress Cataloging-in-Publication Data
CIP data has been applied for.

ISBN: 978-1-138-92444-4 (hbk)
ISBN: 978-0-367-59772-6 (pbk)

Typeset in Sabon
by Apex CoVantage, LLC

Contents

Acknowledgments

As appropriate in a book that calls for a collective effort to move beyond capital, this book is itself the fruit of a collective effort. The authors have benefited from conversations, discussions, and arguments with each other and many others over the years. We are indebted to all those who have helped us with their ideas, time, and goodwill.

A syncretic book like this could not be written without the stimulation of work done by colleagues in several networks, many of whom, but certainly not all, are cited in our chapter references. Of particular importance to us are the students and colleagues with whom we have interacted in visits between Indiana University and the University of Trento. Vincenzo D'Andrea has been an incomparable guide and interlocutor for all of us. Antonella D'Angeli, Giacomo Poderi, Christian Parra, and the members of the InterAction and Social Informatics groups in the Department of Computer Science and Information Engineering at Trento have contributed much to our thinking. Maurizio would particularly like to acknowledge his collaboration with sociologists Annalisa Murgia and Chiara Bassetti, who have provided constant intellectual challenges, as well as Maria Menendez, a graduate student whose intellectual capabilities will soon be recognized by the larger academic community.

At Indiana University, David and Barbara have benefited from the input of a broad group of scholars working in several disciplines. We want to acknowledge the questioning and support of Mike Dunn, Mary Gray, Ilana Gershon, Kalpana Shankar, Steve Schneider, and John Paolillo. Working with Shaowen Bardzell and Selma Sabanovich on participatory design and robots, along with the others in their project groups, has provided a constant source of energy. Jeff Bardzell has enriched our understanding of interactive design and pushed our thinking in new directions. David would like to acknowledge the value of the time spent with both graduate and undergraduate students, particularly Jennifer Terrell, David Nemer, Dong-oh Park, Wynnie Change, Heerin Lee, Alexis Caudel, Rich Knepper, Paula Mate, Tristan Gohring, Alex Mirowski, Emmanuel Udoh, and Anu Prabhakar.

We would also like to thank many members of the large group of international scholars who work in and around participatory design. Tone Brattateig, Ina Wagner, Jesper Simonsen, Pelle Ehn, Liam Bannon, Finn Kensing, Randi Markussen, Joan Greenbaum, Lucy Suchman, and Andrew Clement are among this group of thoughtful people who have been so generous with their time and support. We have learned much from them.

Maurizio's work on this book has benefited from his involvement with the *Journal of Peer Production*. Working with the editorial board has proven an intellectually engaging and educational process with a group of like-minded people. They, as well as other academics and activists like the ones promoting the Italian anti-precarity movement, have provided a window into the combination of scholarship and activism as a compelling way of working and living.

In addition, Maurizio would like to thank his mother Lina, and his sister, Nadia, without whom writing this book would not have been possible. They have been a constant support, and their role in such an enterprise is impossible to overestimate. He is also thankful to long-term colleagues and friends Stefano De Paoli, Manuela Perrotta, Giancarlo Sciascia, and Daniele Pizzolli who, in different times and situations, have contributed to the intellectual development brought to this book. Without the cleverness, affect, and love of Silvia, he thinks nothing would be as beautiful as it is, this book included.

Barbara and David would like to give personal thanks for the long-standing support from Marlene and Bill Fried, Ann Fausto Sterling, Paula Vogel, Carolyn Korsmeyer, and Judith Liben. We are especially thankful for Carlos Dabezies's skill with language (and prepositions). Without the support and encouragement of Nathan Hakken, Laura Hill Hakken, Karl Hakken, Cori Blum, Luke Andrews Hakken, Lavina Lee, and Penny Marie Hakken, the energy to think forward would not have been possible.

1 Thinking about a Future Beyond Capital

PROLOGUE

In early June 2012, David Hakken, Maurizio Teli, and Barbara Andrews were attending the annual Festival of Economics in Trento, a medium-sized city in the northeast of Italy. This event has become a regular part of Trento's summer activities, and it provides a forum where economists, journalists, ministers, and legislators, as well as students and citizens, gather to think about economic issues. On Saturday morning, two of us attended a session led by the British economist Diane Coyle. In arguing for an "economy of enough" as her approach to current dilemmas, Coyle outlined a three-part case on the basis of a parallel with the Industrial Revolution. First, like a good economist, she argued for better measurement of the things we need to measure, e.g., national wealth in general, not just gross national product. Second, in periods of fundamental social change like "today," she argued that there is a need for new institutions; she cited trade unions and cooperative associations as the new institutions characteristic of the Industrial Revolution. Third, to tell us what needs to be valued (measured), as well as what institutions to build, we need values.

In the question and answer period, Hakken questioned her about her thoughts on values. Did they need to be new values, reshaped values, or what we have now? She responded no, old values would serve, and her response was met by a burst of applause from the audience. Indeed, an older gentleman rose to support her, saying that the problem with today's youth was precisely their abandonment of traditional values.

Later, the three of us met for dinner to talk about the sessions we had been to that day. We talked about why we disagreed with Coyle's view that old values were enough. Instead, we felt that new measures and institutions would be born *out of* new values—or at the very least, re-shaped values—but what would those values be? As we tried to answer this question, our book started to take shape. Of course, much of the thinking behind the book began earlier, and is rooted in our previous work. This prologue outlines our backgrounds relative to the problem of new and changed values. The Introduction follows, presenting our thoughts on where we are after wrestling with this problem.

David Hakken's work in anthropology and informatics has led him to write a number of books and articles on digital technologies (DTs), their uses, and their cultural contexts. His most recent Routledge book, *The Knowledge Landscapes of Cyberspace* (Hakken 2003), looks at knowledge and its relationship to DTs. It investigates the so-called "knowledge society," and it has shaped much of the theory of this book in ways that we will elaborate on as we go along. In 1999, Hakken was the first recipient of the American Anthropological Associations The Robert B. Textor and Family Prize for Excellence in Anticipatory Anthropology.

In the mid 2000s, Hakken moved to a new academic appointment at the Indiana University School of Informatics and Computing. He had begun working on a new book about computing, development, and globalization. While the book was ostensibly about "informing," he wanted to show how understandings of globalization and development could be of value irrespective of where "informing" was being practiced. This was true in the remote places where anthropologists had in the past been more likely to spend time, as well as the US and Europe. The book was to serve as an example of what social science and humanities perspectives had to offer to the new field of informatics: the ability to think holistically about particular places, particular technical practices, and the conjunction of transnational forces of all sorts that form the context of any project.

An earlier step in his effort to prepare to write the book and to broaden the geographic scope of research on computing and socio-cultural change was a decision to read the *Financial Times* regularly, which counts itself as a "global" newspaper. Of course, the mid-2000s was also the onset of the financial crisis, and the analysis of its effects increasingly became part of Hakken's interest and questions about finance and globalization. As the crisis developed, there was a noticeable decline in talk about globalization, its demise occasionally being announced in the columns of the *Financial Times*. For a time, attention shifted to concern about whether the crisis heralded the end of capitalism itself, but one or two "green shoots" quickly put paid to the emerging panic. To Hakken, "globalization" began to look more and more like "the new economy," "the network society," and "increase in worker power"—a set of descriptive notions whose value he critiqued in *The Knowledge Landscapes of Cyberspace*. These, too, were conceptualizations implying a computing-induced "fundamental transformation" that were for a time put forward vigorously, but then faded.

Hakken began to re-focus his project back to a perennial one: trying to empirically understand the changes in current social formation reproduction, so that the nature and degree of their relationships to computing practices can be understood. In 2015, as we write this book, there is considerable evidence that the crisis that started then is not over, and it may again become as virulent as it was in 2008, if not more so.

Barbara Andrews has been David's longtime partner in studying and thinking about the uses of digital technologies. Her research has often focused on how technology has been incorporated into educational and work contexts. She has been interested in how the expectations and ideologies of technology have shaped its uses. In particular, she has followed the trajectory of the relationship between women and technology, paying attention to how women have seen opportunities in digital technologies, and how they have dealt with challenges in relating to it. She has studied women's interactions with technology in the US as well as England, Norway, and Sweden.

Andrews has long been interested in patterns of learning, and how both the arts and technology have interacted with teachers and learners in the classroom. For ten years, she collaborated with colleagues involved in Harvard's Project Zero on a number of projects looking at how arts-based learning is used in classrooms and in educating teachers and artists. She has also done research with artists in upstate New York on how artists learn, and how they use their learning strategies to teach others. Most recently, she has been looking at issues of design and particularly critical design in technology contexts.

Maurizio Teli's interest in technology began as a coincidence while he was working on his master's thesis in sociology at the University of Trento. He was investigating how everyday interactions in a supermarket could be a form of resistance to rationalizing processes in consumption. Teli noted how the face-to-face encounters of workers and customers counteracted the rationalization of the computer technologies. Deciding on what software to use on a new computer was what pushed him into further work on technology, specifically free/libre and open-source software (FLOSS). As he studied FLOSS developers, he realized they were changing consumption as well as production. For FLOSS developers, complex things like software packages were created in a collaborative fashion and made available for other people to use. This work was often embedded in narratives of freedom and mutual help.

Teli's dissertation on a corporate-sponsored FLOSS project, OpenSolaris (backed by Sun Microsystems), analyzed how the practices of FLOSS development were intertwined with corporate aims. It focused particularly on how the relation between FLOSS and corporate practices shaped narratives about the practice of freedom. His analysis of corporate FLOSS justified a more critical approach, stressing how corporate power shaped everyday participation. He argued that understanding technology was not enough: sociologists studying technology need to engage in producing and designing technologies to understand the connection between design and use. Subsequently, he has engaged in a number of design projects, from museum exhibitions to civic media. In each instance, he has focused not only on design methods and approaches, such as participatory design, but also on forms of social theory that can provide wider understandings of design projects. Framing a context, providing a direction for action, and allowing design projects to actually intervene in the most relevant contemporary dynamics, the ones of the crisis, are at the core of his interest and what this book is about for him.

As we began working together, we realized that we needed to write a book about the future. We want to respond to a key challenge of our time: creating a new, viable way to be human. We believe that existing ways of being will no longer be adequate, and that they greatly impair the capacity of social formations to extend their reproduction. In our view, future making means not only identifying practices that could make up viable, alternative ways to live; it also means encouraging the capacity of human subjects to be able to live in the new ways. In general terms, this book is an enquiry into what can and should be done to confront what puts a human future at risk. More specifically, it enquires after what computing has to do with these risks, as well as what computing practices suggest about how to deal with them. In writing about the future, we are well aware that some will see our project as utopian. We accept this characterization, but we will repeatedly stress that we do not write to *predict* a better future, but to *imagine* one. As feminist utopian Shaowen Bardzell put it:

> Utopianism is often dismissed as a kind of fantasy, a kind of wishful thinking. Indeed, recent history shows how moments of optimism turn dark: from the promise of scientific rationalism to its horrific realiza-tion in the 'Final Solution to the Jewish Problem' in Nazi Germany, the scientific breakthrough that gave us the atomic bomb, the rise of global capitalism and in spite of its promises the stubborn persistence of global economic injustice, and finally to the looming threats of climate change, mass extinction, and socioeconomic collapse. Worse is the widespread fear that modern systems of governance just aren't up to the problems we face. Yet utopianism is still alive.
>
> (Bardzell 2014)

Along with Bardzell, we believe that writing about the future, researching its possible progenitors in current practices, and imagining its possibilities are all necessary to thinking beyond our present conundrums and crises. For us, this is an act of optimism and imagination, but one tempered by our under-standing of the challenges before us. The philosopher Erin McKenna has writ-ten that utopias embrace "multiple possible futures-in-process," and argued that current choices define what will be possible to pursue in the future. Thus, "we must accept responsibility for creating the future and develop a critical method for directing it, and not wait for it simply to unfold" (McKenna 2001). In the following pages, we take up this responsibility.

INTRODUCTION: BROAD OUTLINES OF THE PROJECT

Steps Toward Making a Future "Beyond Capital"

We begin with the growing scholarly consensus that the challenges facing contemporary social formations are formidable, a consensus we document in Chapter 4. Many suggest that we may not be able to extend our social formations' reproductive capacities sufficiently to achieve a future worth having. These scholars have raised a host of questions about the future, including: Can the environment withstand the levels of environmental degradation humans are creating? Is the apparently global trend toward inequality likely to undermine our current political systems? Is the growing wealth of a few diminishing the capacity for democracy and undermining the idea of capitalism? If (or when) there is another economic-social crisis, how well will nations survive?

Given such issues, we see it as time to think "beyond capital"—that is, about what to do as capitalism's problems accumulate and its social formations becomes less and less viable. Some future will emerge from existing practices and situated knowledges. If we want to *make* a future, we need to have ideas about what we want it to be, how to encourage it, and how to do so. Much needs to be discovered and interpreted. Like many others, we turn to digital mediation for suggestions about what the new values might be.

For us, questions about how to approach the future center on questions of values and valuing.[1] While making a future is partly a matter of discovery and partly invention, it surely involves deliberately choosing among alternative values and intervening to make the pursuit of the values real. While renewal of reproductive capacity is possible, we argue that it will only be extendable if it is based on changed valuing. Thus, what separates this book from others is our attempt to formulate a theory of values and value practices sufficient to making a future. Further, we want to involve as many others as possible in this project. To convince them to participate *now* in going beyond capital, our approach in this book is to specify and to start to address the major intellectual challenges such a project faces. After presenting our general approach in this introduction, we move on to deal with these challenges:

- First, articulating a set of theoretical notions essential to the futuring we engage in;
- Second, explaining why we place computing at the center of our thinking about the future;
- Third, presenting why we think such a project should focus centrally on changes in valuing practices;
- Fourth, selecting appropriate values and fashioning them into a coherent set of alternatives, based on selected computing practices;
- Fifth, evolving from these values new or altered institutions that are able to embody this new value regime, giving it form and structure;
- Sixth, identifying new ways to measure what is important in promoting this new way of life and to track the progress toward the new values made by the institutions.

In short, we present a values approach that is fulsome enough to identify a specific set of possible new values, institutions to support the new valuation practices, and measures to guide institutional practice and to offer ideas for revision. We address the fashioning of new value(s) before taking up the evocation of new institutions and measures, concluding with how these moments may occur together. We also comment on what these things have "in common," in both the general sense of "what holds them together" and in a more specific sense of the extent to which a "commons" approach to social life could be at the center of efforts to make a viable future.

We wrote this book because we think it is the best way to present a persuasive case for our future. In the following sections, we present some themes that recur as we present our case.

Theme One: On the Importance of Value, Values, and Valuation

Because values and valuing are at the core of our case, we want to begin with some of our core ideas about them here. Our main argument is in Chapter 5, where we explain why we see the identification of new values as central to the making of alternative futures. Identifying such values in turn depends on the question of value itself.

In the economics hegemonic in our time, "value" means the quality shared by the things that people create or obtain by taking something from its "natural" context and making it into something humanly valuable. It is this shared quality of being valued that enables a way to compare things, make them commensurable, and organize society around markets. However, there is another important, more transtemporal meaning arena of "value." In the field of anthropology, a "value" is understood to be an articulation of the important mediation *between* something that those sharing a culture collectively conceive—one of their cultural constructs, the things they *can* conceive, or the extent of their cultural imaginary—and something that they do, a characteristic practice. "Values" are notions about basic life orientations, and they involve things that can be articulated, if not always articulated. They make other kinds of comparisons possible.

Encompassing the substantive economic meaning of *value* within the broader and the mediating anthropological meaning of *values* is a central task of *Beyond Capital: Values, Commons, Computing, and the Search for a Viable Future*. We give priority to collective valuation practices—what might be called "valuesing" if it weren't so stylistically objectionable— over mere valuing, assignment of a market value. Valuation practices are the universal human activities that transform things—whether they are material objects or symbolic elements—into something important. We justify this move via critiques of the many ways in which the current market value regime, its institution, and its measures of value are too narrow and inadequate, both descriptively and analytically. Thus, creating new values, institutional regimes, and measures of value are essential to making a viable future.

Theme Two: On Intervening Collectively in SFR

Our work is also based on a further anthropological premise, the idea that humans are capable of intervening collectively and deliberately in social formation reproduction (SFR), the processes that perpetuate their socio-cultural systems. The arguments for this analytic focus are presented in Chapter 2. We also presume that such intervention is more likely to be effective when it is aimed at goals that have already achieved a broad social purview. This is also why "value" and "values" need to be analyzed in the same frame. From this general social analysis, we move especially in Chapters 4 and 5 to argue that:

- The history of the current era can be read as a dialectic between ever more simplified, hierarchical politics, or "value" interventions into SFR and distributed, bottom-up, "trial and error" interventions. These often happen with differently situated peoples acting politically "in common" in relation to multiple values, some derived from previous forms of existence, some newly developed;
- Before a group can decide into which aspects of SFR they want to intervene, and before they can do so successfully, they need to sufficiently articulate an understanding of the ends toward which they wish to intervene. That is, they need to know which new values they want to manifest collectively in their lives. Particularly in times of substantial change, they need to select values that are a likely and logical target for early intervention;
- Moreover, when trying to make new values, a group needs useful, empirical understandings of existing values, their distribution, and how they are reproduced—e.g., through which institutions or practices;
- Many of the key changes in current SFR are associated with the use of digital technologies, so DTs become a key arena in which value regime conflicts are manifested;
- To extend the reproduction of our current social formations successfully into the future, we need to connect the current narrow valuation with why the existing value regime is likely to fail. We include the role of computing in this failure, in order to see how a new regime can be fostered and evolved out of the existing one, including its extensive digital mediation.

We will argue for intervention in human SFR, recognizing that ours is a time in which effective reproduction demands the identification and cultivation of a new value regime.

Theme Three: The Importance of Computing

We see that many of the stresses in current SFR are associated with the use of digital technologies. This is particularly true of those changes that impede or even disable the reproducibility of the prevailing value regime. Successful social reproduction in the future requires turning digital technologies and their uses into extenders of SFR.

Changes in organizing—that is, the getting groups of humans to coordinate their actions—often have a large effect on SFR. Increasingly, organizing is heavily mediated by the use of DTs. In introducing a new *Handbook of Information Technology in Organizations and Electronic Markets*, editors Angel Salazar and Steve Sawyer (Salazar and Sawyer 2007) attempt to generalize what can be said, among other things, about DT use and organizing. They draw attention to the wide and deep array of existing empirical research on which such generalizations could be based. They are enthusiastic about what is known regarding the *potential* for DTs to be associated with changes in patterns of organizing. Salazar and Sawyer conclude nonetheless that there is not much that can be justly said generally about *how much change has actually taken place*, or about the forms that DT-related changes typically take. Michael Barrett, the author of their book's detailed chapter entitled, "ICTs, Organizational Change, and New Modes of Organizing," reaches a similar negative conclusion (Barrett 2007). After a brief discussion of meager consensus findings, he focuses on three equally plausible but incompatible theoretical views—technological determinism, structuration theory, and the practice lens—that dominate the computing/organizing literature. His stress is on how each position draws attention to different factors, frequently producing divergent empirical results.

These are two examples of the scholarly skepticism about the fifty years of popular insistence that computing changes organizing. Organizing is important, but it is only one of the many aspects of SFR that have been implicated in discussions about computing and social change. As we explain in Chapter 3, like the editors of the *Handbook*, we are skeptical of such insistent claims about change. The repeated rhetoric that computers (or currently, artificial intelligence or social robots) "change everything," in popular discourse, is now regularly met with scholarly skepticism. That being said, there are some specific ways in which computing practices can be assigned responsibility for substantial social changes. This can be seen most clearly in negative terms—for example, in how computing undermines a range of practices that were previously important to being human.

Old values are being compromised and computing is involved. We don't accept the idea that all humans have to do is "muddle through" and some new value set will miraculously emerge to replace them and extend SFR. Rather, we have to find new means to defend the social, some set of values and practices that cohere into a new, widely encompassing, technology mediated way of life. Computing is, and likely will continue to be, important to SFR—in complicated ways, but nonetheless necessary-to-be-understood and related to, if we are to make interventions and a viable future.

Theme Four: Information in the Computing/Social Change Relationship

Other aspects of this futuring and computing emerge from what is often called "the information glut." This is the situation arising from the rapidly expanding amount of information made easily available by today's DTs. As information increases with online experience, humans find it hard to cope with the sheer amount of it. Instead of drawing conclusions about what the information means—that is, for constructing knowledge out it—they can only develop strategies to avoid drowning in it (Hakken 2003). Their previous ways of drawing knowledge implications, or concluding what information means, now seem inadequate. But what will take their place? Each day, we struggle with issues like the growing number of emails in our inboxes, unsuccessfully recalling a previous message or locating its reference, or finding a link on the web to something read days or months ago. Sometimes we become aware of a new information resource with potential interest or significance, and we can file away a uniform resource locator (or a url) for a future moment of leisure (which of course never comes). As time goes on and our inboxes gets fuller, we feel like we know less and less.

Such limited control over the information of which we are aware has arguably come to be the distinctive feature of our particular "information society." The inability to extract sufficient knowledge from the information we encounter is common in and even typical of digitally mediated life. Collectively, we digital technology cybernauts understand that our old ways of establishing what is known are outmoded. There exists a wealth of web resources open to those who are looking for answers to their questions, Wikipedia being one obvious example. We often turn to these resources for general information as well as to research topics in depth. But web resources must be verified. Readers, researchers, and students must establish independently the veracity of web-based claims they wish to use as evidence. Whereas in the past, many readers could by and large depend upon the infrastructure of academic journals and publishers to "separate the wheat from the chaff," they now have to do much more of this for themselves, which requires inventing new means to do so. In web content, where the author may be unknown, web users cannot reference past work, or the bona fides of what they read. The effective switch of social attention away from *how we know* and toward *how to get more information* means that we need new ways to extract knowledge from information.

Anthony Giddens has argued that even as experts become more dominant presences in our lives, they are less willing to vouch for any particular set of implications drawn from their expertise (Giddens 1991). In *Bowling Alone*, Robert Putnam details how our membership in institutions is displaced by participation in looser networks where the task of deciding what is actually known has become more individualized (Putnam 2001). The huge piles of new information produced by the computerization of virtually all forms of laboratory and field research led one US National Science Foundation program director to call for all academics to abandon their current preoccupations and turn to handling the data/information glut. This is his sense of what it would take to get us out of our current empiricist trap, identified by others as trying to learn what we can from "mining big data."

A further example of our collective dilemma regarding knowledge is embodied in people who might be called "informationists." That is, when confronted by an issue for which there is no obvious resolution, their default position is to defer judgment and ask for "more information." In the Information Age, more information can always be found. However, such calls for more information generally displace any urgency to resolve the issue at hand; thus, this "informationist" position means indefinitely postponing decisions and not actually dealing with the issue. This leaves to door open for some bureaucratic entity to make a decision that thus renders the issue moot. A similar discourse is at least one part of the call to attend to "big data" and "crowdsourcing" as solutions to the contemporary knowledge problem. As it is currently used, big data is better understood as another name for the problem of continuous data gathering. While crowdsourcing might be useful in certain contexts, say as a market phenomenon, often there is no theoretical explanation offered for how and why it should work more generally as a knowledge strategy. We will return to this question later.

Theme Five: Computing and Crisis

In 2007, there was a notable increase in the worry expressed by writers in the *Financial Times* about a developing crisis. In the reports and opinions of Gillian Tett, the then-deputy editor of the primary finance column, suggested that this crisis was likely to be big, and to reach far beyond the confines of the financial sector, deep into the "real" economy and the broader society. Particularly of interest was Tett's suggestion that the crisis would be greatly exacerbated by a characteristic of our current world economy: that it was only partially globalized. While having developed an international market in capital, neo-liberal, "Washington Consensus" globalization had failed to develop a set of international structures that persuasively "redeemed" or assigned value consistently to bunches of capital as they were migrated across international boundaries. The problem of tainted assets, Tett argued, wasn't just that their value was unknown; it was that, in the absence of appropriate international institutions, it was *unknowable*.

By implication, we were entering a world crisis that would go on until one of two things happened: either capital markets would be effectively re-nationalized, or international/universal institutions for capital evaluation would be developed. Neither of these was particularly likely; indeed, this still remains a problem today. The crisis that followed brought home how any particular "development through computerization" effort would depend greatly on financial/economic as well as other aspects of social context. In Chapter 3, we show how computing greatly afforded the financial innovation and upscaling of capital markets that were central to the crisis. Computational thinking of a certain positivist sort, what David Golumbia calls "computationalism," also played a centrally insidious role in it. Computing was even more central to the crisis, as it afforded the means used for models of financial risk.

Tett reported on what was essentially a developing "capital strike." At a certain point, it became clear that financial institutions had become unwilling to make credit available in the manner and to the degree that they previously had. A result of new commodities badly used, as traced brilliantly in Tett's *Fool's Gold*, this capital strike prolonged the crisis (Tett 2009). The virulence of the capital strike derived in part from institutions having over-relied on computerized models of financial risk, models that had initially given them the confidence to market new financial commodities on a grand scale. The models themselves were flawed because those computationalists who constructed them failed to build into them the possibility of systemic failure. Rather, the models reflected a key computationalist presumption that, as more and more of the available information is integrated into a model, its accuracy approaches 100%. While computers do allow the construction of ever more complex models of phenomena, the models are valid only as long as the phenomena being modeled are indeed systematic. What the models are not designed to do is deal with "long tail" or "black swan" events, the infrequent moment that reveals that what was thought to be real-world systematicity is actually just an assumption of the modeler. In postmodern anthropology talk, there is no system, only practices (Williams 1991).

Summary: Toward a Unified Understanding of Computing and Social Change

These themes are typical of the problems we attempt to deal with in *Beyond Capital*. Central to our approach is the search for good descriptive and analytical ways to frame the computing/social change relationship. A unified interpretation of this relationship provides for us the key to specifying the values we need for constructing new institutions that are viable in an altered world, including the notional one called cyberspace. In the chapters that follow, we present an analysis to explain how and why we reach our conclusions. Our point for the moment is to specify an important aspect of our current cultural condition; namely, that we have lost a shared sense of *knowing how and what to value,* that we lack shared *institutions* through which to realize a shared sense for these values, and that we need refined *ways to measure* the things valued. At best, we have only an inkling of what might replace a narrow reliance on one value—capital—and its institutions and measures, but we need more.

Having lost confidence in our "default" knowledge creation strategies, we humans have temporarily developed a broad set of stances and procedures that allow us to avoid having to commit to any particular understanding of "what is actually the case." This is perhaps a tolerable adaptation to the rapid, often relatively mindless mediation of our social lives by digital technologies, but it is not a long-term strategy. Scholars and writers like Eli Pariser (Pariser 2011), Nicolas Carr (Carr 2011), and Sherry Turkle (Turkle 2011) have recently articulated this conviction. The reproduction of a social formation in which many of the participants have lost their strategies, both individual and collective, for deciding what information means, that is, converting it into knowledge, is clearly at risk. What is to be done to get us out of this position? If we can't go back, what are we to do?

Returning to the disagreement with Diane Coyle at the beginning of this chapter, we will argue that we need to identify a set of new values, create new institutions capable of effectively promoting these values in SFR, and measure what we need to in order to see if our institutions are effectively promoting what we value. Among the institutions we need are those that are capable of extracting effective knowledge from information in digital technology-saturated societies.

But how are we to do this? The work of archaeologists and social historians suggests that new values seldom erupt ex nihilo on their own. Rather, they emerge out of the interplay between representations of extended cultural commentary, like that of artists, and innovative variations on existing practices. Thus, in dealing with measuring, institutional, and value crises, the one thing we surely must do is pay closer attention to what is actually going on now. We can develop much sharper pictures of the current relationship between computing and social change in specific situations. Moreover, we can also build better analyses of the dynamics of this relationship in specific cases, and we can try to construct typologies of the major forms of this relationship.

So, we need conceptual tools to understand how current institutions operate, including how contradictions within them impede but also can contribute to extending SFR. With these tools, it should be easier to build new institutions. Once the current situation is understood, we can choose which dynamics we would like to foster and which to try to discourage. Comparative analyses should also provide important clues regarding what values are best positioned to inform the new institutions, and visa versa.

The Structure of Beyond Capital

In the next chapter, we aim to make clear our perspectives and the basic concepts for our argument, especially those related to both simple and extended SFR. It addresses our commitment to the pursuit of a structural explanation. We are aware of the work of those who claim that ours is a "post-structural" era, and we use some of the concepts often associated with this perspective. These concepts include Actor–Network Theory (ANT, e.g., Latour 2005), which we use although we are aware of its lack of focus on the relevance of history. We appropriate ANT and other post-structural ideas to analyze the practicalities and distributed forms of domination and inequalities that put at risk the reproduction of the current social formation. We also interrogate the problems and perspectives of future studies.

Building on social science and philosophic theory, Chapters 3 and 4 apply this theory to contemporary social formations, especially the computing/ social change nexus in SFR. Chapter 3 begins by critiquing several ways in which this connection is misrepresented. We conclude with a detailed examination of the role of computing in the recent, continuing social crisis and put existing computing practices at the center of it. Our aim with this example is to identify the problematic perspective underlying crisis-causing computing, which we call "computationalism," borrowing from David Golumbia (Golumbia 2009).

In Chapter 4, we explain in detail why pessimism about current SFR justifies thinking beyond capital. We argue that the patterns that dominate current SFR cannot be extended indefinitely at tolerable levels of social stress. Hence, there is a pressing need for an alternative social formation or set of dynamic social relations. What others have written identifies substantial flaws in the current SFR, a system strongly bent to the reproduction of capital. The flaws are such that some form of capital may survive, but the future depends on radically lessening capital's influence on SFR dynamics. The remainder of the chapter identifies specific computing practices that we see as pre-figurative of a different future, which we sometimes call "cyberspace"[2] for short. We explain why we think it likely that any alternative will have to incorporate computing.

Chapter 5 builds on recent anthropological work to present an ethnological theory of values, valuesing, value, and valuing to guide the discovery and creation of an alternative value(s) regime in order to go beyond capital. A key aspect of this theory is the articulation of three basic (that is, cross-culturally applicable) types of valuation practices, which we label the nominal, ordinal, and ratio types. We use distinctions among these three to explain how the dominance of ratio-valuing over nominal- and ordinal-valuing is at the core of SFR risk, and thus how a rebalancing among these types of value practices is essential to recovering the capacity of social formations to extend their reproduction. The chapter also uses anthropological and other forms of theory, including Autonomous Marxism (e.g., Hardt and Negri 2009), to explain why we think humans have the capacity to develop and carry out the project of creating new values, institutions, and measures.

In Chapter 6, we return to the more positive cultural phenomena identified in Chapter 4, the developments connected to digital technology use that point at new dynamics of social formation reproduction. Here, we will restate the developments in terms of the values we see as manifested in them:

General Values:

1. Sustainability
2. Increased and broadened access to the means of cultural reproduction
3. Flexibility in scaling of social formation reproduction
4. A broader understanding of "the economic"
5. Social constructivist perspectives on technology
6. Democracy

Specific Values:

7. A processual approach
8. Informating as the basic goal of computing
9. A "free software" approach to "openness"
10. A service orientation
11. Increased participation

The feasibility of a new cyberspace follows from the premise that interventions promoting new values are more likely to succeed if the values are consonant with phenomena that are already present and likely to loom even larger in the future.

In Chapter 7, we will discuss how the developments and values identified in Chapter 6 might set the ground for transformative practices. In line with sociological thinking, we refer to these as institutions—complex social forms that tend to reproduce themselves. Institutions allow people to engage in socially recognized roles and to create possibilities for transformation, or the emergence of subjectivities (Miller 2007). In other words, the construction of subjectivities takes place between the individual and the role she is supposed to hold, as well as the practices and the relations she is involved in. The practices are possible because certain social arrangements, not immediately visible in the moment, allow for the existence of the institutions, thus constituting their infrastructure. In line with the theory of value presented in Chapter 5, we will consider at the center of our institutional analysis the institutions that reinforce generalized equality. We explain why institutions that support things like common-based forms of livelihood, democratic practices, the equality of class, race, and gender, and human freedoms are especially needed. We say "evolving" because institutions (a term we use in the very general, sociological way) are not invented "out of whole cloth"; rather, they emerge in part out of what already exists.

For our purposes, it is not enough merely to demonstrate how a new complex of institutions could sufficiently support the pursuit of a new value complex. In Chapter 8, we turn to consider how building the new institutions will require judgments about the efficacy of the new institutions. These judgments will include whether the new institutions are functioning properly; if the desired social changes are correlated with the institutions; and whether the new institutions seem to be having the desired consequences, i.e., if their existence seems to support the pursuit of the new values complex effectively. We need measures, because going beyond capital will require humans to make choices, which means we need to be able to compare alternatives against standards. Some of the standards that we will need already exist, but many do not. When using information to make such judgments, one is, in a broad sense, "measuring." Hence, this chapter is about measurement broadly conceived. We aim to be as specific as we can about the kinds of data and information that would allow us to judge how socially efficacious the new institutions are at supporting new values and the subsequent new social formation.

Chapter 9 concludes the book by addressing the plausibility of the transformation we advocate. We envision how the kind of redirection of social formation reproduction *might* actually come about. There are a number of key questions for further consideration, such as, what are the seeds of social change that we have found, and who are some of the thinkers who are already talking about transformation? What role are digital technologies playing, and how are people using them? While we do not think we can design the transformation, we do think we can describe the kind of collaborative design practices, along with appropriate action, that could bring it into being.

NOTES

1. We are quite aware that, especially in the US, where Andrews and Hakken live, "values" is an issue that the political right wing believes it owns. Putting values at the center of our analysis may make us "suspect" to some on the left. The basis of our complaint with Coyle was not her view that we need to reemphasize values, but which values she chose. "Old values" are precisely the one emphasized by the US Tea Party faction and the politicians that pander to it. Our position is different. We need new values, multiple ones, to displace the single thing, called "value," measured in a single place, the market. We provide an extensive theoretical exposition of our position on values in Chapter 5. The point we wish to make here is that it is our intention to join the battle over values by reconsidering values rather than reaffirming the value of markets, the position underlying much right-wing theory and practice.
2. There are some reasonable objections to using the term cyberspace, such as that it has had several distinct meanings, and that it is used less now than in the recent past. (The *New York Times* is rumored to have tried to banish its use from its pages.) We use "making cyberspace" as an occasional substitute for our alternative futures project for several reasons. One is the narrative utility of such a moniker. Another is that the term has already been used as a label for a distinctly different future way of life based fundamentally on digital mediation, so by using it, we are "following the natives," as anthropologists try to do when they can. This is how Hakken used it in *Cyborgs@Cyberspace?* (Hakken 1999). Of course, the popular late-20th century idea that humans were moving rapidly into this new way of life has largely been abandoned. Yet, an important residual of this particular discourse over something like

"cyberspace" is the way in which digital mediation has captured a large part of the transcultural imaginary; that is, the way that people around the world tend to conceptualize the future largely in terms of one set of digital mediations or another, e.g., "the Internet of things." For us, "cyberspace" is a good term for this imaginary, and by extension for our project. We use "cyberspace" with its science fiction connotations to point at an emergent notional arena linked to use of digital technologies, and we see this link as central to being able to articulate alternatives with wide appeal.

REFERENCES

Bardzell, Shaowen. 2014. "Utopias of Participation: Design, Criticality and Emancipation." *ACM Digital Library.* http://dl.acm.org/citation.cfm?doid=2662155. 2662213.

Barrett, Michael. 2007. "ICTs Organizational Change and New Modes of Organizing." In *Handbook of Information Technology in Organizations and Electronic Markets,* edited by Angel Salazar, 39–55. Singapore: World Scientific.

Carr, Nicholas. 2011. *The Shallows: What the Internet Is Doing to Our Brains.* New York: W. W. Norton & Company.

Giddens, Anthony. 1991. *Modernity and Self-Identity: Self and Society in the Late Modern Age.* First edition. Stanford, CA: Stanford University Press.

Golumbia, David. 2009. *The Cultural Logic of Computation.* Cambridge, MA: Harvard University Press.

Hakken, David. 1999. *Cyborgs@Cyberspace?: An Ethnographer Looks to the Future.* New York: Routledge.

———. 2003. *The Knowledge Landscapes of Cyberspace.* New York, NY: Routledge.

Hardt, Michael, and Antonio Negri. 2009. *Commonwealth.* First edition. Cambridge, MA: Belknap Press.

Latour, Bruno. 2005. *Reassembling the Social: An Introduction to Actor-Network-Theory.* Oxford: Oxford University Press.

McKenna, Erin. 2001. *The Task of Utopia: A Pragmatist and Feminist Perspective.* Maryland: Rowman & Littlefield.

Miller, Seumas. 2007. "Social Institutions." http://plato.stanford.edu/archives/fall 2012/entries/social-institutions/.

Pariser, Eli. 2011. *The Filter Bubble: What the Internet Is Hiding from You.* New York: Penguin Press HC.

Putnam, Robert D. 2001. *Bowling Alone: The Collapse and Revival of American Community.* New York: Simon and Schuster.

Salazar, Angel, and Steve Sawyer, eds. 2007. *Handbook of Information Technology in Organizations and Electronic Markets.* Singapore: World Scientific.

Tett, Gillian. 2009. *Fool's Gold: How the Bold Dream of a Small Tribe at J.P. Morgan Was Corrupted by Wall Street Greed and Unleashed a Catastrophe.* Reprint edition. New York: Free Press.

Turkle, Sherry. 2011. *Alone Together: Why We Expect More from Technology and Less from Each Other.* New York: Basic Books.

Williams, Brackette F. 1991. *Stains on My Name, War in My Veins: Guyana and the Politics of Cultural Struggle.* Durham: Duke University Press Books.

2 Theoretical Orientations

INTRODUCTION

To make our case for attending to what should happen beyond capital, we rely heavily on contemporary social theory. This chapter presents the general social theory that we use—a theory that applies to all social forms. We aim to make explicit here the general conceptual and theoretical presumptions that underlie our argument, based on our research and reading of the literatures on the dynamics of social life. We focus especially on those presumptions that enable us to distinguish between simple and extended social formation reproduction (SFR). In our theory, we are committed to:

- Non-essentialist, structural, ethnological explanations of social and cultural reproduction in general;
- Distinguishing systematically among the data, information, knowledge, and wisdom moments of what we will call the DIKW cycle;
- Considering humans and non-humans and their actions in the same frame, as cyborgs;
- Finding motivations for pursuing change—through multitudes, for freedom, desire, and love—in many social formations;
- Attending to futures, utopias, ethics, and being responsible.

While this chapter presents an abstract theory relevant to these five general themes, the following three chapters use the theory to explicate the current situation and its practices to suggest how SFR might be extended.

GENERAL THEORETICAL COMMITMENTS

Certain general theoretical commitments are important for a project to influence the direction of social change. We want to articulate non-essentialist, structural, and ethnological explanations of changes in SFR. In this chapter, we explain why we think it necessary to discuss social dynamics in these terms.

Social Formation: This term, which denotes the fundamental unit of sociality, has come into analytical use as an alternative to "society." The term "society" carries the essentialist implication of being a social totality, and similar to the current notion of "nation." Thus, to use "society" for the basic social unit is to presume that nations are normal and that social formations, unlike nations, are abnormal. "Social formation" is a broader term, applicable to both the vast (like the global political economy) to the small (like a network of friends). A society is thus one of many types of social formations.

Non-Essentialist: Being "essentialist" is often a characteristic of rigid forms of thinking, such as literalist interpretations of texts, bibles, or constitutions. The notions making up a social theory are essentialist when the content of their elements is unchanging, the same in each social formation. Hence, explanations are *non*-essentialist when they are constructed with flexible elements and interrelations, those whose content changes as the elements and their relations change. "Social formation" is an example of a non-essentialist entity with such flexible elements. We return to the problems of essentialist theory in our discussion of ethnological perspectives below.

Social Formation Reproduction: Social formations, no matter their type, must be reproduced (Hakken 1987). This is because what social formations share is the condition of being "extra-somatic." While they are carried by (human) life forms, they are not extended from one moment to the next by biology. Instead, social formations must be actively reproduced to persist. Although this reproduction might occasionally look like mere replication, to be perpetuated by something analogous to "momentum," this is not the case. They must *be extended*, not merely replicated. Social formations typically face reproducing themselves under conditions that have changed, both from when they originally came into existence and from the recent past. A social formation is at risk if it cannot extend its practices to cope with the changes. Whether the results of the changes extend or fail to do so, or are progressive or regressive and authoritarian, they unfold in history, which in essence is an account of how the people in them cope with the necessity to reproduce actively.

Social formation reproduction is structured through the relations among the different social groups in a social formation. Recognition of the likelihood of change in SFR forces attention to how humans engage collectively with the forces of reproduction. In order to intervene in SFR, and to decide when and where to do so, human beings need to share understandings of the ends of an intervention; that is, to know what values they wish to manifest collectively in their lives, which practices are a likely and logical target for such intervention, and its likely results. Even deciding to do nothing about the dynamics of SFR requires discussion and decisions.

Cultural Reproduction: SFR in turn rests on cultural reproduction, the extension in time of the constructs and practices through which people apprehend, talk about, and act on their social formation and its dynamics.

If a group wishes to influence the trajectory of the reproduction of its social formation, a good place to intervene is trying to change these cultural categories, including the means by which SFR is perceived and thus how it might be manipulated. The creation of such means, and the struggles over how to get others to adopt new or keep old means, is at the center of cultural reproduction. When trying to make new values, a group needs a useful and empirical understanding of existing values, their distribution, and how they are reproduced—e.g., through which cultural constructs and institutions.

Conditions like social inequalities, whether in work or in knowledge construction practices, affect the opportunity of each group to influence cultural reproduction, and in this sense, things like inequalities have structural properties that are implicated in SFR. For example, inequality can inhibit collective processes of decision-making and reinforce hierarchical decision-making, especially about what to value and how to value.

Structuralist: As described in the preceding chapter, a goal of this book is to demonstrate the need for new values, institutions, and measures in order to achieve a life beyond capital. We want to present and argue for new things as central to extending SFR. This presumes certain assumptions about the properties of social formations—that they exist, that it makes sense to conceptualize them as socio-cultural-material wholes, that there are certain types of them, that each type has certain characteristic dynamics, and so on. Such presumptions are structural, and our use of them makes our account a structural one, of the type normally associated with terms like "political economy." It accepts the *plausibility* that trajectories of general social change exist and that they can be affected directly by conscious, collective intervention, or indirectly, as by adopting new technologies.

Contemporary social thought is suspicious of talk of a structuralist sort as, for example, it is difficult for a theory to be both structuralist and anti-essentialist. We are aware of the work of those who claim that, in theoretical terms, ours is a "post-structural" era.[1] Brackette Williams is typical of those anthropologists who, in a postmodern register, are skeptical of the idea of structure, claiming that there are only people and their practices (Williams 1991). Sociologist Craig Calhoun similarly uses "post-structural" to describe his influential social theory (Calhoun 1994). Before people can decide *which among* the structural accounts best accounts for the likely direction of future social reproduction, they need good reasons for interest in *any* structural analysis, such as a political-economic one.

Some writers have attempted to develop Marxism in a post-structural way, following the reflections of Michel Foucault, Gilles Deleuze, and Felix Guattari (Deleuze and Guattari 1988; Foucault 1977). Others, such as Autonomous Marxists, e.g., Michael Hardt and Antonio Negri (Hardt and Negri 2001), Christian Fuchs (Fuchs 2015), and advocates of Open Marxism, e.g., John Holloway (Holloway, Varney, and Gosden 2010), try to keep structuralism but reframe its arguments in a manner informed by critiques of overly structural presumptions. We, too, use some concepts often associated with post-structuralisms. We think Actor–Network Theory (ANT) (e.g., Latour 2005) helps clarify the relation between material artifacts and symbolic elements. We use ANT and other post-structural ideas in conjunction with structural explanations to analyze some of the risks to SFR associated with computing. When a social formation is at risk, a possibility for radical change often emerges, but the changes possible are not determined just by the properties internal to the social formation. In reframed structural terms, there is room for planning to intervene and to leverage possibilities, as by trying to change the way people conceive of their actions. As such actions are situated (Suchman 1987), it is possible to ground action, to change the situation specifically while aiming it toward progressive social change (Suchman 1987).

Put a bit differently, we aim for an account of SFR that can be of value to a political program as well as to description and analysis. We want something similar to the account of Adam Smith's economics offered by David Graeber (Graeber 2011), or the careful evaluations of the Hobbes-Boyle conflict, highlighting its political dimension carried out by Shapin and Schaffer (Shapin and Schaffer 2011). Bruno Latour (Latour 1993) and Donna Haraway (Haraway 1988) demonstrate the structural properties of scientific scholarship, while still acknowledging the importance of interpretive flexibility. Debates in science, technology, and society (STS) also acknowledge how scientific programs have politics, as in the work of Langdon Winner (Winner 1980), Bruno Latour (Latour 2005), and Bernward Joerges (Joerges 1999). Like all these scholars, we acknowledge the relevance of the political dimension of technologies, but we also acknowledge that it can take multiple forms.

Another example of a way in which structural accounts remain relevant to the social sciences is the 1990s claims of a knowledge change-induced transformation of society, an idea that is both structural and political economic. The recent prominence of such accounts requires us to develop alternatives to be used as a pragmatic answer to their overt optimism or pessimism. Consider Peter Drucker's articulation of "The Rise of the Knowledge Society" (Drucker 1993). In his view, this rise profoundly decreases the social power of particular occupational groups (e.g., manufacturing workers), and he predicts the ushering in of a "postcapitalist" social formation. Drucker's notion of a post-capitalist knowledge society is "structural" in that it articulates a fundamental change in the character of social reproduction. Analyses like his usually include an element of compulsion, evoking social determination by large "systems." While talk about the future sometimes stresses its voluntary character, a new framework for social life or a set of widely influential social relations is more typically posed as central. For example, Yochai Benkler (Benkler 2006) sees the character of digital goods combined with the preference for reduced transaction costs as a push toward forms of "social production." Such imagined new social relations are usually influential, as well as greater in scale than local community, organizational, or even regional relations. They are the kinds of forces that limit human volition, both individual and collective; that is, they are structural.

Both Anti-Essentialist and Structural: The typical slogans for the primary social formation in waiting—"information society," etc.—frequently deploy the structural speech forms characteristic of economics. Despite occasional demurrals about how, e.g., it is "the local" where it is actually manifest, this talk often has a strongly foundational or essentialist quality, as often in the uses of the term "globalization." The ease with which structural terms can become foundational opens them to critiques of essentialism, which indicate that they erroneously identify as permanent characteristics things that are better understood as transient or contingent. In anti-essentialism, features normally considered to be part of an object's "nature" are instead understood as artifacts of particular interpretive framings of actual conjunctions of contexts. Discomfort with "structure talk" also follows from its frequent association with discourses of mastery, whose hegemonic concepts facilitate domination. Postmodern critiques of ideas of knowledge build on various criticisms of the structuralism of classical social theory (Hakken 2003). An example is what Hakken calls knowledge regression, where one begins with embodied knowledge, rather than with "raw data." In sociology, such critiques include the symbolic interactionism of George Herbert Mead (Mead 1934), the ethnomethodology of Harold Garfinkel (Garfinkel 1967), and the social constructivism of Berger and Luckman (Berger and Luckmann 1966).

Scholars like Brackette Williams (Williams 1991) acknowledge structure theoretically, but they see its impacts as only taking place "behind peoples' backs." That is, the impacts are irrelevant to experiential analyses, privileging explanation in terms of human perceptions as mediated by cultural constructs over all others because structure is beyond perception. It is only what we try to do that matters, not whether our actions have the desired consequences. Concluding that the structure of social life is not discernible means ultimately that analysis itself is largely beside the point. In contrast, we think it possible to ground structure talk non-essentially through reproductionist readings of social dynamics (Hakken 1987). As we have said, in social reproductionist accounts, frequent intervention is necessary if existing social arrangements are to be extended in time, since human social arrangements don't perpetuate themselves automatically. Therefore, the study of deliberate actions to promote the continuation of social arrangements from one period to the next is useful, as it provides insight into how continuity (or change) is accomplished, denied, or mitigated. Such insight makes clear how social arrangements are a consequence, among other things, of deliberate acts of constructing the social, acts that can be evaluated on the basis of the strength of the construction, such as its ability to endure over time. To paraphrase the language of Latour, the connections between structural forces and people's immediate actions or experiences are highly mediated by the chain of material objects that populate everyday life. This is what enables structural forces to reach beyond the specific locality, nation state, or other wide agglomeration. It is part of what makes humans unique when compared to other species (Strum and Latour 1987). Since social arrangements emerge from collective, widely shared dynamics, acting on them requires an equally collective, widely shared approach. We hope our book contributes to promoting this approach.

The key analytic step in a reproductionist account that wants to be structural while avoiding essentialism is to distinguish between practices that merely replicate macro-social relationships—simple reproduction—from those that transform them in relation to their contexts—extended reproduction (for more see Hakken 1987). In terms of objects and technologies, this kind of account distinguishes between *intermediaries*, which carry on a current practice, meaning, or symbol, and *mediators*, which act transformatively, translating the same practice, meaning, and symbol into a new one (Latour 2005). Practices do sometimes have dynamic, structure-transformative implications, but these are to be accounted for in terms of the conjunctions of particular circumstances, not essences. In our understanding of the relationship between contingencies and structures, structures can be conceived as relatively stable over a long period of time and across different configurations of contingencies. Like change, such structures need to be accounted for historically.

Ethnology and Ethnography: A loose notion of structure is implicit in the idea that there are legitimate analytic moments in social studies. Taking the idea of social transformation seriously enough to examine the evidence relevant to it means admitting at least *the possibility* of something like structure (Hakken 2003). If things are to change, they must do so from one thing to something else. This same minimum notion of structure is necessary to ethnography. To do ethnography, one must presume that general practices are present in enough social formations that their different manifestations can be compared. To communicate across languages and cultures, ethnographers must have available categories with substantial overlap in meaning, the kind of overlap that enables meaningful talk about what is or is not generally the case. That is, they need ethnology, the theoretical counterpart to ethnography.

Ethnography is a social scientific way of knowing that describes particular phenomena by placing them in relevant contexts. Ethnology is a more general explanatory effort, one that aims to *account for* the specific practices described by ethnography in terms of more general socio-cultural processes. Ethnological thinking requires attending to discourses about things in general, like those of the last several pages. Ethnography needs ethnology, for it is the latter that provides the terms for comparison that make ethnographic description communicable. For example, it is common to speak of "ages," "eras," or "information societies" outside of specific places or spaces. Differences between "times like these" and "times like those" are frequently explained in terms of the dynamics indexical of or at least indicative of different types of social formations. The use of such general discourse phrases points at a desire for broad understandings of past and present.

Ethnographers, like other social theorists, use terms that presume the existence of things that have structure-like regularity, the development of terms being an important ethnological task. People arguing for one or another public policy also need notions about why things are as they are, and therefore they, too, deploy such concepts. The cost to social life of labeling as essentialist all discussion of regularity in social dynamics is too high. To do so leads to unending ad hoc accounts of discrete events. Knowledge then can only be "local," a presumption about knowledge that is itself essentialist. Further, an "only local knowledge" claim is rhetorical, because it cannot be demonstrated to be true: to establish that every social formation's reproduction has total local autonomy, one would have to engage in structural discourse. Without identifying structures that generally support local autonomy, the latter idea remains a mere premise. Attempts to avoid theorizing structure end up merely masking it.

Additional Justifications for Structure Talk: An almost tautological justification for talk about structure is that a large proportion of humans/cyborgs currently extend their own social reproduction by using concepts that presume structure. Relating on the basis of presumed structure engenders structure-like effects. For example, since the late nineteenth century, public intellectuals in the West have used models of social formation reproduction framed in the formalisms of neo-classical economics. An essentialist notion of "productivity" developed within these models that has migrated outside its original realm—e.g., into social policy. Similarly, talk about cyberspace "causes" certain connections to be made, or talk about a "knowledge society" engenders quasi-formal, must-be-related-to-as-structural effects. Structure-presuming practices, like policies based on the "human capital" notions critiqued later in the book, influence experience irrespective of the concepts' analytical validity. To address the possibility that there may be a gap between talk and reality, ethnographers must generate possible alternative accounts. To open space to criticize dominant discourses, one must hypothesize alternative structural narratives, rather than reject political economy a priori.

The arguments for structural narratives made thus far follow from meta-discourse over the *possibility* of structural talk. They are ethnologically "weak," not derived from demonstrated structural regularities in the reproduction of actual social formations. There is a "stronger" case for thinking structurally, which begins by recognizing a human proclivity to develop structural accounts. This is what C. Wright Mills called the sociological imagination or the ability to connect biography with wider discourses (Mills 2000). Human action, especially when supported by self-conscious, collective articulations, produces cultural structures and artifacts. This is why human interventions often appear to have something like inertia, because deliberate interventions can foster sustained practices, in ways that have momentum or a cumulative, material impact on social formation reproduction. In

Actor–Network Theories of technology, as particular technology actor net-works become central to social reproduction, they incline SFR in some directions, while making others less likely (Latour and Woolgar 2013). Langdon Winner thus argues that technologies do have politics (Winner 1980). To explain the problems in SFR directed only at value, we will have to be able to imagine how change *might* result in new reproductive dynamics. (We elaborate more in Chapter 5.) At the same time, we need ways to talk about change that *don't presume* that change automatically results in new dynamics. Structure talk exists, and when humans coordinate action through talk, it matters. We need general talk—discourses capable of accounting for first, the notions about the structural with which people operate, second, the consequences of these notions, and finally, the inertias and momenta that are potentially manifest at the social formation level, that is "systems as wholes."

Structuralism and Computing: We also need to be alert so that our talk does not presume what needs to be examined. There are reasons why it is important to avoid presuming that what exists now is what should be paid attention to, or that what *did* happen is what *should have* happened. This is why we insist on using "digital technologies" (DTs) rather than just "information technologies" (ITs),[2] because we are embracing the notion that digital ones are just one kind of technology of information, that is, that "ITs" take a variety of historical and cultural forms. Likewise, simplistic references to "how computers change society" while ignoring how social actors change computing are widespread (see Bannon 1989). Ignoring social action and actors reinforces and is reinforced by what Edward Said called "naïve Orientalism," based on presumptions like, e.g., that the US is typical of and/or a "model" for all societies, or all future societies (Said 1979).

Rather than talking as if the contemporary social formation is the only one with information and communication technologies, the definition of technology needs to include other kinds of information and communication technologies, like books and storytelling. Then information and communication technologies can be properly considered as apparatuses, the ensemble of objects and meanings that allow the circulation of information and the practices of human communication. When one does so, all social formations appear to be heavily mediated by technological apparatuses. For some authors, technologies and artifacts are what distinguish human societies from animal ones, e.g., Strum and Latour (Strum and Latour 1987). The specific architectures of the apparatuses doing the mediation work are often important indicators of how one social formation is different from another, as different technologies often have different social correlates and different social formations have different technological correlates.

This epistemological stance forces any analysis to be specific about the particular technologies and social changes one has in mind when wanting to make a causative argument. We give significance, for example, to the specific way in which computer-based technologies "process" information and signals. They do so automatically; that is, they are a form of social action that really does take place "behind the backs" of those who run them. The result is that users are often ignorant of the manipulations of data and information that a computer makes, making digital technologies an invisible infrastructure for human action (for the concept of infrastructure, see Susan Leigh Star, 1999). The speed that follows from the automatic character of these manipulations is one of the important reasons for using computers. There are trade-offs, as the ease of gathering, storing, and manipulating information with DTs has also led to the withering of important social institutions for certifying knowledge. For some time it has been clear that the cultural correlates of computing are varied. We are interested in *how much* they vary and even more how to *account for* the variation. Only when we have a better grasp of how the computing/culture nexus works can we move on to how much it matters, and how to account for it in the design and development of DTs.

Our futuring project depends upon a clear understanding of the importance of social formation reproduction at the time we finished writing, in early 2015. Changes in these dynamics are often correlated with the use of digital technologies, now used so extensively as to make it hard to imagine returning to the prior state of SFR. Our analysis of the current moment in SFR is in the following chapter.

THE DATA-INFORMATION-KNOWLEDGE-WISDOM CYCLE (DIKW) AND SIMPLE VERSUS EXTENDED SFR

Our accounts of the present moment in SFR attend primarily to computing and its relationship to social change. Computing may (or may not) have changed the character of preexisting extrasomatic ways of dealing with signals and feedback, or how agency (acting in the world in a way that has consequences) is manifest, or any number of other SFR forms. Approaching change as being about different SFR dynamics means paying attention to ways computing gives entities new means to engage with information-loaded contexts, but more than this. To see what more is needed requires us to return to the differences between physical and social reproduction.

Humans, like other life forms, reproduce physically. Unless drastic changes in genetics (mutation) or context (e.g., catastrophic climate change) prevent it, the physical reproduction of life forms seems to take place rather "automatically" from one generation to the next. In contrast, the social formations on which human existence is dependent have no such physical trajectory; they require cultural production and reproduction. If institutions are not created to pass on culture from one generation to the next, a social formation is unlikely to reproduce itself and will probably disappear. Such institutions are also extrasomatic means of dealing with feedback. As part of the collective infrastructure for human existence, they are essential to social life.

In particular, educational institutions play an important part in cultural reproduction. They practice a kind of societal cybernetics—i.e., collecting information (e.g., through research) and responding to it, whether by new means or old. Recognizing that educational institutions were cybernetic *before* computers came along means that questions about the impact of computing on education should be about how computing changed educational cybernetics. One should not presume that computers are the first manifestations of cybernetics. Moreover, humans are capable of intervening collectively and deliberately in SFR, for example, by creating educational institutions. They can do this in order to achieve goals, especially if there is a broad social consensus about the value of the goal.

In order to intervene collectively in SFR, humans need to develop knowledge about the needed changes, and this knowledge is discursively related to the information they have. They also need to deal with related concepts like data and wisdom. It is therefore important to be clear about how these four things relate to each other. "Data" can be used to refer very generally to things that exist and can be noticed by people. "Information" exists when these data are placed in some kind of context that is potentially meaningful. Another way to say this is that information is contextualized data that is thought to be potentially meaningful, but the meaning is still unclear. "Knowledge," then, is information whose meaning is understood, at least by the people willing to affirm this to be the case. We can think of "wisdom" as knowledge whose meaning has been existentially justified. Interestingly, wisdom is not talked about much in digital contexts.

Thinking together about data, information, knowledge, and wisdom (DIKW) in this way provides procedural language to frame any intervention, including with regard to computing. The four words—data, information, knowledge, and wisdom—can make a continuum seeable as cyclical. It is expressible as a procedure, although the cyclical properties are often ignored in uses of the terms (e.g., when they are used as synonyms for each other). We refer to this as the human information cycle, or procedure for short. In general, narratives about knowledge and wisdom involve more complex procedures that the more basic ones, data and information (Hakken 2003). The elements are sometimes theorized as a progressive procedure, as in many positivist accounts of how data turn into information, and information into knowledge. Others theorize the continuum as a regression, as in deconstructionist accounts of how knowledge is what is always embedded, so information is abstracted from it. Looked at empirically, it is often difficult to distinguish progressive from regressive DIKW.

Considered as a continuum of distinct phases, the DIKW process affords an understanding of important differences in procedural relationships among the four phases. Information is more complex than data, knowledge more than information, and wisdom more than knowledge. Each phase is also central to humans' capacity for culture. Some aspects of these phases, such as the capacity to recognize data and act contextually upon it, are shared with other species. Among humans, the procedures are more elaborate, involve more steps, and in other ways are different from other species' informational practices. In many species, sexual reproduction involves information, as in sexual selection by females in many bird species, where sense data clearly impacts the selection of appropriate mating partners. The mechanisms of physical reproduction—which became a part of the genetic heritage of species via evolution—can be accounted for without explicit recourse to steps 3 (knowledge) and 4 (wisdom) of the human informational procedure. We need not presume that "knowledge" and "wisdom" are necessary to physical reproduction among humans, but they exist. K and W are profoundly cultural DIKW moments, and it is in these that computing's social correlates are most evident.

Cultural ways are not reproduced automatically, as the means of sexual reproduction seem to be in non-human species. Rather, they need to be reproduced consciously, which often involves a great deal of reflective communication among the members of the group about the significance of changes in their environment. In the absence of this communication, the survival of the cultural forms, and thus potentially that of both the individuals and the group, is put at risk (Hakken 2003). This is the fate today, for example, of many "orphan" languages, forms of human communication that are seldom used, especially by young group members. There is, indeed, a likely connection between use of the Internet in its dominant English modality and the increasing frequency of language orphanage (see the work of John Paolillo (Paolillo 2005)).

Simple and Expanded Cultural Reproduction: We can conceive of cultural reproduction as involving the phases of the DIKW procedure. In certain contexts, data becomes information, knowledge can be achieved from information, and wisdom from knowledge. The distinction between simple and extended reproduction is as relevant to cultural reproduction and DIKW as it is to social reproduction, for which Karl Marx argued in Volume 2 of *Capital* (Marx 1967). One can speak of simple cultural reproduction via the process of socialization—that is, through the immersion of individuals in cultural and social contexts that provide them with face-to-face opportunities for (essentially unequal) communication. An example of this kind of socialization is the way a master teaches an apprentice, where roles are often taken on via observation, mimicry, and rote learning. Expanded cultural reproduction is a more collaborative way where more complex information procedures can be perpetuated. Here, cultural objects are endowed with new attributes. These objects extend the communicative abilities of a population in space and time (Strum and Latour 1987). A simple example would be putting female and male symbols on restroom doors. A more complex example is the expansion of computing access to the means of cultural reproduction that we will discuss in Chapter 4. Cultures differ in the relative importance of these two modes of reproduction, but all are profoundly dependent on the expanded information procedure.

Because contexts often change, SFR's being extended to meet new conditions is its normal state. Extending SFR often depends on extracting some knowledge from information, and knowledge extraction depends on values. Likewise, values need to be analyzed in terms of the valuables (symbols, objects, cultural artifacts) that sustain the process of social formation reproduction.

CYBORGS: CONSIDERING THINGS AND HUMANS TOGETHER

Cyborgs are best understood as life-form-based entities (organisms) whose capacities have been substantially increased via the addition of extrasomatic elements. The obverse form of cyborgs—mechanical or other non-somatic forms enhanced by biological supplements—is a conceptual possibility, but rarely occurs. Robots are purely extrasomatic, and thus differ from cyborgs. The term "cyborg," a shortening of the notion "cybernetic organism," now generally refers to well-integrated combinations of the human biological and the mechanical.

We use the history of the use of "cyborgs" to afford a perspective from which human beings and things are framed together, as both have agency in SFR. "Cyborg" entered popular discourse in the mid-twentieth century, in conjunction with the disputed founding of the field of cybernetics (Wiener 1948). As a general science of feedback, cybernetics focused on the capacity of entities to deal with feedback. "Cyborg" was invented to describe enhancements of human physical capacities when dealing with a hostile environment (Clynes and Kline 1960). Based on a recognition of the similarity and linkages between human and machines, the term "cyborg" also came relatively quickly to be used to describe a human whose ability to use feedback was greatly enhanced via artificial means (e.g., as depicted fictionally by things like the "bionic leg"). Over time, cyborgs have become increasingly thought of as potentially having a co-constructive relationship between their biological and mechanical features. Via feedback loops, they can respond more extensively and actively to new information, and such co-construction enhances cyborgs' capacities for agency.

"Agency" is a philosophical concept with both metaphysical and ethical aspects. An entity or group with agency is able to affect its/their experience. Thus, single-celled protozoa have a degree of agency, since they can move themselves around via their flagella. However, as flagella are somatic, their presence does not make protozoa into cyborgs. In the late twentieth century, the term "cyborg" re-emerged in popular discourse with the recognition that computers offered additional means to enhance human capabilities. We conceive of computers formally as electronic devices for the automatic, rapid storing, processing, and communicating of information. The term "cyborg" never really disappeared, even though "computer science" displaced "cybernetics" as the label for the field. In a parallel to the usage in popular discourse of "information technology" to apply only to computer-mediated information technology, "cyborg" came to refer to entities that used computing to process and deal with feedback. Non-computer entities, those that are extrasomatically enhanced by non-digital things (like non-digital technology-mediated DTs), do not count as cyborgs.

The narrative exorcism of non-computered cyborgs follows from a prevailing tendency to presume that changes in social processes are primarily a result of new technologies (Hakken 1999). Donna Haraway is largely responsible for re-stimulating academic interest in the cyborg through her work "A Cyborg Manifesto" (Haraway 1990). In this essay, Haraway points to the possibility of rethinking essentialism through recognition of the hybrid, cyborgic characteristics of the entities inhabiting the world. She provided an important theoretical lens that reinforced a major STS insight, that humans share with things capacities to act responsibly, to have agency. Cyborgs, a single unity of thing and human, came to exemplify this shared capacity. This exemplification led to a number of questions about computing and social change, such as how cyborgs realize their potential to alter agency, and whether cyborgs' abilities to influence their own actions produce substantially different results.

In Chapter 3, we will critique as facile several presumptions about how computing is a general source of social change. However, we use the cyborg as an entity that maintains transformative potential. As unified entities, they hold a strong potential for changing SFR. Thinking through cyborgs also helps situate concerns about agency in specific times and places. We are grateful for the renewed focus on how a cyberspace of Haraway's cyborgs might be different, but we use the term more broadly than she did. We use it also to draw attention to how humans' actions in the world have always been supported and mediated by extrasomatic entities, from language and shared modes of production through gasoline-powered vehicles and self-driving cars.

Recognizing that we have always been cyborgs provides additional purchase on the complex questions of causality that arise when considering computing and social change. Before concluding that the existence of a new entity, a computer, is the cause of a concurrent historical event, we need to consider other possibilities. The uses of new computing forms occur at the same time, and often in conjunction with, a number of other contemporary phenomena. For example, many of the financial innovations of the decade of the period 2000–2009, such as sub-prime mortgage-based securities and collateralized debt obligations, could hardly have emerged without computing. Nor were they likely to have mattered nearly so much without the computing-enabled contraction of national markets in capital at the same time as the expansion of international markets. Although these events would have been less likely without computing, they nonetheless are not the same thing as computing.[3] We should be cautious when considering cause and agency, keeping in mind the many causal claims about the good social consequences of computing made by "experts" in the quest for a "new-new thing" or in what have been called "computerization movements" (Kling and Iacono 1995).

Computing and social changes can take place in the same time frame, suggesting the possibility of causality but not itself constituting evidence for it. At the same time, acknowledging the cyborgic characteristics of all human action should protect us from the essentializing danger of acting as if it is only purely biological humans who have agency. The nexus between computing and social change needs to be investigated through a wide lens. This lens should also include the economic and the commodity forms, a point explored in later chapters.

THE SOURCES OF THE MOTIVATION FOR INTERVENTION: THE MULTITUDE, FREEDOM, AND LOVE

We are aware that our project of trying now to think beyond capital is ambitious, not least because it will need to attract a large number and a broad range of humans/cyborgs. Identifying those who could have the motivation for projects like this is a task taken up by others trying to develop a structuralist but non-essentialist Marxism. Christian Fuchs's work on "digital labour" (Fuchs 2013) updates the social dynamics model of Marx's theory of modes of production so that they apply to motivation in the present. As a prelude to this task, Fuchs develops a general (in our terms, ethnological) theory of things like forms of ownership, the powers of coercion, mechanisms of allocation/distribution, and forms of division of labor. Social change typically happens when one of these four aspects is changing. Social relations are present in all modes of production, but each takes a specific form that influences its potential as a source of resistance or of relevance to other counter-narratives.

In their own rethinking of Marxism, Michael Hardt and Antonio Negri also strive for a more general (ethnological) account of motivation (Hardt and Negri 2009). Their recent restatement of the Autonomous Marxism (AM) tradition begins with a new take on the Marxist tradition of placing revolutionary primacy on the working class. They identify this not as an essential quality of industrial workers, but as something that follows from Marx's identification of the labor-capital struggle as the key element in the promotion of social change in the nineteenth century. AM frames in time the prioritizing of the specific form of the industrial working class struggle, taking it as an example of a more ethnologically general struggle. This general struggle is the one for freedom in relation to power—as well as resistance to imposing the will of one group on free subjects. Hardt and Negri de-essentialize the struggle by enlarging on how these elements are to be understood differently in different eras. They also broaden Marx's concepts of historical and ethnological purchase. They re-conceptualize the working class as one of many forms of what they call "the multitude." In this way, they open up space for an account of all forms of living labor. Further, the agency of the working class in production is also changed in terms of its position. By relocating the positional agency as that of "the poor," Hardt and Negri revive the concept of "the multitudes of the poor" in Baruch Spinoza's *Ethics* (Spinoza 2005). Being part of the multitude for them means more than having the potential of inducing fear in rulers, as Spinoza thought. It also carries the positive power of the capacity to be a subject or to have agency, what Michel Foucault called "bio-power" (Foucault 2010). Hardt and Negri acknowledge both bio-power and bio-politics, the former the power *over* life, the latter the power *of* life. In their view, the central issue for social change is not to identify structurally whether a group of people is a component part of the multitude. Rather, the key question is who is engaged in *making* the multitude or, in our terms, participating in creating active, political subjectivities to influence particular moments of SFR.

Hardt and Negri's approach fosters a re-thinking of subjectivities in stratified social formations, past and future. The bio-political struggle over re-making the multitude can reconstruct the configuration of bio-power in each social formation. For example, through its implementation and expanded interpretation, the Magna Carta became a document that reshaped individual freedoms and limited the power of the monarchy. In capitalist social formations, the defining feature of bio-power is the ability to create commodities, including the transformation of people into commodities. Under these conditions, the main political struggle is for free subjects to de-commodify the world. This implies, for example, constructing a world where resources are pooled commonly (Ostrom 1990). A bio-political "event" is one that pushes the boundaries of bio-power and reshapes it. More recently, the encampment strategy enacted by Occupy Wall Street strove to break the constituted power over spaces through the physical presence of living bodies (Hardt and Negri 2012). At least for a time, it opened up scenarios for alternative uses of civic spaces. With the destruction of boundaries, new conditions of existence can be created, and changes in the bio-political domain can enable the extension of SFR. Of course, possible forms of agency are limited by each social formation's particular characteristics, and one should be careful, as Slavoj Žižek stresses, not to use the multitude to create new myths (Žižek 2004).

Why might such theoretical broadenings be useful? For Negri and Hardt, no "multitude" (or class) can redefine the conditions of existence and extend SFR if freedom does not have priority over power. Negri and Hardt see this emerging by drawing on one of Foucault's last interviews, in which he declared, "[I]f power is everywhere, it is because freedom is everywhere" (Foucault 1984). Foucault suggests a casual nexus: in order for freedom to prevail over power, resistance to power must sufficiently expand freedom. The example Negri and Hardt offer to illustrate this dynamic is slavery.

Despite being subjected to what Orlando Patterson defined as a form of social death (Patterson 1982), slaves continuously resist the hierarchy in which they live. The slaves' fight for freedom is not anti-modern, in that they do not reject modernity as a whole, but *alter-modern*, because they strive to extend the claims for freedom typical of modernity to the entire population. In resistance, they extend and expand the dynamics of the reproduction of the social formation in which they live. Such practices of constructing alter-modernity can be primary extenders of SFR.

Negri and Hardt recognize that not all the practices of alter-modernity by the multitude are oriented toward liberation. Some are oriented toward new hierarchical and expropriation-based forms of social organization. To know if liberation is the inclination of a practice, a criterion is needed. For this, Hardt and Negri reconceptualize "love" as the power to think and act in association with other human beings (Hardt and Negri 2009). They invoke Spinoza to differentiate among *conatus*, the fight for one's own existence, *cupiditas*, the desire expressed through affection, and *amor*, the desire affirmed through reason. Amor is the affirmation through reason of the desire for association and for a common future. (Love can, of course, go badly, becoming the basis for hate, when it becomes love for one's own identity over that of others.)

Our task in the following chapters is to identify social dynamics that make sense and provide a basis for intervention. We do this by identifying some already-existing efforts of multitudes, efforts in computing, to extend social formation reproduction, drawing out values and corresponding institutions and measures that can create and sustain a common future.

FUTURES, UTOPIAS, AND COMPUTING; ALSO, ETHICS AND RESPONSIBILITY

In the Prologue, we acknowledged that ours is a form of utopian thinking. Here, we acknowledge as well that it fits into what in social science is calling "future studies."[4] Analyses of future possibilities necessarily walk a fine line. On one side of the line understanding of current conditions should inform such work, but one cannot merely extrapolate from what exists. On the other side, while a utopian task involves thinking about the future we desire, it cannot turn into fantasy. To avoid both these dangers, we try to locate what we are doing in relationship to future studies (FS) in social science, and pragmatist and feminist utopianism (Bardzell 2014).

Future studies scholars try to answer questions about what social forms will be more characteristic of times to come and which will be less characteristic. The emergence of FS can be attributed to several factors, including the needs of policy makers to give their recommendations more weight than can be derived from their mere desirability. Predictions about the future need to be plausible. The rise of FS was also a response to the general problem of prediction in social science. The middle part of the twentieth century was marked by an effort to model social science on natural science, including the adoption of "predictability" as a criterion of scientific value. The digital computer enabled the construction of models with much more complexity, and this promise provided a strong boost to FS optimism. (This optimism was not unlike that currently surrounding the pursuit of "big data.")

The task of making social science predictive, however, faces a huge "open feedback loop" (cybernetic) obstacle, namely the fact that humans can and do change their behavior in response to researchers' findings. Moreover, such changes in behavior can be emergent; that is to say, changes grow unobserved for a long time and then emerge suddenly. Thus, they are very difficult to predict. These are only two of many reasons why "simple" futurism—the mere extension of current trajectories of change into the future—is likely to have little predictive value. Given such problems, those willing to call themselves "futurists" developed various approaches to disciplining their future imaginary. These are illustrated in, for example, the journal *Futures*.

One method widely used in FS is the Delphi method (Dalkey and Helmer 1963). This uses panels of experts in particular fields to predict aspects of the future. The experts are asked to first identify their "best case" scenario, then their "worst case," and finally, the scenario they consider "most likely." These last are combined into a collective "most likely," which is then presented as likely to be a reasonably close approximation of what will be. There are, of course, many reasons to critique the Delphi approach, including biases possible in the selection of experts and problems of inter-rater reliability. To our knowledge, the futurist community of scholars is yet to settle on a preferred methodology. Similarly, the initial optimism about computer modeling, which flowed so pervasively in the early days of artificial intelligence, ebbed rather suddenly (Turkle 2012). Like other computer science "trends," they come and go more or less regularly. This is especially true of approaches, like some to big data, that chase correlations without developing an accompanying theoretical apparatus.

We acknowledge that "futuring" is hard to do, and that we are not aware of a "mainstream" futurist approach that is reliable or predictive. Yet, we will try to "future" anyway for several reasons. First, implicit in our main argument is the understanding that continuing along the current paths of social formation reproduction is unlikely to yield a viable future. Environmentalists are predicting changes in our ecosystem that threatens life, and economists argue that increasing inequality will result in a marginal existence for the majority of the world's population. These are not the futures we think people would choose, but we must intervene if the trajectory is to be changed.

We have confidence that humans have the ability to reformulate problems, look to new values, and intervene deliberately to change the dynamics of SFR. We would further argue that such intervention is more likely to succeed if it first builds on identifiable, existing dynamics and second if the reasons for intervention, and the justifications of the intervention strategy and tactics, are widely understood and shared. We think it ethnologically demonstrable that "really existing" human cultures have regular dialogues regarding ultimate ends or values. These dialogues are the proper loci of interventions, and we see our task as entering into the ongoing debate over values in our social formations. Our intervention aims to build consensus behind values connected to computing, something that has for some time now strongly influenced the general cultural imaginary.

Discourses about cyberspace sometimes identify empirical approaches that are more promising than reliance on panels of experts. In *Computing Myths, Class Realities* we recognized that existing cultures don't realize the potential of what a general cyber-culture could be (Hakken and Andrews 1993). However, certain cultural forms, such as those prominent among information systems developers, online gamers, and proponents of community informatics, could be seen as suggestive precursors of cyberspace. Via ethnographic fieldwork, there are already some useful understandings of the cultural potential of cyberspace (see *Cyborgs@Cyberspace?* Hakken 1999).[5]

Another argument for a futures/utopian project is an ethical imperative. Given the predictions about the trajectory of life on earth, not to give thought to the future is irresponsible.

Ethnographers of the future have a responsibility to articulate a preferred future, or at least the values that could provide a basis for a future. All ethnographers have an ethical responsibility to present understandings of the cultural patterns they study that are as accurate as possible, the articulation that best explains the existing patterns of culture. For those studying cultures that are emerging or may be emerging, what we refer to as cyberspace, the patterns are only partly formed. One can, however, provide an account of the kinds of future SFR dynamics that one would prefer. As this provides criteria with which to place the scholar's account of patterns in relation to aims, we think that it is irresponsible not to provide it. Moreover, studies of the dynamics of possibly emerging cultures can be and often are directly implicated in their creation. Those fostering the new can use research and studies. The uses of the work of Larry Lessig (Lessig 2004) are important examples of such studies about cyberspace. An articulation of the cyber-vision informing this work is essential to the process of debating its merits.

Feminist utopians have often aligned themselves with philosophical pragmatists, especially John Dewey. This is in part because Dewey embraced responsibility for imagining a future as a philosophical imperative. He argued, "Faith in the power of intelligence to imagine a future which is the projection of the desirable in the present, and to invent the instrumentalities of its realization, is our salvation"(Dewey 2015). Dewey was writing to, in his words, "forward the emancipation of philosophy from too intimate and exclusive an attachment to traditional problems."

Initially, cyberspace was envisioned as an arena for egalitarian practices and values, as well as democratic practices. For all these reasons, we feel a positive responsibility to articulate our vision of the future and to articulate its values. This must be done if we are to identify the institutions and measures that are likely to help bring a viable social formation into existence. We now turn to identifying such understandings and drawing alternative futures out of them.

NOTES

1. The term "post-structural" is an example of an annoying tendency in current social theorizing, that of attaching the "post-" prefix to any new form of a phenomenon arising after the current one. This would be probably be alright if the author really meant, say, "post-structural" to mean "non-structural," but this is not normally the case. "Post-modern" does not mean the complete eclipse of modernism, much of which is still around in the periods labeled "post-modern," just as there is still a great deal of industry in a "post-industrial" age. And, most egregiously but thankfully, "post-human" does not mean all the humans are dead. In general, such terminological coinages are a consequence of an academic penchant for "newness," not much different from the same penchant regarding soap powders. Thus, "post-structural" tends to mean "structural with a twist." To avoid such misdirection is another reason we call our theory "structuralist."

2. As Hakken frequently points out to his students, they use the terms "information technology" or "IT" as if the present ones are the only social formations with such things. However, books and even stories are also information technologies. Thus, their usage is both deeply ethnocentric and also gets in the way of the kinds of comparisons necessary to ground things like "computer revolution" talk (Hakken 1999). This is why we avoid using "ITs" or "ICTs" and instead talk of digital technologies when we mean to refer to contemporary, computer-based information or communication technologies.

3. Today, the continuing rapid development and adoption of new computing artifacts remains dependent upon their sale in new and existing markets, ones expanding quickly in both capitalization and geographic scope. Greater access to non-national capital and large increases in the communicative exchange among cultures were and are still both necessary in order for computing to spread. The same is true of the transmission—indeed, on occasion, the amplification—of financial and economic distress.

4. Many well-researched and accepted attempts to synthesize a framework for future studies have appeared, including Wendell Bell's *The Foundation of Future Studies* (Bell 2011); James Dator's *Advancing Future Studies* (Dator 2002); Eleonora Masini's *Why Future Studies* (Masini 1993); Ziauddin Sardar's *Rescuing All of Our Futures* (Sardar 1999); Richard Slaughter's *New Thinking for a New Millennium* (Slaughter 2002).

5. In *Cyborgs@Cyberspace?: An Ethnography Looks to the Future* (Hakken 1999), Hakken used this approach. In his more recent *Futures* article, he tried to identify whether work is "re-socialed" as a key criterion regarding computing's socially transformative potential (Hakken 2000). He used a similar approach to address "The Future of the Journal in Asia" (Hakken 2009).

REFERENCES

Bannon, Liam. 1989. *Discovering the Human Actors in Human Factors*. Aarhus, Denmark: Aarhus University, Computer Science Dept.

Bardzell, Shaowen. 2014. "Utopias of Participation: Design, Criticality and Emancipation." *ACM Digital Library*. http://dl.acm.org/citation.cfm?doid=2662155. 2662213.

Bell, Wendell. 2011. *Foundations of Futures Studies: Human Science for a New Era: Values, Objectivity, and the Good Society*. Piscataway, NJ: Transaction Publishers.

Benkler, Yochai. 2006. *The Wealth of Networks: How Social Production Transforms Markets and Freedom*. New Haven, CT: Yale University Press.

Berger, Peter, and Thomas Luckmann. 1966. "The Social Construction of Knowledge: A Treatise in the Sociology of Knowledge."Soho, NY: Open Road Media.

Calhoun, Craig. 1994. "Social Theory and the Politics of Identity." In *Social Theory and the Politics of Identity*, edited by Craig Calhoun, 9–36. Oxford, UK: Blackwell. http://eu.wiley.com/WileyCDA/Brand/id-35.html.

Clynes, Manfred E., and Nathan S Kline. 1960. "Cyborgs and Space." *Astronautics*, 26–27; 75–76.

Dalkey, Norman, and Olaf Helmer. 1963. "An Experimental Application of the Delphi Method to the Use of Experts." *Management Science* 9 (3): 458–67.

Dator, James Allen. 2002. *Advancing Futures: Futures Studies in Higher Education*. Santa Barbara, CA: Greenwood Publishing Group.

Deleuze, Gilles, and Félix Guattari. 1988. *A Thousand Plateaus: Capitalism and Schizophrenia*. London: Bloomsbury Publishing.

Dewey, John. 2015. *The Need for a Recovery of Philosophy*. Accessed April 18. https://deweypragmatismo.wordpress.com/texto-2/.

Drucker, Peter F. 1993. "The Rise of the Knowledge Society." *The Wilson Quarterly* 17 (2): 52–17.

Foucault, Michel. 1977. Discipline and Punish: The Birth of the Prison. New York, NY: Pantheon.

———. 1984. "L'ethique de Souci de Soi Comme Pratique de La Liberté." *Concordia. Revista International de Filosofia*, no. 6: 99–116.

———. 2010. "The Birth of Biopolitics: Lectures at the Collège De France, 1978–1979." http://www.openisbn.org/download/0312203411.pdf.

Fuchs, Christian. 2013. *Digital Labour and Karl Marx*. New York, NY: Routledge.

———. 2015. "Internet and Society: Social Theory in the Information Age (Paperback)—Routledge." Accessed March 30. http://www.routledge.com/books/details/9780 415889926/.

Garfinkel, Harold. 1967. *Ethnomethodological Studies*.Englewood Cliffs, NJ: Prentice-Hall.

Graeber, David. 2011. *Debt—Updated and Expanded: The First 5,000 Years*. Updated Exp edition. Brooklyn: Melville House.

Hakken, David. 1987. "Reproduction in Complex Social Formations." *Dialectical Anthropology* 12 (2): 193–204. doi:10.1007/BF00263324.

———. 1999. *Cyborgs@Cyberspace?: An Ethnographer Looks to the Future*. New York: Routledge.

———. 2000. "Resocialing Work? Anticipatory Anthropology of the Labor Process." *Futures* 32: 767–75.

———. 2003. *The Knowledge Landscapes of Cyberspace*. New York, NY: Routledge.

———. 2009. "The Future of the Journal in Asia: An Information Ethnographer's Notes." In *The Future of the Academic Journal*, edited by Bill Cope and Angus Phillips, 301–18. Oxford, UK: Chandos Publishing.

Hakken, David, and Barbara Andrews. 1993. *Computing Myths, Class Realities: An Ethnography of Technology and Working People in Sheffield, England.* Boulder: Westview Press.

Haraway, Donna. 1988. "Situated Knowledges: The Science Question in Feminism and the Privilege of Partial Perspective." *Feminist Studies* 14 (3): 575–99.

———. 1990. *Simians, Cyborgs, and Women: The Reinvention of Nature.* First Thus edition. New York: Routledge.

Hardt, Michael, and Antonio Negri. 2001. *Empire.* Cambridge, MA: Harvard University Press.

———. 2009. *Commonwealth.* First edition. Cambridge, MA: Belknap Press.

———. 2012. *Declaration.* New York: Argo-Navis.

Holloway, John, Wendy Varney, and Richard Gosden. 2010. *Change the World Without Taking Power: The Meaning of Revolution Today.* Third edition. London: Pluto Press.

Kling, Rob, and C. Suzanne Iacono. 1995. "Computerization Movement and the Mobilization of Support for Computerization." In *Ecologies of Knowledge: Work and Politics in Science and Technology*, edited by Susan Leigh Star, 113–53. New York: State University of New York Press.

Latour, Bruno. 1993. *We Have Never Been Modern.* Translated by Catherine Porter. Cambridge, MA: Harvard University Press.

———. 2005. *Reassembling the Social: An Introduction to Actor-Network-Theory.* Oxford University Press.

Latour, Bruno, and Steve Woolgar. 2013. *Laboratory Life: The Construction of Scientific Facts.* Princeton, NJ: Princeton University Press.

Lessig, Lawrence. 2004. *Free Culture: How Big Media Uses Technology and the Law to Lock Down Culture and Control Creativity.* New York, NY: Penguin Press.

Marx, Karl. 1967. *Capital: A Critical Analysis of Capitalist Production.* Edited by Friedrich Engels. New York: International Publishers.

Masini, Eleanora. 1993. *Why Future Studies?* London, UK: Grey Seal Books.

Mead, George H. 1934. *Mind, Self, and Society from the Standpoint of a Social Behaviorist.* Chicago: University of Chicago Press.

Mills, C. Wright. 2000. *The Sociological Imagination.* Oxford University Press.

Ostrom, Elinor. 1990. *Governing the Commons: The Evolution of Institutions for Collective Action.* Cambridge University Press.

Paolillo, John. 2005. "Language Diversity on the Internet." In *Measuring Linguistic Diversity on the Internet*, edited by UNESCO Institute for Statistics. 43–89. France: UNESCO.

Patterson, Orlando. 1982. *Slavery and Social Death: A Comparative Study.* First edition. Cambridge, MA: Harvard University Press.

Said, Edward W. 1979. *Orientalism.* First edition. New York: Vintage.

Sardar, Ziauddin. 1999. *Rescuing All Our Futures: The Future of Futures Studies.* Santa Barbara: Praeger.

Shapin, Steven, and Simon Schaffer. 2011. *Leviathan and the Air-Pump: Hobbes, Boyle, and the Experimental Life (New in Paper).* Princeton, NJ: Princeton University Press.

Slaughter, Richard A. (ed.). 2002. *New Thinking for a New Millennium: The Knowledge Base of Futures Studies.* London, UK: Routledge.

Spinoza, Benedict de. 2005. *Ethics.* Translated by Edwin Curley. London: Penguin Classics.

Star, Susan Leigh. 1999. "The Ethnography of Infrastructure." *American Behavioral Scientist* 43 (3): 377–91.

Strum, Shirley S., and Bruno Latour. 1987. "Redefining the Social Link: From Baboons to Humans." *Social Science Information* 26 (4): 783–802. doi:10.1177/05390188 7026004004.

Suchman, Lucy A. 1987. *Plans and Situated Actions: The Problem of Human-Machine Communication*. Second edition. Cambridge University Press.

Turkle, Sherry. 2012. A*lone Together: Why We Expect More from Technology and Less from Each Other*. First Trade Paper edition. New York: Basic Books.

Wiener, Norbert. 1948. *Cybernetics*. New York: J. Wiley.

Williams, Brackette F. 1991. *Stains on My Name, War in My Veins: Guyana and the Politics of Cultural Struggle*. Durham: Duke University Press Books.

Winner, Langdon. 1980. "Do Artifacts Have Politics?" *Daedalus* 109 (1): 121–36.

Žižek, Slavoj. 2004. "The Ongoing 'Soft Revolution.'" *Critical Inquiry* 30 (2): 292–323. doi:10.1086/421126.

3 Views of the Computing and Social Change Nexus

INTRODUCTION

In the previous chapter, we presented the analytical concepts that we will use in the rest of the book. This chapter and the next address the specifics of our current times with regard to the computing social change nexus. In this chapter, we use our concepts in multiple ways. First, in the spirit of Raymond Williams's *Key Words* we begin with two issues of terminology, one regarding information technology, or IT, and the other about our "information society" (Williams 1985). Clarifying these terms helps prepare for the chapter's primary task, specifying the ways digital technologies (DTs) both are and are not of importance to current social formation reproduction (SFR).

After clarifying terms, we present an analysis of a specific event, namely the role of computing in the recent (and in many ways, continuing) crisis that began in 2007. This analysis offers an example of a useful way to delineate the relationships between computing and change in SFR. We then critique several problematic ways that other scholars and popular writers have framed computing events and specified the social significance of computing phenomena from about 1990 to 2010. Three ways concentrate on economic or political-economic trends: the new economy, the networked society, and the rise of cyberfacture. The following five ways offer more social or socioeconomic analyses: globalization, virtual organization, non-instrumental computing (e.g., Web 2.0), big data, and the sharing economy.

These framings generally share a "society transformed" perspective, where computing is believed to have engendered a new way of life. Each framing shares the presumptions that a transformation was caused by digital technology mediation, implying more generally that social changes are driven by the nature of digital technology and that the changes are inevitable—a form of technological determinism. These analyses also share the position that David Golumbia identifies as "computationalism" (Golumbia 2009). In philosophy and psychology, this term is used to characterize any theory of mind where thoughts are seen as computations. Golumbia extends the term to include views where computation is seen as the appropriate way to frame any problem, including social ones.

Our aim in these critiques is to show how technological determinism and computationalism undermine the value of these analyses, resulting in simplistic, causative accounts of social change. These approaches obscure, rather than account for, the important changes in the dynamics of SFR. Our critique does not mean that we see *no* relation between computing and social change, including change in SFR. Our book is based on understandings that this relationship is important but also complex.

- As in the crisis beginning in 2007, computing can and does play a very important role in certain changes in SFR dynamics.
- In the future, forms of computing can be structured to embody values whose pursuit can change SFR dynamics fundamentally.
- The mere demonstration of a simple correlation between computing and some other event is not sufficient to demonstrate that computing *caused* the event. More compelling arguments need to be made if one is to make that claim.

In short, the social role of computing can be accounted for, but not if the analysis is essentialist or simplistically identified as a single cause. Detailing this is the task of the bulk of the chapter. In Chapter 4, building on assessments of computing-related social transformation and social non-transformation, we go on to identify specific transformational potentials in some selected computing practices.

THE FIRST TERMINOLOGY PROBLEM: INFORMATION TECHNOLOGY, INFORMATION AND COMPUTING TECHNOLOGY, OR DIGITAL TECHNOLOGY?

In their abbreviated forms, "IT" and "ICT" (which stands for information and computing technology) seem to refer to different things. However, there is little point in digitizing something (that is, turning it into the kind of information represented by 1s and 0s) unless one wants to do something with it, which requires sending it somewhere (i.e., communicating it). Conversely, knowing what to do about a message generally requires context awareness (i.e., how it became information). Hence, "IT" and "ICT" differ little in meaning, and thus their generally interchangeable use makes sense.

There is however a problem implicit in the way the two terms are normally used, which is to equate the digital forms of IT and ICT with all their forms, thereby terminologically obliterating ITs and ICTs that are not digital (Hakken 1999). Implicit is the notion that digital forms are the only information/communication technologies worth bothering about. Previous ITs/ITCs, like stories, books, newspapers, speeches, telephones, etc., fall from consideration, not worth attending to empirically, or are considered to be of value only as a foil for digital technologies. The frequent contrasting of the current "revolution" in ITs/ICTs with the previous "revolutions," like the one associated with industrialization or with the Gutenberg press, appear to contradict such "DT only" usages. This contradictory usage pattern suggests it performs important ideological functions, such as to establish ITs (or ICTs) as ontologically distinct entities, things that exist on their own, without a history. Among other things, this ideology affords campaigns to sell digital commodities.

The usages have important implications. One is that non-digital solutions need not be attended to. In the academic field of human-computer interaction, for example, there is often support for the presumption that the only appropriate solutions worth considering are digital ones (Hakken 2004). At a conceptual level, the presumption inhibits empirical inquiry into what is both shared by and what separates digital from non-digital ITs/ICTs, what actually makes the latter unique.

We can avoid ambiguity in using both "IT" and "ICT," as well as the disappearing of non-digital information and communication technologies. All we need to do is refer to the now-dominant computer-based forms of such technologies as digital technologies. This allows us to use "ITs" and "ICTs" more broadly, to mean more that just DTs and to include all the ways humans have developed to represent information and communicate it, both non-digital and digital technologies. Recognizing all these as ITs encourages attention to what distinguishes DTs from ITs, as well as allowing us to understand their actual social correlates, rather than the potential ones.[1]

THE SECOND TERMINOLOGY PROBLEM: THE DIKW CYCLE TODAY: AN INFORMATION SOCIETY, OR A (TOO MUCH) INFORMATION SOCIETY?

Another consequence of the common usage of "IT" and "ICT" is the implication that it is DTs that create information societies (ISs), and thus that all previous societies were not ISs. Yet this would only make sense if previous societies had experienced no informational moment—if there were no times when data attained the aura of significance. That would mean no second stage (and thus no third or fourth) in the data-information-knowledge-wisdom (DIKW) procedure discussed in Chapter 2. But the DIKW process is present in *all* of the social formation types of which we have anthropological knowledge (Hakken 2003). Thus, all human societies are "information societies," in that the informational moment, like the data, knowledge, and even wisdom moments, is an important moment in the DIKW cycle. Characterizing only ours as an "information society" is ethnocentric, ideological, and of little use in social theory. Further, it encourages a conception of current social formations as being ontologically distinct, while at the same time discouraging thinking about how such conceptions might be validated.[2]

In Chapter 1, we pointed out how our current "info-glut" means the label "information society" does not make current sense. Spread of the use of DTs means that current social formation reproduction, and the people caught up in it, would face an impossible task if the knowledge quality of each item in the growing pile of communicated information had to be evaluated. This glut of information problem is of course a direct consequence of the increased use of digital technologies—desktop PCs, laptops, tablets, "smart" phones, etc.

We want to place our current social formations with their info-glut problems in a long-term historical, ethnological context. Over time, some social formation types have reached a kind of stability that enables them to exist for a long time. This can be true even when more complex social formations have developed alongside them, which has been the case for what anthropologists call "hunting and gathering," "horticultural," "pastoral," and "agricultural" social formations. It is arguable that an important aspect of their stability derives from having achieved proportionality among the DIKW moments. Data can be contextualized, and subsequent information can by and large be evaluated, then knowledge evaluated experientially. This is not the state of current social formations. Proportionality among the DIKW moments is *not* characteristic of them, in that they are *un*able to evaluate much information, not able to say what it means. A primary task of contemporary humans is figuring out how to live despite having too much information, the meaning of which is not clear. Yet we humans are also encouraged, by those we called "informationists," to treat "information" as something that is quasi-sacred: now that there is so much more information out there, it all needs to be considered before taking action. Informationists commonly deal with info-glut by postponing decisions while "more information is gathered," thereby often avoiding decision-making altogether. Informationism amounts to a preference for staying in the informational moment, inhibiting a commitment to collective interpretations because there is always more information to be gathered. It is a problematic attitude particular to social formations highly mediated by DTs.

The differentiation between simple and expanded reproduction made in Chapter 2 is suggestive of a way to deal with, rather than surrender to, info-glut. This problem is a breakdown in the normal movement from one step in the DIKW cycle to the next. An example of a "simple" form of this breakdown is when an apprentice fails to hear specific instructions necessary to her knowing how to replicate the master's practice. An example of an extended, more difficult expanded breakdown form would be the failure of a group to continue a discourse over how to adapt existing procedures to new conditions, or a failure to produce new ways to specify the significance of some new information. In either case, the breakdown produces the incapacity to proceed from the information to the knowledge stage in the DIKW cycle, which is problematic in the same way a failure to move from the knowledge to the wisdom moments of the procedure would be. There is reason to worry that the current moment is one of extended breakdown, that a key characteristic of today is a general difficulty in going from information to knowledge. Specifically, while the amount of information has increased greatly, growth in effective ways to assess information in terms of its meaning, to turn it into knowledge, has not kept pace.

There is indeed reason to believe that this situation has arisen only recently. This problem is now so extensive that it gives an ironic twist to the much-hyped, popular name for our social formation type, that of being an "information society" (Beniger 1986; Masuda 1980). "Information society" would be a useful label if it were being used to draw attention to how the information step in the human information procedure has expanded so much—its importance so exaggerated as to take up such a large portion of social activity that it threatens social formation reproduction. The arrival of an "information overload"—that is, having masses of information we don't know what to do with—is a matter of a disproportionality (Eppler and Mengis 2004). What profoundly extends our social formations' reproduction problems is not just a surfeit of information. It is also an extended breakdown in shared techniques to identify its meaning, i.e., to create knowledge.

We are stuck in the informational moment of the DIKW cycle. The emergence of the (too much) information society is clearly connected to overwhelming success in developing, and getting aspects of SFR dependent on the use of, new digital information technologies. Digital informing has not been accompanied by a concomitant development of knowledging, digital or otherwise. Not only have we not developed new "knowledging" institutions (Hakken 2004) sufficient in scale to the huge amounts and the new forms of information, we have also marginalized many of the knowledge creation means, like encyclopedias and academic journals, on which we relied until recently. (In Chapter 7, we address creating new knowledge institutions to address this problem.) This state of imbalance between informing and knowledging is one reason why we find one popular current theory of value, the knowledge theory described below, so unpersuasive. While we might *like* to be a knowledge society, we are too overwhelmed by information, much of it unprocessable with the currently accepted knowledge means, to justify even pretending to be one. Consider again the common problem of the contemporary human: having to act in the face of a great deal of information without effective knowledge extraction tools.

The terms "information," "knowledge," and even "data" are often used interchangeably. The situation described above is the reason we think it is important to differentiate systematically among them. That is, something is "known" only when a socially significant group is able to articulate the significance of some information, and a large proportion of the relevant individuals agree to act as if it were known, in concert with this articulation—that is, to perform, not attack, the expression of the knowledge (Hakken 2003). The emergence of digital technologies has greatly afforded the informational moment. While in some cases, it may have contributed to knowledge,

DTs have mostly merely expanded humans' capacity to structure data. DTs often exacerbate rather than help us cope with the ambiguities that follow frequently from increased informational moments. These moments hint that juxtaposing some data points may be meaningful, but about the actual meaning, there is no consensus. This is why the "Information Age" might just as legitimately be called an "Age of Ambiguity" or, in Langdon Winner's terms, the era of "Mythinformation" (Winner 1986).

The academic response to the data deluge, the creation of programs on "big data" (or, named more respectfully, "data science") is at the time of writing presented as the most pressing task for informatics. (In the US, the use of this term as a label indicating a renewal in computer science is of interest, as it is pointing toward information rather than knowledge.) The data science label is, to us, terminologically and thus substantively inappropriate. In our understanding, the pressing need is not to double down on the creation of even more information via more formal attention to data. Rather, what is needed are new, more robust institutions for evaluating existing information from a knowledge-creation perspective. If what we need is more and better institutions for creating knowledge, we don't need to go *back* on the DIKW continuum from the study of information to the study of data, but rather forward. We need knowledge studies rather than data science (see Chapter 8 for an extended treatment of this issue).

THE ILLUSTRATIVE CASE: THE ROLE OF INFORMATION TECHNOLOGIES IN THE SOCIO-ECONOMIC MELTDOWN OF 2007

As is often the case during one of the transnational crises that periodically afflict capitalist political economies, a large body of literature regarding what to do about it quickly emerged in the US.[3] The crisis talk focused mostly on what to do "right now," downplaying reflection on what caused it. We want to analyze the crisis and highlight the intimate links between computing and the emerging crisis in current SFR. This will orient us toward a discussion of values, and a new set of values, later in the book.

Generally, the literature manifested what C. Wright Mills called the "crackpot realism" of American public discourse (Mills 2000). The length, virulence, and distinctive features of this crisis eventually evoked a deeper examination of causes. The broadly spread meltdown, and the changes in SFR associated with it,[4] became the subject of social science and humanities scholarship. Often, the argument advanced was that fundamental changes were taking place in global work, economic, and political structures. Writers on the crisis often connected it causally to computing and the emergence of a computer-related value regime (McLean and Nocera 2010). Even these accounts failed to specify the actual connections among the three trends—computing, the value regime, and the crisis.

In broad-brush terms, three specific aspects of computationalist computing played a central role in the 2007 socio-economic crisis. First, computing played a key role in the creation and marketing of new financial instruments. Computer professionals who became known as "quants" (Patterson 2010) created the financial instruments that gained the most public attention: the sub-prime mortgages (largely in the US). They also created new financial commodities that collateralized debt in new forms. These forms were engineered by mixing several financial components into complex and largely opaque new entities. They were sold via new international markets in securities, along with parallel, equally non-transparent credit default insurance. Computing was implicated in the emergence and trade of all these commodities. Given their complexity, none could have existed without it, but computing also helped create both their opacity and their general acceptance. As they were computed things, only computer professionals were expected to understand them.

Nor was the role of computing merely that of creating *the possibility* of doing such things. Only a few of the many things that could have been done with computers were actually done (Tett 2009). The financial instruments were developed with what computer people call "affordances"—the pushes or possibilities that, given pre-existing developments or "path dependencies," are likely to happen unless action is taken to prevent them. The prior computing that made these new commodities possible was done in order to *create things like them*, a consequence of the mix of the particular entrepreneurial and technical practices built into contemporary financial computing. In the sense that new financial commodities were central aspects of the crisis, and that computing was central to their creation, computing brought about the crisis.

Second, computing forms were developed that afforded the transformation of pre-existing, mostly national capital markets into an international, demi-global one. Just as the desire for more profit via new commodities to trade drove more computing, so too was the development of international computing networks incentivized by the desire to widen and release capital markets from national regulation. Indeed, the two go together. Prospects for profitable trading in new financial instruments were directly related to the extent to which the reach of the capital market could be made bigger. However, the modalities of this market were formed without the creation of a parallel set of governance tools to regulate trade. In *The Wealth of Nations*, Adam Smith long ago pointed out the importance of governance when extra value was to be realized in new forms of capital (Smith 1863). The problems of weak governance were exacerbated in the current crisis by the fact that these financial commodities were largely conceptual. They were not part of what economics refer to (delightfully!) as the *real* economy. A consequence of the implementation of a computing-enabled but institutionally underdeveloped capital market was increased volatility and market fluctuation, another way in which computing caused the crisis.

Finally, there were the widely adopted, computer-generated models of the risks to sellers and buyers associated with trade in the new financial instruments, also central to generating crisis. These too were created by quants. As the instruments were new, there was no "track record" of actuarial data on which to base judgments regarding trading risks. One consequence was major difficulty in pricing them, a difficulty exacerbated by the absence of international governance forms or experience with their use. Markets in the new commodities, and global trade in them, might well have remained marginal if not for the development and adoption of complex, algorithm-based computer risk models.

These computer-based risk models were not well understood, but were widely adopted anyway. They were complex and based on the computationalist assumption that detailed models would capture relevant risk factors, and risk would follow statistically normal distributions. They became the basis of price setting and were treated as reliable. In retrospect, the models failed, as has been pointed out by numerous scholars and commentators, most famously in the black swan metaphor of (Roubini and Mihm 2010). The risk models did not, in fact, incorporate the risk of a general "systemic" failure—the one that actually occurred. In the computationalist mindset, models presume that modeled phenomena have systemic properties. Algorithmic models must presume systematicity and thus could not incorporate the impossible to quantify "black swan/long tail" risks, like general system failure. This reliance on information filled computationalist models that presumed that systemic properties also caused the crisis.

THE CRISIS, COMPUTING, AND PRICE UN-KNOWABILITY

The creation and marketing of new financial instruments, the semi-globalization of financial markets, and the computer-generated risk models were necessary to the financialization that by 2008 mediated upwards of 80% of the US economy (Tett 2009). The absence of any one of them might have rendered the others less important. All three were central to a computing regime, a computing socio-technological system in the sense of Thomas Hughes (2011), or a computing technology actor network in the science, technology, and society language of Callon and Latour (Callon and Latour 1992). In the absence of such a computing regime, there may have been a crisis, but it would likely have taken a different, probably less virulent form. As such, it would have been more easily dealt with by previously understood, Keynesian means, rather than the extraordinary interventions of bank nationalizations and the $800 billion Troubled Asset Relief Program.

These affordances of computing emerged during the high points of two influential context factors. One was neo-liberal economics and politics, which by the time of the crisis had become a significant influence in many nations. Neo-liberalism generally aimed to maximize the role of markets in the reproduction of social formations. The other was globalizationism. While not so much an intervention initiative like neo-liberalism, globalizationist rhetoric was more a presumed analytical perspective. It discouraged attention to the specific geographical ambit of markets, presuming they all tended toward being global in scope. While neo-liberalism led to increases in the influence of already powerful economic actors (e.g., corporations), globalizationism made substantial increases in the scale of some (but not all, or even most) aspects of contemporary SFR. Globalization made it appear "natural" and not to be resisted. Increased corporate power enabled a broader international reach, while a broader reach enabled increased corporate power—a symbiotic relationship.

Both neo-liberal economics and globalizationalist rhetoric were enabled by and mediated by the computing practices described above. The combination of these neo-liberal and globalizing changes in power and scale amplified the crisis consequences of the forms of computing described above. Consider first the unevenness of upscaling, a kind of demi-globalization. While some practices have been greatly upscaled (e.g., the switch from largely national to an essentially global trading of/in capital), several others have not (e.g., regulation of enforceable procedures for converting commodities back into investable resources, or capital). The co-occurrence of the forms of computing described above *with* demi-globalism led some sharp observers (e.g., Gillian Tett 2009) to identify a problem early on that is quite distinctive of this crisis: namely, the existence of a large class of purported assets where, while the *past* value was known, the current value was not. Indeed, in at least three important senses, their current value was *unknowable*.

The un-knowability derived first from how traders ascribe a value to an asset. The way to do this, according to the European Basel II accounting conventions, is to "mark to market," that is, to ascribe as the value of an asset the value the asset fetched when last traded. Marking to market makes sense and works well as long as markets are active. However, when in 2008 many markets (such as sub-prime mortgages) seized up, it was no longer possible to mark to market. As there were few, if any, "free market" sales of the "troubled" assets, one could only, in the words of one trader quoted by the *Financial Times*, "mark to myth."[5]

Second, when the difficult to value or "troubled" assets were sold, the buyer was generally some government or government-controlled entity. The sale prices had mainly to do with the state's desires to save financial institutions that were "too big to fail" and/or to concentrate the assets in a "bad bank." The value of the asset then becomes what is convenient/desirable for a state, not a market, to make it—a poor guide to its "real" worth.

Third, discovering prices was, and remains, difficult, because while capital in the form of computered information markets has become globally fungible, there are no global practices capable of certifying value in even these weak ways (mark to myth or state-dictated) outlined above. In order for a market in capital to give useful prices, an infrastructure of social institutions is needed, including laws, regulatory agencies, and institutions to certify requisite skills. Further, there need to be ways for buyers to meet sellers, e.g., a marketplace. In the absence of an infrastructure operating on a global scale, all that can be done is to make up new stories or "myths" about what value would be in a notional global market and hope that people collude in them.[6] The International Monetary Fund estimated in March 2009 that the crisis had destroyed something like 50 trillion dollars in value, leading Gillian Tett to estimate that many assets would ultimately be redeemable for only 5% of their face value (Tett 2009). The accuracy of *any* such estimate is doubtful, because current values are either a) unknowable because of the inability to mark them to market or, b) have been assigned arbitrarily to meet some state objective, or c) the prices are concocted by and colluded in by a group of people for whom any price is better than no price.

The unique characteristics of this crisis, then, are precisely these huge, persisting socio-economic spaces of *un-knowability*. The lack of fit between the particular forms of computer-mediation of financial assets on the one hand, and the substantial upping of the scale at which some aspects of social formations (but not others) reproduce on the other means there is no way to discover the value of "troubled" assets. Having to deal with *un*-valuable assets stymied the considerable efforts of many governments around the world to "unfreeze" seized-up credit markets. *This truly is a more general crisis in the ability of social formations to reproduce, and not merely an economic crisis.* More neo-liberalism, in the form of "austerity," and "globalization" of the sort that has narrowed the ability of states to intervene in SFR (e.g., the Euro) have extended rather than lessened the crisis, in part because forms of computing require people to act as if they know what cannot be known.

We have presented here a computing-related analysis of change in the dynamics of recent SFR, an analysis that, while complex, allows us to be precise about how this form of computing relates causally to the form of change in SFR. The rapid generalization of market control of SFR fostered by neo-liberalism and afforded by globalizationist thinking was the starting point. Into these contexts were introduced specific forms of finance-related computing that fostered deep crises in several markets. In particular, the forms of computing made the identification of prices close to impossible, which made loosening up the markets even harder. The form of computing can be seen as bringing SFR to the brink of breaking down altogether, which raises questions about the ethical responsibilities of computer professionals. No wonder *Financial Times* columnists began questioning the future of capitalism.

The crisis indeed changed the dynamics of the dominant value regime, but not because of changes in the basic relationships among owners, managers, workers, and consumers. What changed was the ways important cultural constructs, including legal instrumentalities, were deployed. Analytically, the crisis should be linked to a daring effort to commodify "thinking stuff," (i.e., intellectual property-IP).[7] This occurred at the same time as a powerful alternative, a commons-type, anti-commoditization regime (i.e., free/libre and open-source software, or FLOSS) grew in the heart of the DT realm. FLOSSing, and the broader, open cultural imaginary that it exemplifies, undercut the IP move and thus also contributed to the crisis.

What was "wrong" with how computing was done before and as the crisis was breaking? The failure of the new property regime and the instruments it generated were at the heart of the crisis. In later chapters, we will argue that we need to compute differently if we are not to experience repeating crises like the one that occurred in 2007 (and is still ongoing). We need to look to ideas incubated in alternative traditions in computing, and we need to put away the computationalist imperative that computers will magically solve problems. Socially robust forms of computing derived from what we will call the strong program[8] in social computing need to be developed and implemented more. Some computer practitioners have ideas about how to pursue socially robust and enduring computing (Hakken, Teli, and D'Andrea 2010). Their ability to thrive, however, depends inter alia upon changed valuation practices (see Ostrom 1990).

PROBLEMATIC FRAMINGS TYPE 1: ECONOMIC AND POLITICAL ECONOMIC

With this example of a specific way in which computing contributed to the crisis in SFR in mind, we turn to a discussion of what is less compelling about several other attempts to capture the computing/social change relationship. Unlike our example, the perspectives we are about to examine do not aim to explicate specific computing/social change connections; instead, they aim to analyze computing and social change in general. For example, in the 1990s, the trope that the adoption of DTs moves us beyond an information society to a knowledge society spread widely. This amounted to the contention that change in the process of going from information to knowledge was the dominant mediator of SFR. To illustrate the breadth of the articulations of this idea, we examine three diverse economic approaches. Each one gives causative centrality to knowledge as driving change in SFR dynamics, but none of them offer an explanation of the dynamics as powerful as the example above.

Computing and the New Economy

The spread of digital technologies quickly became associated with the idea of a "new economy." A review of the business sections of large-circulation Western newspapers during the late 1990s would have established the importance in popular thought of the "new economy," as well as DT's role in it. The notion of a "new" economy implies a pre-existing, "old" one. In the second half of the 20th century in the US, a case for a new economic dynamic emerged from the simultaneous presence of several positive economic phenomena, including continuing expansion, fast growth, low inflation, and low unemployment—thus, the "permanent" or "the Great Moderation," as it came to be called (Bernanke 2000). According to the "old" neo-classical economics that were academically regnant in the US, these factors couldn't co-occur for long periods of time. Many social theorists championed and mainstreamed this "new economy" idea (Pupo and Thomas 2010; Shepard 1992). A related "old" law was that of the inevitability in business cycles of alternating growth and decline. Since the co-presence of the first four phenomena, and the absence of the last, indicated that the old "laws" of economics no longer applied, the new economy demanded a new economics.

DTs were generally treated as one, if not "the," important factor responsible for the new economy. If productivity rose faster than income via use of DTs, profits could continue to increase, allowing for continuous economic expansion. However, attempts to empirically justify such connections between the new economy and computing were stymied for a long time by the so-called "IT productivity paradox." From at least the 1960s, increased investment in technology was associated with *declining* rather than increasing productivity statistics (Attewell 1994). In the words of Nobel laureate Robert Solow, "You can see the computer age everywhere but in the productivity statistics" (Solow 1987).

The embarrassing absence of the expected increase in productivity was poorly explained by various ad hoc means, including the "old" idea of technology "convergence" (Korotayev and Zinkina 2014). In convergence theory, to be a leader in adopting an application is risky, because costs are high and others can quickly take advantage of your efforts with less capital. Such economic calculations mean that the advantages of applying new technologies would tend to dissipate quickly, so it would be easier, and much cheaper, for most producers to wait to innovate until a few have worked out the bugs. Convergence would predict a slow pace of technology deployment. In fact, firms continued to deploy DTs massively *in the face of* the declining productivity statistics—Attewell's productivity paradox (Attewell 1994). Moreover, convergence predicts declining profits, but profits were generally increasing. From a convergence perspective, the actual correlates of DTs look even more paradoxical.

In about 1995 US productivity statistics started to increase, and the embarrassing "IT productivity paradox" was (temporarily, it turns out) put to rest. In particular, "new economy" advocates seized upon the argument that increased productivity was at last a consequence of the latest corporate knowledge technologies. These included inventory control/enterprise resource planning systems, demand forecasting, and the flexible scheduling of production, computer-supported collaborative work, intranet knowledge bases, and interorganizational data sharing. They were held to have narrowed the gap between supply and demand so much that an epochal productivity surge had overcome whatever had previously held it back (Pupo and Thomas 2010).

British sociologist Anthony Giddens argued that the emergence of a new economy, namely, the "knowledge economy," is structural "proof" that we are now a "knowledge society" (Hutton and Giddens 2000). Giddens exercised a substantial theoretical influence over Tony Blair's "new" Labour as well as Bill Clinton's Democratic administration. In a debate with Will Hutton in 2000, Giddens highlighted "the new role of knowledge as a factor of production" (Hutton and Giddens 2000, 4). He spoke of a "new knowledge economy," which, he argued, "[a]lmost certainly operates according to different principles from the industrial economy." He went on to claim this was "changing the very character of how we live and work" (Hutton and Giddens 2000, 5).

Giddens accounted for this transformative change in terms of increased information flow:

> [M]ost companies know pretty quickly what other companies are planning, because of the general profusion of information. Secrecy is much more difficult. Given the global nature of contemporary communications, there is no geographical isolation any longer.
>
> (Hutton and Giddens 2000, 26)

Giddens blurs the difference between information and knowledge. He also invokes popular, but simplistic, space/place contrasts. More problematic is that he ignores that the one overt primary task of corporate knowledge DT initiatives was to *prevent* general dissemination of company knowledge! In other words, world-transformative changes were to be traced to the abject failure of knowledge management technologies to accomplish a major intended goal.

Still, in his speech to the Federal Reserve in 2002, even the skeptical Federal Reserve Chairman Alan Greenspan spoke of DT-induced productivity increases (Greenspan 2002). The idea of a "new economy" was no longer treated as hype, because increase in productivity really did indicate new dynamics, including characteristics/functions of knowledge brought about by DTs. However, declining rates of productivity emerged again later in the 2000s, undermining the "new economy" theory. Following the social crisis of 2007, talk of a new economy was displaced by talk of the Great Recession.

Computing and the Network Society

The most influential scholarly articulation of the links between DT-induced change in knowledge and thus broader social change was that of geographer/urban sociologist Manuel Castells. His ideas were influential in scholarly and politically liberal policy circles, particularly, again, through his influence on both Tony Blair's and Bill Clinton's policies.

Castells's notion of the "network society" (Castells 1996) strove both to name and to account for the general dynamics of a new type of social formation, one that he believed had come (again) to dominate social reproduction.[9] After the turn of the century, Castells substituted "network society" for what he had previously called "information society," his term for the new social formation type. He did so on the anthropological ground that "knowledge and information were central in all societies" (Castells 2000); thus, he concluded that the "information society" label was misleading.[10] For Castells, the new dynamics derive from a profound shift in the locus of social process. A "space of flows" displaces the grounding of human activity in "particular places"—or, in the phrasing we prefer, space is "decoupled" from place. The salience of units like cities or nations to social reproduction was seen as decreasing. If geography is no longer a particularly meaningful framework against which to organize accounts of social relation and interaction flows, what alternative framing should replace it? For Castells, "networks," replace a topographic framing with an alternative topological one.

Castells's justification for the new "network society" label is not that networks themselves were socially new. Rather, networks were *re*-emerging in new forms, and displacing the centralized, hierarchical forms characteristic of organization and governance in the industrial society. The new networks were coming to dominate SFR because of DTs. Under conditions of capitalism, DT use disperses activity, distributes intelligence, and unhinges knowledge from place. "Network enterprises"—intra- but especially inter-organizational networks—replace firms as the chief unit of capital accumulation and replace states as the chief units of governance, creating a new, globally operating economy. A network society, he argued, has very different dynamics from an industrial society. Electronic networks facilitate more individuated identifying formation that replaces the collective units of organic solidarity so important to Marx, Weber, and Durkheim. The result is consummately Blairite and Clintonite, capitalism with neither a capitalist nor a working class:

> In the last analysis, the networking of relationships of production leads to the blurring of class relationships. This does not preclude exploitation, social differentiation, and social resistance. But production-based, social classes, as constituted, and enacted in the Industrial Age, cease to exist in the network society.
>
> (Castells 2000, 18)

Castells's model of contemporary social dynamics is similar in many was to the contemporary sociology of Barry Wellman (Wellman 2001), but its history is different. Initially and for a very long time, networking had been seen as the most typical form of human interaction, until it was displaced by the rise of hierarchies like states and corporations. By undermining these latter forms, DTs compel the re-emergence of networking. "But for the first time, new information/communication technologies allows (sic) networks to keep their flexibility and adaptability, thus asserting their evolutionary nature . . . Networks de-centre performance and share decision-making" (Castells 2000). It is difficult to ignore the parallel between Castells's view on the return of networking and Marx's view on the return of communism from its primitive forms when writing about pre-capitalist modes of production.

For all its academic popularity, a Castells's network is an oddly autonomous, quasi-biological, even self-determining entity:

> It works on a binary logic: inclusion/exclusion. All there is in the network is useful and necessary for the existence of the network. What is not in the network does not exist from the network's perspective, and thus must be either ignored . . . or eliminated. If a node in the network ceases to perform a useful function it is phased out from the network, and the network rearranges itself—as cells do in biological processes.
>
> (Castells 2000, 15)

The only way this description has empirical resonance is if Castells's networks are conceived as essentially informational rather than as organic-like entities. "A network is a set of interconnected nodes. A node is the point where the curve intersects itself" (2000, 15). These quotations capture the essentialist, "foundational" quality of Castells's account of the implications of DTs for SFR. Liberated from the inefficiency and ineffectiveness of hierarchy on the one hand and place boundedness on the other, DT-compelled networks manifest their underlying potential to evolve and remake SFR in their own image. The resulting social formation is driven by a "flow, flow, flow!" imperative, replacing the "accumulate, accumulate, accumulate" of Marx (Marx 1967).

Like other cyber-enthusiasts, Castells views these changes in epic terms, as a ". . . greater change in the history of technology than the technologies associated with the Industrial Revolution" (2000, 10). Like Giddens, Castells assigns a key place in the ascension of the network society to change in the social functioning of knowledge:

> [Characteristic of] this new technological paradigm is the use of knowledge-based, information technologies to enhance and accelerate the production of knowledge and information, in a self-expanding, virtuous circle. Because information processing is at the source of life, and of social action, every domain of our eco-social system is thereby transformed.
>
> (Castells 2000, 10)

Note again the way that any differences between information and knowledge are elided: ". . . knowledge-based information technologies . . ."

Knowledge changes, fudged to include informational ones as well, generalize their social impact via the network enterprises described above. These new forms are found "[at] the heart of the connectivity of the global economy and of the flexibility of informational production" (2000, 10).

In Castells argument, we can see a clear example of David Golumbia's idea of computationalism:

> Compuationalism manifests in messianic claims about sudden, radical, and almost always salutary changes in the fundamental fabric of politics, economics, and social formations . . . in the belief that computers inherently create distributed democratic forms; and more abstractly, in claims that we can ignore any number of pressing social problems by dint of some kind of unnamable change . . .
>
> (Golumbia 2000, 9).

We do not aim to diminish the importance of computing to social change, as manifested in our analysis of computing and the crisis. What we reject is these essentialist accounts that sweep away all before it, as if computing has one overwhelming, all-engrossing impact, rather than multiple complex correlates that are often contradictory. Similar problems are at the root of some overtly political leftist accounts of the computing/social change nexus, also mediated by knowledge, as in the ones we turn to now.

Computing and the Rise of "Cyber-Facture," a Cybernetic Revolution That May Increase Worker Power/ Revolutionary Potential

In 1994, once-New Leftists Carl Davidson, Ivan Handler, and Jerry Harris launched *cy.Rev: A Journal of Cybernetic Revolution, Sustainable Socialism & Radical Democracy*. In contrast to leftists critical of DTs-related knowledge changes (e.g., Aronowitz and DiFazio 2010; Noble 1999; Stoll 2005), *cy.Rev* celebrated the computer revolution. For it, the key to the revival of an American left was not to critique cyber-knowledge rhetoric, but to embrace it as a new social form:

> [A]n important revolution going on in the world today . . . [is] being driven by new developments in information technology . . . Digitalized knowledge has now become the major component in the production of new wealth. The information society is supplanting industrial society as surely as industrial society replaced agrarian society. The depth of these changes, however, has been largely ignored by much of the left community.
>
> (Davidson, Handler, and Harris 1994)

Once the change is recognized, previous Marxist notions have to be revised in light of these changes in knowledge.

There are new social divisions being created along with a realignment of classes and strata around many critical issues. The ground for organizing the class struggle is shifting; there are new dangers of prolonged joblessness, repression, chauvinism and war. But there are also new opportunities creating new possibilities for a democratic and ecologically sustainable socialism.

(Davidson, Handler, and Harris 1994, 4)

Like Castells and so many others (e.g., the National Science Foundation, or NSF), Davidson and his co-writers elide the information/knowledge distinction. They cited Alvin and Heidi Toffler's idea that the microchip was "changing everything" and argued that the change was "on the order of the agricultural revolution," going on to enthusiastically proclaim:

Intellectual capital, developed and held by knowledge workers and encoded in software and smart machines, is the key element of wealth in today's information capitalism. Physical labor and industrial machinery are now secondary to the value added by information.

(1994, 6)

We note the easy acceptance of the problematic notion of "intellectual capital," which we will explore further in Chapter 6. Following from the change in class structure are challenges to Marxism and radical theory. Knowledge workers have displaced the industrial proletariat. Hurry, progressives! Embrace the new order!

While to our knowledge, *cy.Rev* is no longer being published, its structural arguments influenced debate in several places, for example, the turn of the century anti-globalization movement. To develop effective alternative structuralistics to the dominant neo-classical ones, we want to be cautious of the political economism of Davidson and his colleagues.[11] We need to be empirical about computing and social change, avoiding both anti- and pro-capitalist techno-determinism (Hakken 2003). In Davidson's version, knowledge-change-inducing DTs cause a revolution in the forces of production, which in turn moves social dynamics onto new terrain. This parallels the argument of the Organisation for Economic Co-operation and Development that "[d]igitalized knowledge has now become the major component in the production of new wealth" (Hakken 2003). Its naive positivism about DT echoes Bernal and other inter-war socialists committed to a scientific-technical revolution, for whom this "way forward" substituted policy for politics.

We need to go beyond the more obvious problems of conceiving contemporary social formations as "knowledge societies," which is a poor way to characterize social formations unable to cope with an "information glut." The arguments for a "new economy," or "networked society," or "cyber-facture" all depend on the presumption that DT mediation makes us better able to extract knowledge from information. All three enthusiastically support a deterministic cyber worldview where computerization will solve all problems, rather than becoming arguably a problem itself. We submit that what needs to be attended to instead is the question of how the DT use-induced information glut actually makes knowledge creation more difficult.

Globalization and Computing

> *I am a technological determinist! Guilty as charged . . . If you can do it, you must do it, otherwise your competition will . . . [T]here is a whole new universe of things that companies, countries, and individuals . . . must do to thrive in a flat world.*
> —Thomas Friedman, *The World Is Flat*

Thomas Friedman's book is arguably the text with the most impact on popular understanding of globalization (Friedman 2007). In it, Friedman articulates a common, influential understanding of the role of computing, namely that it causes globalization. Technology (specifically computing technology) forces societies to develop, and in the process, to globalize. As the above statement acknowledges, such a position is determinist, holding that societies do what they must do. To be a determinist means there is no other option. And what must they do? They must globalize, but in order to do this, they must first implement necessary technology, most of it computer-based. Why? Because DT use has made the world flat—it has globalized, or at least it will in an inevitable process of globalization.[12] The position is analogous to Adam Smith's view on the necessity of law (Smith 2014), and could be read as meaning that any society failing to implement DTs (the rule of law) would not develop (would not become more wealthy than its neighbors). This deterministic view—that the use of DTs makes the world flat, and a flat world is highly competitive, which means competing to the broadest extent possible—is arguably the standard one in contemporary cultures.

The prominence of this determinist view is also a good reason for attending closely to globalist and the related upscaling discourses in a book on computing. This strident globalization rhetoric re-emerged in the 1990s.[13] It was "globalizationist" in that it presumed a one-way process of scale enlargement, a process inclined toward the most important social processes operating generally on a transnational, universal scale. Like Friedman, the new globalizationists usually see digitization as doing more than just accompanying globalization. Observable upward trends in scale were seen as the inevitable consequence of the use of digital technologies. The two processes were presumed to be tightly and inextricably linked, in a reinforcing, deterministic, causal loop, one in which digitization fosters globalization, and globalization further affords digitization.

This rhetoric confuses a process, that which is called globalization (a tendency toward massive social upscaling) with an end state, that of globality (where social relations generally operate at the global level). The existence of the trajectory is presumed to be the same as its end point. We can illustrate the confusion with the market in capital, a "best case" scenario for globalizationists. A major change upward *has* taken place in the scale of markets for capital, and therefore the reproduction of capital has scaled upward (that is, resources either invested or available for investing). It makes sense to characterize this as a change from largely national markets in capital *towards* a global market. Before the end of World War II, if one wanted access to capital—e.g., money to invest in a venture intended to make a profit—one normally got it from formal institutions within one's nation, via a market sphere set up for this purpose, such as national banks or national stock (share) markets. Colonialism was different because the capital was extorted from the colonized. Subsequently, a number of developments have contributed to the increasingly transnational character of access to capital via trade in, and therefore the reproductive scale of it (Dimson, Marsh, and Sutton 2002). They include:

- Creation of the Bretton Woods international institutions (including the World Bank and the International Monetary Fund);
- The development of a market in Eurodollars (that is, a located-in-Europe fund of US currency from which one could borrow);
- The spread of TCP/IP-based electronic communication (Transmission Control Protocol/Internet Protocol);
- Neo-liberal "reforms" that eliminated various national limits on the movement of capital, both foreign and domestic;
- The creation of crypto-currencies like bitcoin, which are money in new, non-fiat forms. (Fiat currencies are those issued by a state, which declares, in effect, "This is money," and it is generally treated as such, at least within the state's boundaries. A limitation of fiat moneys is that the value can be manipulated by the issuing state.)

Yet despite all these developments, there remain substantial limits to global capital markets/capital reproduction on a global scale. They include:

- Remaining formal and informal limits to foreign direct investment;
- Currency and currency-trading differences, to say nothing of currency trading manipulations—even for bitcoin, although for distinct reasons;
- Entire nations or sectors of nations where the infrastructure to handle capital is weak or non-existent.

While the moment of capital reproduction is more global, there are many obstacles to it becoming truly global. This is even truer for other aspects of contemporary SFR. Regulation remains largely national or at most, regional (e.g., the European Union). Even the relative closeness to having global capital markets is not enough to attain globality. There is not a single, worldwide capital reproducing SFR dynamic, one that has displaced national, regional, and other sub-global dynamics. Indeed, because of the 2007 Great Recession, capital markets are *less* global now than they were in 2006. For some, capital reproduction on a global scale—where capital relations in virtually every place on earth are subject to the global reproductive dynamic—may be a goal, but it has not been accomplished.

Many writers, including at least some *Financial Times* writers, seem to think that truly global capital may not be such a good idea. They agree with Adam Smith that capital markets have to be regulated, and they point out that only nations are currently equipped to regulate effectively (e.g., Tett 2009). We can imagine that global governance might replace national governance, perhaps via a state that exercises effective global sovereignty. Political theorists disagree about whether this is possible, let alone desirable. Moreover, as implied by Joseph Stiglitz's distinction between "governance" and "government," one needs to differentiate the process of how things are to be run from the formal institutions where that might take place (Stiglitz 2003). Technocrats tend to prefer governance via technologies. Their designed rationality provides channels of action distanced from the vagaries of human sentiment. On the other hand, democrats tend to be suspicious of such instrumentalities. So government need not be global to talk of global governance. Still, the failure of rapidly upscaling, "free" capital markets to foster strong, universal, democratic governance is a strong reason to stress the need for government and to keep in mind the gap between current globalization and true globality.

As manifested in the current controversies over immigration, the degree to which labor has become global does not match that of capital. Partly this is due to government policies—free movement within the European Union constituting an exception, albeit one constantly under threat. The location of some labor can be easily dispersed, e.g., "outsourced" or made virtual, but much of it cannot. Fields must be plowed, children bathed, and health care delivered in place. Indeed, scholars argue that the physicality of many forms of labor limit its capacity to move, and thus make it more difficult to lower the cost by migrating it to another nation (Stiglitz 2003). Could interventions that "free" capital while keeping labor "in (national) chains" have a purpose different from globalization? Might they be understood as intended to increase return to capital at the cost of labor, rather than as a "progressive" movement toward general upscaling? A relative reduction of the return to labor is achieved by such partial or "demi-"globalization, even as it is also a source of increased difficulty in the reproduction of capital. There is a strong correlation between the stagnation of wages and the lack of demand manifest in deflation (Wolf 2014).

Considering this actual demi-globalization from the perspective of DTs, it is possible to see a strong correlation between their recent use and the globalization of capital markets. DTs have afforded global markets, but do they necessarily or even primarily foster more general globality? Authors like Friedman confuse one correlation/affordance relationship, that of DTs and capital globalization, with a general relationship. In adopting for himself the label of "technological determinist," Friedman reveals simplification as the source of his confusion. Transnational capital long preceded the use of DTs. Admittedly, the scale at which this is happening is now much bigger, as discussed by Saskia Sassen (Sassen 2001). Nonetheless, it has been possible to transfer capital "instantaneously" since the late 19th century via telegraph, and the market in Eurodollars so central to the spreading ambit of transnational corporations after World War II *preceded* the institutionalization of electronic funds transfer. Moreover, there remain considerable differences in technological systems, both within and between nations. The differential uptake of proprietary and "open source" software is a good example of systemic difference. Likewise, bitcoin, which *could* play the role of a "global" currency, is not subject to state manipulation or to regulation. In practice, the primary use of bitcoin has been as an investment itself, even as a medium for speculation (Kostakis and Giotitsas 2014).

The correlates of technology are always manifesting within particular social contexts. This is the fundamental problem with technological determinism. A fundamental insight from analyses of techno-science, based on the Actor–Network Theory, is the need to differentiate the so-called "impacts" of a set of technical artifacts from the "correlates" that make up their context (Latour 2005). This limits the explanatory value of technology as the motivator of changes in SFR. Of course, there are occasions when a technological artifact should be examined on its own terms (e.g., when troubleshooting), and there are examples of how the use of a technology can reasonably be seen as having a strong exogenous impact on work or the economy (e.g., computerization of an office routine, or credit default swaps). These occasions, including the role of computing in current crisis, do not demonstrate that DT use compels globalization, nor that globalization *necessarily* compels DT use.

There is a reason for the recent, radical decline in comments on globalization in the pages of the *Financial Times*. It is clearer now that there is no pell-mell charge to globality. It appears further away than it was ten years ago. The scaling correlates of SFR dynamics are diverse and relate to each other in complex ways; certainly, they cannot be understood in terms of technological determinism.

PROBLEMATIC AND/OR UNDERDEVELOPED FRAMINGS PART 2: ECONOMIC AND SOCIAL AND SOCIO-ECONOMIC PERSPECTIVES

Virtual Organization

The phrase "the rise of virtual organizations" (VOs) is often used to describe how the changes in current organizations are induced by the use of DT. This means that VOs are a good lens to approach questions about the ways in which computing actually relates to organizational change. In 2008, the US National Science Foundation released a call for a new research initiative on VOs as social systems. This call defined a virtual organization as a group of individuals whose members and resources are dispersed geographically but function as a coherent unit through the use of cyber-infrastructure. This was only one of several efforts to define and describe VOs (Travica 1998).

Attention to computing and organization is surely warranted, but this NSF definition is inadequate for a number of reasons. At its baseline, it never specifies what a cyber-infrastructure is. It also seems to suggest that there is something unique about VOs gaining coherence despite the fact that they are in multiple locations, but multiple-place organized activity existed long before the invention of DTs.[14] Coherent outcomes among dispersed people have long been a significant part of capitalism, despite complex sets of relationships. The NSF concept also fails to include temporal dispersion, operating at different times, as also characteristic of VOs.

Today, organizations coordinate through computing, whereas previous large-scale, dispersed organizations coordinated through other means, like mail, phone, and meetings. Hence, the NSF definition suggests that the computing infrastructure (capable of handling all an organization's information and communication needs) is centrally important to making VOs different. A clearer conception of what a cyber-infrastructure is would help in evaluating this claim, but so would examining where VOs, and other new forms correlated with DT use, fit in relation to the history of organizations and organizing. Classic social theories about organization (Taylor 1914; Weber 2003) concentrated on control of work (labor process) and workers (bureaucracy). While not always framing difference in location/ time as important issues *per se*, control was nonetheless clearly theorized as being exercised *across* place and time. After World War II, organization studies (OS) began to argue that all organizations, including states, non-governmental organizations, and not-for-profits were importantly similar. This led OS to re-conceptualize the latter as being like the corporate form, which remained the approved model. Sociological OS therefore renamed itself "complex organizations."

The successes and failures of new forms of DT-enabled organizing in dealing with persistent problems should be key areas of research in OS. To what extent are new ways of organizing becoming actualized? Do those associated with or afforded by computing manage to organize with less formal structure? What makes these alternative forms effective? By the end of the 20th century, several concerns about the problems of corporate-style, complex organizations were being raised in OS. Their large sunk costs (e.g., wages, salaries, benefits, inflexibility, costs of building and idle time for expensive machines, etc.) pushed sociologists to form alternative ideas about how to organize. New models, such as social movements and networking, encouraged a shift in focus away from Taylorist ideal structures back to the process of organization itself. The OS name morphed again from the sociology of (complex) organizations (things) to the sociology of organization or organizing as a process (Clegg 1990).

Whatever the name, OS has since then become preoccupied with the problem of organization, whether it is single-spaced/timed or virtual, as well as focused on changes in organizing dynamics traceable to computing. Large-scale computing continues to fall short of its promise (productivity paradox), while long-standing work practices (e.g., "waterfall" software development) persist, in spite of being subject to critique (Clegg and Walsh 2004). OS scholars are now concerned with the search for alternative process forms, such as "business process engineering" (Hammer and Champy 2009). They ask if there are ways to achieve coordination without having to enforce control, and thus avoid all the problems of formal organization. In effect, can we organize without organizations? OS theorists attended to the considerable "anti-complexity" experimentation within formal organization, for example, matrix structures vs. bureaucracy that turn employees into sub-contractors. Some theorists examined relations between organizations as networked organizations, porous boundaries, and still others looked outside organizations at outsourcing, offshoring, etc. In the work of some scholars, there are clear examples of de-placed and out-of-same-time "virtual" entities that now are regularly "organized" or mediated by the use of linked DTs (e.g., Heaton 1999; Kogut and Metiu 2001; Mowshowitz 1994). Specific computing approaches, like computer-supported collaborative work and participatory design, and the tools in use (e.g., shared electronic whiteboards, multimedia conferencing systems, etc.) are designed to support experiments in organization.

FLOSS projects take the most advantage of such tools and approaches and thus are arguably the most developed alternative organizing practice. As "really existing" VOs, FLOSS projects offer an empirical basis for deciding whether computing significantly affords important new organizing dynamics. Stephen Weber has carried out one of the more sustained enquiries into FLOSS and its organizational affordances. For him,

> Standard arguments in organizational theory predict that increasing complexity in a division of labor leads to formal organizational structures ... In contrast ... much recent literature on the Internet and the 'new economy' argues that Internet technologies radically undermine organizational structures because they reduce the costs of communication and transaction toward an asymptote of zero. This is *supposed to* enable the formation of 'episodic communities on demand,' so-called virtual organizations that come together without friction for a particular task and then redistribute to the next task just as smoothly. [emphasis added]
>
> (Weber 2005, 171)

Weber is skeptical of the overstatement of this line of argument, which is vulnerable because of its technological determinism. Some DTs do seem to afford particular social patterns (Davis et al. 2005). According to Weber, this appears to be the case with FLOSS computing, that it is possible to identify configurations and conditions that *generally* afford alternative, less formal organizing, achieving effective organization virtually. Interest in computing-mediated virtual organization is piqued by the hope that better-designed computing tools will eventually be able to extend organization without having to extend organizations, the kind of change with the potential to give SFR a different dynamic. Identifying how broadly FLOSS-type mechanisms can be deployed and thereby actualize this potential should be the major goals of VO research. Can computing-enabled virtual organizing enable us to move beyond capital as well? To say that VOs *may* be transformative is not to say that they are; we need to be wary of the computationalist imperative. Nonetheless, understanding the organizing implications of FLOSSing may point the way toward VOs that are transformative.

Web 2.0 and the Semantic Web 3.0

In the early 2000s, there was significant buzz about Web 2.0, alluding to how it was different from Web 1.0. The old web, the one that emerged in the decade from 1993 to 2003 following the widespread adoption of World Wide Web standards (use of html, etc.), was a less interactive complex of websites, blogs, and e-commerce. Among the "new" phenomena identified as characteristic of Web 2.0 were:

- Social networking (first MySpace, then Facebook, and then, and then . . .);
- New online forms of gaming, especially those played massively;
- FLOSS projects, which are perhaps the most prominent of several innovations associated with an "open" cultural imaginary;
- Social computing, including things like "crowdsourcing."

Enthusiasts for these phenomena, even when they were only concepts, insisted that their use would be "game changing." Such enthusiasms continue: Trento recently attempted recently to promote itself as the home of "Web 3.0," a "semantic web" as different from Web 2.0 as Web 2.0 was from Web 1.0.

Questions about the difference between Web 2.0 and Web 1.0 have animated books and academic articles, presentations, and projects. We want to focus on what can be demonstrated empirically about how the relationship of computing to the social has actually changed, and on what such demonstrations suggest about the future. Most claims of Web 2.0 transformativeness that concentrate on social networking focus on the role it takes in creating monetary value. Many of the corporations with the most valuable stock in the world are either social networking entities (e.g., Facebook and Twitter) or those supporting them (Google, Apple, and Microsoft). This form of computationalism is linked to capital through the quantification of social relations and the claim of a new, computer-mediated-and-created market economy (van Dijck 2013).

In *Alone Together,* Sherry Turkle expresses concern about the effects social networking has on social relationships (Turkle 2012). In some regards, social networking is similar to other ways people relate to their social relations and try to make them stronger. Some researchers see this activity, including online gaming, use of programs like "Second Life," and time on social networking sites,[15] as largely non-instrumental. Turkle sees a difference in how the activities create solitude and possibly asociality. Further, these frames ignore the role of how the activity creates monetary value, for example, by the selling of advertising. When a person makes a video and posts it, Google makes money through the aggregate transformation of personal behavior into marketable data (Fuchs 2012). In these ways, Web 2.0 reinforces the reproduction of capital. The precise balance between the extent to which Web 2.0 entities afford alternatives vs. reinforce capital reproduction is yet to be determined.

Playbor and Other New Forms of Economic Activity

Ted Castronova (Castronova 2008) suggests that an economy based on the sale of commodities is being replaced by a new one based on "attention." Tapscott and Williams's *Wikinomics* claims that the older preoccupation on workers producing commodities for markets is being displaced by new, generally non-waged, collaborative activities, e.g., volunteering for Wikipedia and FLOSS projects (Tapscott and Williams 2010). Jeremy Rifkin has recently claimed that such peer-to-peer activities will over time replace capitalist social relations and cause them to whither and die (Rifkin 2014). In some new economic forms, value is also being created by the very acts of living, but is being appropriated by corporations outside of the employment relationship (Morini and Fumagalli 2010). In "ludo-capitalism" (Dibbell 2007), gaming shifts social reproduction away from industrial capitalism, where the prime sources of value production are labor, capital, or both. All of these are potential grounds for a new system, one where consumers produce value non-instrumentally and producers consume new forms—e.g., "knowledge" rather than commodities.

Consideration of activities like these has spawned a new vocabulary of terms like "playbor" and "prosumer," where neo-classical economics is replaced by "Wikinomics," and labor is carried out both by "prosumers" and, presumably, "conducers" (Tapscott and Williams 2010; Toffler 1980). Several scholars involved in the book *Digital Labor* (Scholz 2012) argue that despite appearances to the contrary, Web 2.0 and things like it are now the primary loci of value creation. We first encountered "playbor" as part of a critical discourse at the 2009 Digital Labor Conference (Hakken 2012). Some participants extended the Marxist language of exploitation to unpack playbor, arguing that, as these "play laborers" get no money in exchange for the results of their work, they are the most exploited. At the playbor conference, much of the ire directed at those exploiting playbor had an ethical valence— for example, the claim that such a condition was not "fair." The critiques were often framed in terms of "intellectual property," for the creation of which conducer/prosumer creators were given no, or poor, compensation. These analyses claim the existence of a major disparity between what those engaged in the activities think they are doing and the actual consequences of their activities, making the former an important new form of false consciousness. In playbor readings, for example, the video maker is being exploited. While value is being created, the creator is not being compensated by the entity that reaps the value.

These forms clearly change the activities through which contemporary social formations reproduce. Do they induce broad changes in political economy, including the creation of new types of capital, such as "bio-capital?" Are such claims indexical of major shifts in the locus of value production? If so, does it make sense to see what is created in this manner as a surplus? Is this similar to or very different from what results when an ordinary worker produces commodities that are more valuable than the wages she is paid? The spread of voluntary virtual organizations, the expansion of the number of the working poor, and free labor in the form of non-paid internships all suggest that important economic shifts are taking place. What is not clear, however, is whether they change in a fundamental way the dynamics of SFR, or if they are merely new ways that accompany the basic wage relationship. An associated question is to what extent it makes sense to see these new patterns as "exploitation."

In classic Marxism, value is created by the sale of commodities, but one commodity, labor, or the capacity to do work, is unique. Labor is unique because owners have a monopoly on access to the means of production, workers can be forced to produce more value than they are given in wages. Out of the unpaid work of reproducing labor power, as by housewives doing housework, or the worker acquiring the new skills needed to keep a job, a surplus is created, which becomes value. Might these new activities of bio-capital, prosumer, etc. be just new forms of non-compensated work to reproduce labor power, as opposed to a fundamentally new political economy? This is one way to think about, for example, the need in many intellectual professions today to have a high reputation, forcing professionals to spend time on the web to build it, e.g., not being hired because of a low "Klout Score".[16] Moreover, the peasant was forced by the enclosure of the commons to either migrate to the cities or starve. The househusband cooks for his wife so she can survive another day on the job. Those whose pay is being exploited as if it is unpaid work can often choose to stop. If they need the income, they can become online gold farmers or take on jobs on Mechanical Turk.

Capitalism has long responded to the need to reproduce itself by extending commoditization to ever more arenas of social life. The woman who once was a housewife now works in a low-paid job, but must buy fast food to feed her children because she doesn't have time to fix it herself. However, the commoditization process is not endless, and it is even possible that an economy based on Web 2.0 practices might create less overall surplus value or fewer valuable commodities in the long run. Many Web 2.0 activities look to be "disintermediation" (i.e., tending toward the elimination of intermediate stages of labor processes and thus lessening the need for labor). This eliminates more opportunities to realize value than it creates. A tendency toward disintermediation is recognized as a likely correlate of computerization. At least conceptually, this phenomenon has as much potential to undermine capitalism as to sustain it. Many people now book their own flights and hotels, using their time to do the things that travel agents used to do. As we do more things for ourselves, others lose jobs and income, and the gross domestic product shrinks.

In general, the economic phenomena of this section are indicative of shifts in economy, and some of them have the potential to change SFR substantially. It is not clear that they actually do, as they have no clear overall direction. As in previous examples, what is needed is a close examination of specific cases, and to establish what causal relationship they might have with computing.

The Sharing Economy, Including the Emergence of Online Reputation Systems

One development of recent years has been the emergence of a set of new activities sometimes labeled the "social" or "sharing" economy (Sacks 2011). These activities involve the creation of websites where people who want something done can connect with people willing to provide the service. Often, the website claims only to provide a matching service, not itself providing the actual thing desired. These developments are of particular interest to us, as we look to identify and build on digital initiatives that operate at a substantial distance from the value-oriented marketplace away from the ambit of the reproduction of capital. Initiatives like Airbnb and Uber claim to enable the mobilization of resources that exist but are not being used much. Airbnb, among others, has built on the tradition of allowing a visiting friend the use of an air mattress or a bed in a spare room. Car services build upon lending a friend the use of a car we are not using at the moment. The websites of these services present themselves as a means to extend acts of sharing to those we don't know, giving them a place to stay while the owner earns money for unused space. As we need some prompting to extend to a stranger what we would do for a friend, the elements of the sharing economy have also developed reputation systems. Ex post facto, the stranger can comment on the quality of the place where they stayed or the ride with a provider, while the provider can also comment on the conduct of the stranger. As such, the systems are a way for the platforms to promote quality without having to provide their own evaluation system.

But is it actually unused space and provided travel that is mobilized? Recent research suggests otherwise; a majority of the accommodation offered is *un*inhabited places, often one of multiple properties owned by a single individual, recognized by Airbnb as a "super-host" (Slee 2014). Such provisions are more short-term rentals by a landlord than sharing with a friend. In many cities, the hosts of the properties are in conflicts with those who would be long-term renters, and some cities are moving against these services because of housing shortages or the lost hotel tax revenues (Streitfeld 2014). Similarly, Uber drivers often provide rides as their primary way of making a living.

What about the reputation systems? According to Tom Slee's research, the modal response to such systems is around 4 on a 1–5 point, bad to good, scale. Most raters are just polite when they enter a rating into the system. A minority of users gives bad ratings, and it is in the interest of providers to avoid them. Often, the provider can also poorly rate a client. The reputation systems can become a battleground on which providers and users are vulnerable, rather than an accurate reflection of how close the market transaction comes to being an act of friendship. Such reputation systems actually create scarcity when they are supposed to encourage participation and resources sharing. Importantly, in these reputation systems, there is no overall editor to function as "umpire" or referee. An allegedly neutral platform, they discipline those providing the commodity, which makes the social economy more like the market, rather than modifying markets in a "commons" direction. For example, in places such as the US, Uber will assist some of its drivers to get a loan on a new car. However, if such drivers start getting poor ratings on the Uber reputation system, Uber will drop the driver and withdraw its purchase support, leaving the driver to bear the full cost of the car loan (Slee 2014).

Airbnb and Uber are not the only examples of the social economy. Later in the book, we will discuss common and commons. Are these things fundamentally the same? Not all social economy initiatives manifest the same dynamics. For example, the European initiative BlaBlaCar refused to enter the US market in 2014 to avoid these issues. At this point, it appears that, whatever un- or under-used resources the social/sharing economy may mobilize, it does more to reproduce capital than to be a dynamic alternative to it.

Big Data

As witnessed by massive media coverage, there is no phenomenon that better captures the place of computing in the contemporary social imaginary than big data (BD). BD is based on the reality that much social interaction is now digitally mediated, and thus information about it is easily harvestable. We now have unprecedented opportunities to study social dynamics, understand them, and use these understandings as a basis for whatever interventions we wish to make. The main tools so far used to analyze big data sets are network analysis and visualization. Some see the things afforded by BD as so promising that they justify the creation of a new scientific discipline devoted to it, often labeled data science (DS). Colleges and universities in the US and elsewhere are rushing to create graduate programs in DS or data analytics.

While the amount of BD hype continues to increase, there are several reasons to suspect that its promise will be difficult to realize (Boyd and Crawford 2012). One reason is conceptual. By and large, BD work assumes that online behavior is similar to behavior in general, and so inferences about general behavior can be drawn directly from BD behavior. However, the extent to which online behavior is indicative of offline or general behavior is not clear. For example, very different behaviors are encouraged by differently designed digital media, so there is ample reason to expect that the characteristics of digital behavior also vary greatly. Establishing the extent of similarity or difference is not on the BD agenda, nor can it be, as long as BD analysis remains restricted to the online world. Amazon, for example, algorithmically analyzes a user's previous purchases not just to suggest additional items that might be purchased. The price of the suggested item can be raised in proportion to the algorithm's calculation of the user's purchase predilection. Whatever claims to science BD advocates make, commercial uses like this are, for the moment, the main purpose of BD. Hence, the broader BD discourse is at least for the moment vulnerable to the charge of being ideological camouflage for capital reproduction.

Many of the data science advocates would use it to address social problems. Their argument for such applications is often couched in terms of a general critique of previous social science as not being "real science." It is not real science because it has yet to deal with big enough numbers to sustain statistical analysis, and thus there is no need to attend to its analysis of, say, social problems. BD, in contrast, holds out the possibility of creating a real social science, because it can deal with big enough numbers. Such attitudes undermine possibilities of using BD to contribute to multi-disciplinary efforts to further understanding of social dynamics, as they marginalize the research and expertise of those in the social sciences.

Consider the creation and dissolution of communities, where humans create and destroy social relationships out of social relations. This is a long-standing issue of importance in social science research, including network analysis (see, e.g., Mitchell 1974; Wellman 2001). However, the research on community projected in a BD survey on the DS literature does not engage with this research (Fortunato 2010); (see also Hric, Darst, and Fortunato 2014). Rather, Santo Fortunato constructs social networking models out of a variety of BD corpuses. He scans the model to identify areas in which the connections among nodes appear to be denser than average, calls such areas "communities," and proceeds to mathematically analyze their comparative denseness properties. Nowhere does he offer a substantive definition of community. Although he makes several claims about the relevance of his analysis to real human communities, his network models abstract from most data—other than whether a node exists and if it is connected to other nodes. Hence, most of what social science has found about the significant differences in types of social interaction—the strength of ties, the density of different types, the degree of overlap among the networks of individual nodes, etc., is absent. Scholars of community try to figure out the conditions that contribute to the existence of a social relation turning into a social relationship, or visa versa. When pressed to indicate at what point his work might be of value to existing community scholarship, Fortunato argues that it will be able to say something about when smaller clusters of connection density can be grouped under some larger entity. He supposes that this will allow inference regarding hierarchical relations in communities (Fortunato 2010).

The current DS approach ensconces itself in an almost 19th-century empiricist approach to science. DS scholars do not articulate theoretically expressed hypotheses in response to research questions about how well-defined variables are related to each other. Nor do they then test hypotheses against data that are demonstrably relevant to the questions being asked. Instead of following the scientific method described in natural science, these scholars apply a particular visualization tool to data gathered fortuitously, then run a number of statistical tests until they find something striking or "interesting." Then they give it a common name without justifying the naming, and run further manipulations, hoping their methods don't create too many Hawthorne effects—results more a consequence of method than theory. Once again, the technology determines what will be studied and how it will be analyzed.

Additionally, corporations like Facebook hold data sets as proprietary resources. This data is either impossible to buy or too expensive, but it is occasionally released to the research community, presumably because of the expectation that the research benefits the companies. Twitter, in contrast, is providing more and more data for research, in its attempt to become an information infrastructure. Still, as shown by José van Dijck, what data will be available is determined by the profit motivation of these corporations (van Dijck 2013). It would be difficult to find a stronger case of research activities being bent to the reproduction of capital.

CONCLUSION: CAN "COMPUTATIONALIST" COMPUTING SOLVE THE CRISIS IT HAS PARTLY CAUSED?

We doubt it. We began by arguing that computing added momentum to precisely those changes in SFR that exacerbated crisis dynamics. We have several times referred to David Golumbia's label "computationalism" for the conceptual basis of the standard, formal approach to computing (Golumbia 2009). This involves using algorithms to manipulate existing data in order to extract information, in the belief that the information can be used to arrive at more and better knowledge. In computationalism, the more data incorporated into the information extraction engine, the greater the likelihood of a fit between computational model and the real world. This means that computationalism only makes sense as a basis for research or planning if the world itself is both rational and predictable enough to be treated as such.

The role of computing in the crisis demonstrates the grave limits of computationalism. Within the field of economics, we can see the beginnings of a critique of the rationalistic assumptions of neo-classical economics, e.g., Greenspan's auto-critique. Some analysts foresaw the likelihood of the crisis, if not necessarily the specific forms it has taken (see, e.g., Galbraith 2014; Kuttner 2008; Marglin 2008; Shiller 2015). It is clear that it is not more data, nor more manipulations of it that are needed. We need new evaluative standards, or, more precisely, new agreed-upon standard-making procedures for getting knowledge out of information.

Computing practices like those associated with the Internet Society, the World Wide Web Consortium, and the Internet Engineering Task Force suggest ways to get us to "sing a new song." The innovative social arrangements characteristic of some FLOSS projects also suggest alternate directions. Additionally, new practices have been developed in participatory design work and other user-oriented activities carried on within standard computing. Some social networking sites, and the creation of entities like Wikipedia, imply a different way of computing. A "new song" would also need to be performed by those creating the dynamics of the crisis. They cannot do so if they are blinded by data assumptions, or if they are compelled to do so, or if they are tricked into doing so, but they can otherwise participate in its creation.

Professional/Ethical Responsibility of Computing Professionals in Light of the Crisis

Computing professionals who articulate or benefit from computationalism share responsibility for the crisis. To the extent that they benefit, "fellow traveler" users of computers, those of us involved in any way in the world of computing, also bear responsibility. This includes those writing the code and implementing the systems, and those choosing to implement them. It includes those of us who study what happens when computers are used, that is, those in social informatics. Our acts of research and study are implicated in creating the world we study. Further, we need to understand what was wrong with the design and use of the tools, but even more, to identify possible alternatives. In the following chapter, we draw upon the alternative traditions and analyze how to make different tools and/or use them differently. In an important sense everything following in this book is about developing such alternatives. Since computing helped collectively to shape the context of use, computing professionals have an obligation to participate in reshaping the social context where the new tools will be designed and used. In the following chapter, we lay the basis for such an alternative.

NOTES

1. There remains a set of conceptual issues around what a "technology" is and what to include in its definition. Science, technology, and society approaches like the Actor–Network Theory encourage the inclusion of more that the machine or artifacts alone, to include the actors that work (with) it in their practices. We take up this issue in detail while discussing the value of social constructivist rather than technological determinist approaches in Chapter 6.

2. In *Cyborgs@Cyberspace?* (Hakken 1999), Hakken develops a typology of the different degrees of social change, from those associated with being "just another technology" to the elimination of human life (e.g., the replacement of "wetware" with "software"). He also points out that social transformations can "devolve" back to some prior stage, as technology-related change is not necessarily progressive.

3. There is a strong connection between the date given to important events in social formation reproduction, such as a crisis, and how one conceptualizes the character of the event—its basic outlines and "nature." Dating thus has implications for what is done about the crisis—how to end it or at least mitigate its consequences. We date the crisis from late summer to early fall 2007. This is the point when problems in the US housing and financial markets led to a radical tightening of access to credit. The effects of these development quickly led to a general crisis, substantially enabled by the recent financialization of the US and other "developed" economies. "Ownership" of a substantial proportion of assets were transformed into (or at least closely linked to) "innovative financial products" like collateralized debt obligations and credit default swaps. In short, the crisis began when a transformation of the character of asset ownership began to have substantial negative impacts on wide swathes of commodity production, leading to a crisis in the reproduction of capital.

4. As the use of "social formation reproduction" connotes that our argument is located within an intellectual terrain which concentrates on the ways in which human social and cultural relations are perpetuated. Social formation reproduction theory begins with a contrast between the way individual life forms and human social arrangements perpetuate themselves. Life forms follow a course dictated by the way in which genetic potentials interact with particular material conditions. Social arrangements are perpetuated through deliberate collective actions, both individual and collective. Social formation reproduction is more contingent than physical reproduction. To understand the crisis, we concentrate on changes in either the forms through which or the conditions under which such deliberate reproductive effort takes place (see Hakken 1987).

5. The "mark to market or mark to myth" problem persisted, as evidenced by the decisions made surrounding the "stress tests" of bank assets initiated in spring 2009 by the Obama administration in the US. (The stress test remains a central feature of regimes to protect capitalism from further crisis.) In the face of more or less non-existent "free" (i.e., non-governmental) markets for troubled assets, one alternative might have been to rely on a panel of outside experts to assign their "best guess" evaluations. Instead, the Treasury Department used the values that the banks in question chose to assign to their own untradeable assets. Consequently, no bank was determined to have "failed" the stress test.

6. This is a dilemma. Two resolutions seem possible. One is to move from demi- to real globalism in capital market support infrastructures. The second is to de-globalize and then re-nationalize capital markets, or go back to the

institutional pattern that existed between the World Wars I and II. The first would require the surrender of national sovereignty over a broad range of national institutions. The lack of coordination thus far among nations regarding the proper policies for dealing with the crisis, as well as the ongoing trials of the Euro, suggests that this option is highly unlikely, e.g., the difficulties of creating consensus on policy in the United Nations, NATO, or the European Union. Those who believe that one can have global governance without global government, and are willing to try to solve such problems technocratically rather than democratically, can draw little confidence from the experience of entities like ICANN (Internet Corporation for Assigned Names and Numbers) that controls the IP number system and WIPO (World Intellectual Property Organization) that offers arbitration and mediation services with regard to intellectual property disputes. Alternatively, several nations have maintained structures that place limits on international capital flow (e.g., the Chinese control over currency exchange rates and foreign direct investment). Still, there is no effort to reestablish strong, general national boundaries to the movement of capital among nations; even in China, the role of Taiwanese capital continues to be a critical element of economic development.

7. To the best of our knowledge, the term "intellectual property" emerged in US jurisprudence in the late 19th century, but largely disappeared from public discourse until recently. Use of the concept was revived late in the 20th century, in conjunction with efforts to make software patentable by those who felt that copyright wasn't sufficiently strong enough to protect their interests.

8. The term "strong program" is a critical, descriptive advocacy notion widely used in science/policy circles. It is normally used to refer to an existing program that the critic believes has insufficient substance to reach its intended goals. We are most familiar with the term's use by David Bloor in relation to efforts to develop the sociology of knowledge (SK). From an SK perspective, social process, rather than their inherent, transcendent truth-value, explains why some perspectives are treated as "known" while others are not.

9. At least, Castells usually does. In line with the title he gives his *British Journal of Sociology* article (Castells 2000), one could read his intervention as more tentative: "Materials for an *exploratory* theory of the network society" (emphasis added). There is thus some ambiguity in Castells's theoretical project. However, for some twenty years he has been making statements like the following: "The network society is the social structure characteristic of the Information Age . . . It permeates most societies in the world . . . as the industrial society characterized the social structure of both capitalism and stateism for most of the twentieth century" (Castells 2000, 5). Similarly, he characterizes his recently republished three-volume book *The Information Age* as making the empirical case for this analysis.

10. See Chapter 2 of *Cyborgs@Cyberspace?* for an extended development of this point. For Castells, it was not deemed misleading enough to require renaming (e.g., from *The Information Age* to *The Network Age*). The "network society" might more accurately be called the "digital technology network-driven society."

11. Scholars are right to frame their work as in terms of evolution (e.g., the Tofflers), but the specific sequence of technological forms they offer is questionable. Like many sociologists, they foreshorten human history prior to the "Industrial Revolution" into one long, effectively a-technological, "traditional" period. A metaphysical leap in dialectics brings them into an antithetical, "modern, technological" era, the synthesis being the "third wave." Chapter 2 of *Cyborgs@Cyberspace?* outlined a more varied set of evolutionary options for

cyberspace: as a new, cyborgified, species; a new mode of production or social formation; a new, "fourth" form within the labor/commodity mode of production/ social; or merely another, perhaps more concentrated, manifestation of the existing machinofacture stage of the labor process. Equally important was the notion that cyberspace might just as logically be "devolved back" to a prior form. This framing provides much more space to capture the many possible nuances of change than the Castells or Davidson/Toffler options. More nuanced structuralism enhances our capacity to identify which account best describes the actual, empirically observable relationship between DT-based actor networks and broader, cyberspace-related social changes. Are these highly correlated? If so, what are the implications of their most likely causal links?

12. More precisely, the most relevant relationships are no longer topographical, to be found among points on a map, but topological, among the nodes of a network. Put simply, spaces have been decoupled from places.

13. Globalization rhetoric "re-emerged" in the sense that it is a recurrent trope. Perhaps the most important previous period from this perspective was around the turn of the 20th century, at the height of European colonialism.

14. The intervention that many see as having consolidated business/organizational sociology, what we will call organization studies, was Alfred Chandler's work, especially *Strategy and Structure* (Chandler 2013). Chandler locates the superiority of the complex corporate form in the divisional structure invented by General Motors. This structure, despite being geographically dispersed, had in his view apparently limitless capacity for upscaling.

15. Combined with certain forms of online commerce, either "business to business" or "business to consumer," these activities are often referred to as Web 2.0. Web 2.0 is usually distinguished from the earlier form of the World Wide Web as being more interactive, some of its forms less similar to earlier "broadcast"-like activities like blogging, creating listservs, and selling things. As it is the Web 2.0 activities that seem least similar to the previous commercial ones that are usually regarded as being most generative of change, we concentrate on these here.

16. https://klout.com/corp/score[0]

REFERENCES

Andrey Korotayev, and Julia Zinkina. 2014. "On the Structure of the Present-Day Convergence." *Campus-Wide Information Systems* 31 (2/3): 139–52. doi:10.1108/ CWIS-11-2013-0064.

Aronowitz, Stanley, and William DiFazio. 2010. *The Jobless Future: Second Edition.* Minneapolis, MN: University of Minnesota Press.

Attewell, Paul. 1994. "Information Technology and the Productivity Paradox." In *Organizational Linkages: Understanding the Productivity Paradox*, edited by Douglas H. Harris, 13–53. Washington, DC: National Academy Press.

Beniger, James. 1986. *The Control Revolution: Technological and Economic Origins of the Information Society.* Cambridge, MA: Harvard University Press.

Bernanke, Ben. 2000. *Essays on the Great Depression.* Princeton University Press.

Boyd, Danah, and Kate Crawford. 2012. "Critical Questions for Big Data." *Information, Communication & Society* 15 (5): 662–79. doi:10.1080/1369118X. 2012.678878.

Callon, Michel, and Bruno Latour. 1992. "Don't Throw the Baby out with the Bath School! A Reply to Collins and Yearley." *Science as Practice and Culture* 343: 368.

Castells, Manuel. 1996. *The Rise of the Network Society.* Malden, MA: Blackwell.
———. 2000. "Materials for an Exploratory Theory of the Network Society." *British Journal of Sociology* 51 (1): 5–24.
Castronova, Edward. 2008. *Synthetic Worlds: The Business and Culture of Online Games.* University of Chicago Press.
Chandler, Alfred D. 2013. *Strategy and Structure: Chapters in the History of the Industrial Enterprise.* Mansfield Centre, CT: Martino Fine Books.
Clegg, Chris, and Susan Walsh. 2004. "Change Management: Time for a Change!" *European Journal of Work and Organizational Psychology* 13 (2): 217–39. doi:10.1080/13594320444000074.
Clegg, Ian. 1990. *Modern Organizations.* London: SAGE Publications.
Davidson, Carl, Ivan Handler, and Jerry Harris. 1994. "The Promise and the Peril of the Third Wave." *cyRev* 1: 28–39.
Davis, Gerald F., Doug McAdam, W. Richard Scott, and Mayer N. Zald. 2005. *Social Movements and Organization Theory.* Cambridge University Press.
Dibbell, Julian. 2007. "The Life of the Chinese Gold Farmer." *New York Times,* June 17, sec. Magazine. http://www.nytimes.com/2007/06/17/magazine/17lootfarmers-t.html.
Dimson, E., P. Marsh, and M. Sutton. 2002. *Triumph of the Optimists: 101 Years of Global Investment Returns.* Princeton, NJ: Princeton University Press.
Eppler, Martin J., and Jeanne Mengis. 2004. "The Concept of Information Overload: A Review of Literature from Organization Science, Accounting, Marketing, MIS, and Related Disciplines." *The Information Society* 20 (5): 325–44. doi:10.1080/01972240490507974.
Fortunato, Santo. 2010. "Community Detection in Graphs." *Physics Reports* 486: 75–174.
Friedman, Thomas L. 2007. *The World Is Flat 3.0: A Brief History of the Twenty-First Century.* Third edition. New York, NY: Picador.
Fuchs, Christian. 2012. "With or Without Marx? With or Without Capitalism? A Rejoinder to Adam Arvidsson and Eleanor Colleoni." *tripleC: Communication, Capitalism & Critique. Open Access Journal for a Global Sustainable Information Society* 10 (2): 633–45.
Galbraith, James K. 2014. *The End of Normal: The Great Crisis and the Future of Growth.* New York: Simon & Schuster.
Golumbia, David. 2009. *The Cultural Logic of Computation.* Cambridge, MA: Harvard University Press.
Greenspan, Alan. 2002. "Remarks by Chairman Alan Greenspan." *Federal Reserve Board.* http://www.federalreserve.gov/boarddocs/speeches/2002/20021023/default.htm.
Hakken, David. 1987. "Reproduction in Complex Social Formations." *Dialectical Anthropology* 12 (2): 193–204. doi:10.1007/BF00263324.
———. 1999. *Cyborgs@Cyberspace?: An Ethnographer Looks to the Future.* New York: Routledge.
———. 2003. *The Knowledge Landscapes of Cyberspace.* New York, NY: Routledge.
———. 2004. "Recent Information Technology Events in the West: A Memorial for the Economy Formerly Known as 'New'." *Anthropologi Indonesia* 73 (Hakken): 76–81.
———. 2012. "From Labor to Playbor? A Fundamental Shift in Social Formation Reproduction or Merely a Catchy Slogan?", Presented at Fourth STS Italia Conference, Rovigo, IT.
Hakken, David, Maurizio Teli, and Vincenzo D'Andrea. 2010. "Intercalating the Social and the Technical: Socially Robust and Enduring Computing." *PDC*: 231–34. http://ojs.ruc.dk/index.php/pdc/article/view/1919.

Hammer, Michael, and James Champy. 2009. *A Reengineering the Corporation: Manifesto for Business Revolution*. New York: Harper Collins.

Heaton, Lorna. 1999. "Preserving Communication Context: Virtual Workspace and Interpersonal Space in Japanese CSCW." *AI & SOCIETY* 13 (4): 357–76. doi:10.1007/BF01205983.

Hric, Darko, Richard Darst, and Santo Fortunato. 2014. "Community Detection in Networks: Structural Communities versus Ground Truth." *Physical Review E* 90 (6). doi:10.1103/PhysRevE.90.062805.

Hughes, Thomas P. 2011. *Rescuing Prometheus: Four Monumental Projects That Changed Our World*. New York: Knopf Doubleday Publishing Group.

Hutton, Will, and Anthony Giddens, eds. 2000. *Global Capitalism*. New York: New Press.

Kogut, Bruce, and Anca Metiu. 2001. "Open-Source Software Development and Distributed Innovation." *Oxford Review of Economic Policy* 17 (2): 248–64. doi:10.1093/oxrep/17.2.2.248.

Kostakis, Vasilis, and Chris Giotitsas. 2014. "The (A)Political Economy of Bitcoin." *tripleC: Communication, Capitalism & Critique. Open Access Journal for a Global Sustainable Information Society* 12 (2): 431–40.

Kuttner, Robert. 2008. *The Squandering of America: How the Failure of Our Politics Undermines Our Prosperity*. Reprint edition. New York: Vintage.

Latour, Bruno. 2005. *Reassembling the Social: An Introduction to Actor-Network-Theory*. Oxford: Oxford University Press.

Marglin, Stephen A. 2008. *The Dismal Science: How Thinking Like an Economist Undermines Community*. Cambridge, MA: Harvard University Press.

Marx, Karl. 1967. *Capital: A Critical Analysis of Capitalist Production: The Process of Capitalist Production*. Edited by Friedrich Engels. New York: International.

Masuda, Yoneji. 1980. *The Information Society as Post-Industrial Society*. Bethesda, MD: World Future Society.

McLean, Bethany, and Joe Nocera. 2010. *All the Devils Are Here: The Hidden History of the Financial Crisis*. Reprint edition. New York: Portfolio Hardcover.

Mills, C. Wright. 2000. *The Sociological Imagination*. Oxford University Press.

Mitchell, J. Clyde. 1974. "Social Networks." *Annual Review of Anthropology* 3: 279–99.

Morini, Cristina, and Andrea Fumagalli. 2010. "Life Put to Work: Towards a Life Theory of Value." *Ephemera: Theory & Politics in Organization* 10 (3/4): 234–52.

Mowshowitz, Abbe. 1994. "Virtual Organization: A Vision of Management in the Information Age." *The Information Society* 10 (4): 267–88. doi:10.1080/01972 243.1994.9960172.

Noble, David F. 1999. *The Religion of Technology: The Divinity of Man and the Spirit of Invention*. New York: Penguin Books.

Ostrom, Elinor. 1990. *Governing the Commons: The Evolution of Institutions for Collective Action*. Cambridge University Press.

Patterson, Scott. 2010. *The Quants: How a New Breed of Math Whizzes Conquered Wall Street and Nearly Destroyed It*. New York: Crown Business.

Pupo, Norene, and Mark Preston Thomas. 2010. *Interrogating the New Economy: Restructuring Work in the 21st Century*. University of Toronto Press.

Rifkin, Jeremy. 2014. *The Zero Marginal Cost Society: The Internet of Things, the Collaborative Commons, and the Eclipse of Capitalism*. New York: Palgrave Macmillan Trade.

Roubini, Nouriel, and Stephen Mihm. 2010. *Crisis Economics: A Crash Course in the Future of Finance*. New York: Penguin.

Sacks, Danielle. 2011. "The Sharing Economy." *Fast Company*. http://www.fastcompany.com/1747551/sharing-economy.

Sassen, Saskia. 2001. *The Global City: New York, London, Tokyo*. Second edition. Princeton, NJ: Princeton University Press.

Scholz, Trebor, ed. 2012. *Digital Labor: The Internet as Playground and Factory.* First edition. New York: Routledge.

Shepard, John Carl. 1992. *Redefining "Place": Community and Vitality in the New Economy.* Denver, CO: Center for the New West.

Shiller, Robert J. 2015. *Irrational Exuberance.* Revised and Expanded Third edition. Princeton, NJ: Princeton University Press.

Slee, Tom. 2014. *The Future of Workers in the Sharing Economy* Presented at Digital Labor 2014. New York, NY.

Smith, Adam. 1863. *An Inquiry into the Nature and Causes of the Wealth of Nations.* London, UK: Adam and Charles Black.

Solow, Robert. 1987. "We'd Better Watch Out." *New York Times Book Review*, 36: July 12.

Stiglitz, Joseph E. 2003. *Globalization and Its Discontents.* First edition. New York, NY: W. W. Norton & Company.

Stoll, Cliff. 2005. *The Cuckoo's Egg: Tracking a Spy Through the Maze of Computer Espionage.* New York: Pocket Books.

Streitfeld, David. 2014. "Some Setbacks for the Sharing Economy." *Bits Blog.* April 23. http://bits.blogs.nytimes.com/2014/04/23/some-setbacks-for-the-sharing-economy/.

Tapscott, Don, and Anthony D. Williams. 2010. *Wikinomics: How Mass Collaboration Changes Everything.* Expanded edition. New York: Portfolio.

Taylor, Frederick Winslow. 1914. *The Principles of Scientific Management.* New York: Harper.

Tett, Gillian. 2009. *Fool's Gold: How the Bold Dream of a Small Tribe at J.P. Morgan Was Corrupted by Wall Street Greed and Unleashed a Catastrophe.* Reprint edition. New York: Free Press.

Toffler, Alvin. 1980. *The Third Wave.* First edition. New York: Morrow.

Travica, Bob. 1998. *New Organizational Designs: Information Aspects.* Stamford, CT: Ablex Publishing Corporation.

Turkle, Sherry. 2012. *Alone Together: Why We Expect More from Technology and Less from Each Other.* First Trade Paper edition. New York: Basic Books.

Van Dijck, José. 2013. *The Culture of Connectivity: A Critical History of Social Media.* Oxford University Press.

Weber, Max. 2003. *From Max Weber: Essays in Sociology.* Edited by Hans H. Gerth and C. Wright Mills. Reprinted in 1998 edition. London: Routledge.

Weber, Steven. 2005. *The Success of Open Source.* Cambridge, MA: Harvard University Press.

Wellman, Barry. 2001. "Physical Place and Cyberplace: The Rise of Personalized Networking." *International Journal of Urban and Regional Research* 25 (2): 227–52. doi:10.1111/1468-2427.00309.

Williams, Raymond. 1985. *Keywords: A Vocabulary of Culture and Society.* Oxford University Press.

Winner, Langdon. 1986. "Myth Information: Romantic Politics in the Computer Revolution." In *Philosophy and Technology II*, edited by Carl Mitcham and Alois Huning, 269–89. Boston Studies in the Philosophy of Science 90. Springer Netherlands. http://link.springer.com/chapter/10.1007/978-94-009-4512-8_20.

Wolf, Martin. 2014. *The Shifts and the Shocks: What We've Learned-and Have Still to Learn-from the Financial Crisis.* New York: Penguin Press.

4 Computing and Social Change Relationships

INTRODUCTION

We began Chapter 3 with an example of a specific analysis of the relationship between the use of digital technologies (DTs) and social change relevant to the dynamics of social formation reproduction (SFR). Our extended example was the role of computing in the crisis beginning in 2007. We also offered critiques of several other framings of this relationship, framings that generally present the relationship as simple, one directional, and causal. In these analyses, computing causes social change and the impacts of computing on society need to be examined, but the impacts of society on computing can be ignored. We identified two key premises, technological determinism and computationalism, whose premises were closely associated with these framings.

We accept that there is often a relationship between a form of computing and some social change at a general level. We see this relationship as highly mediated and often different from one computing form to another. After many years of trying to make empirical sense of these relationships, we understand that computing is so imbricated in SFR that it will likely be a central aspect of any future social formation. Likewise, SFR is imbricated in computing. This co-relationship makes it even more important to "get right" the specifics of any particular DTs/SFR relationship. This is particularly true in cases like the crisis of 2007, when the role of computing became *generally* relevant to SFR. Computing practices associated with the crisis can be described as having *specific* roles in causing it. Identifiable computing practices, such as risk models and algorithms, were central to the crisis. In the crisis, computing was visibly connected to social forms such as complexly engineered financial instruments that could not have existed otherwise. These forms were directly connected to changes in SFR, changes that challenged the ability of current social formations to reproduce themselves, let alone extend their reproduction. The digital mediations leading to the crisis, like all digital mediations, were not inevitable. They followed from choices made by humans, both actively by the quants, and passively by the bankers who chose not to examine the premises built into quant models. While these computing practices were necessary for the crisis to develop as it did, they were not on their own a sufficient cause of the crisis, nor did they single-handedly determine its characteristics. Other forms of computing existed whose use instead would have, at a minimum, led to a different crisis. Within a different policy context, the other forms may even have meant the crisis was largely avoided, as was the case in Canada. Because these other forms were not chosen, computer people at least potentially share in the ethical responsibility for the crisis. These analyses, of course, reflect our rejection of simplistic technological determinism.

In this chapter, we want to stress the *contingency* of the potential causative inter-relationships between computing and social change, how form and presence are dependent upon specific practices and their context. We also want to come at the question from a different direction. The primary aim of this chapter is to present different analyses of specific computing/social change nexuses. These examples are chosen to illustrate the affordances for alternative SFR that some existing forms of computing possess. These forms are selected because they are ethno-generative; they are rich in the capacity to generate new cultural forms suggestive of alternative futures beyond capital. The interventions we describe later in the book afford values that are different from the reproduction of capital, while also avoiding other effects and dynamics. There is a pressing need for a project to construct an alternative social formation/set of dynamic social relations, and a need for available, good examples of what to promote.

Before we focus on these forms and their ethno-generative potentials, it is important to address why the patterns that dominate current SFR cannot be extended indefinitely at tolerable levels of social stress. Part of this general understanding follows from our analysis of the 2007 crisis, but not all of it. SFR problems, when bent so heavily to capital reproduction, were present before the crisis, but the crisis made very clear the *un*likelihood of SFR extension when so bent. While many digital technology uses increasingly mediate them, the forces undermining the adaptability of current SFR *are* distinguishable from DT use. Computing is not the cause of this dim future for current SFR. Rather, we think it possible to advance DTs whose social correlates would extend SFR adaptability.

Our arguments to this point are:

- Computing is around for the long haul; it will continue to mediate major aspects of SFR;
- Computing does not inevitably cause social change;
- Computing can impact social changes, but the causal connections are complex and need to be understood in specific contexts;
- While computing can be done in ways that undermine prospects for extending social reproductive capacity, there is nothing that makes this necessarily the case;

- There are substantial characteristics of current social formations that generally undermine prospects for extending their reproduction;
- Computing is often correlated with these characteristics but need not be; indeed, there are selected forms of computing with alternative practices that might be interventions to extend SFR.

We begin this chapter by focusing on the characteristics of the current social formation, explaining why we are pessimistic about the future of social formations whose social reproduction is heavily bent to capital. It is this pessimism that leads us to commit ourselves to exploring alternative options for SFR, to take on the tasks of identifying and carrying out some of the intellectual work necessary to develop an alternative SFR dynamic. Any alternative will likely incorporate computing, given its place in the collective cultural imaginary. In the main part of this chapter, we will identify forms of computing that can serve as signposts for what an alternative that might be encouraged might look like. Before we can get to the values, institutions, and measures that might describe this alternative, we need to discuss the conceptual problem that impedes the creation of alternative forms of computing, and thus an alternative SFR dynamic. In the last part of this chapter, we explain why we reject the several theories of value developed to explain or justify bending social formations to the reproduction of capital. What we need are theories of multiple values—values different from market maximization.

RESTRICTED PROSPECTS FOR CONTEMPORARY SOCIAL FORMATION REPRODUCTION

We are pessimistic about the long-term reproductive prospects of existing social formations. Seeing why this is so requires us to set aside the misrepresentations of the DT use/social change nexus that we critique in the previous chapter. We have referenced Anthony Giddens's claim that the use of DTs led to a revolution in knowledge that in turn drove many other social changes (Hutton and Giddens 2000). Giddens's interlocutor, Will Hutton, offers a different analysis of the SFR dynamics. For Hutton, knowledge's influence is not causative, but highly mediated through what he, following Edward Luttwak, calls "turbo-capitalism." Turbo-capitalism is identified as a variety that emerged from the historical conflict with communism, and took a triumphant form, a variety of capitalism:

> . . . that is much harder, more mobile, more ruthless and more certain about what it needs to make it tick. . . . Its overriding objective is to serve the interests of property owners and shareholders, and it has a firm belief . . . that all obstacles to its capacity to do that—regulation, controls, trade unions, taxation, public ownership, etc.—are unjustified and should be removed . . .
>
> (2000, 9–10)

To show how strongly this "turbo" form of capital dominated SFR, Hutton notes how in its victory over state communism, it has also eclipsed other forms of capital (Catholic, social market, and stakeholder) alternative to it. "I would say that communism, although it failed, did have one good impact; it kept capitalism on its guard—in a sense it kept it aware that it had to have a human face . . ." (2000, 9).

Hutton acknowledges a connection between this resurgent capitalism and DTs, but, unlike Giddens, he argues that turbo-capitalism was driving technology rather than being driven by it. Steroidal capital is in a position to take advantage of the opportunities to extend its reproductive ambit that were opened by technological change, and it has. In a Schumpeterian register, Hutton argued that turbo-capitalism became more influential in times of technological change because it allowed "a sort of quantum leap" to spread the influence of capital (Schumpeter 2008). We will return to Hutton's argument later in this chapter.

HOW WE CAME TO REALIZE THAT THE EMPEROR OF THE GREAT MODERATION HAD NO CLOTHES

It is a commonplace that social formations bent to the reproductive demands of capital—that is, capitalist social formations or capitalism as a social system—are inclined to periodic crises. In neo-classical economics, such crises are usually related to as "down" periods in a regular business cycle of (greater) expansion and (lesser) contraction. Much macro-economic theory is dedicated to explaining why the peak of each cycle should be higher than the last (Weisskopf 1979). Theoretically, the long-term tendency of capitalism is to improve the quality of life through each boom/bust cycle, resulting in a widening and improving of the range of use values available as commodities through markets. An example of how this macro-economic analysis is faulty is the characterization of the time preceding the crisis as "the Great Moderation." In his book *Capital in the Twenty-First Century*, Thomas Piketty critiques the inequality that ensued as the general case, the decline in inequality after World War II being the exception (Piketty 2014).

Turbo-capitalism, with its ideological cover, neo-liberalism, was, for a time, arguably demonstrative of capital's general robustness (Comaroff and Comaroff 2001). The Asian crisis of the late 1990s and the dot-com bust of 2000 hardly impacted the explanations of and justifications for the regency of capital. Perhaps those most characteristic of the first part of the first decade of the 2000s were the exuberant paeans to the Great Moderation, in which the problems of periodic crises were no longer to be feared because "we know how to manage them." Technical economics had purportedly identified a range of tools, such as those deployable by national central banks, which would substantially moderate, perhaps even eliminate, the down periods of the cycle, while also raising the "ups" peaks.

Soon, however, "the Great Recession" put paid to the Great Moderation. The causes of the broad socio-economic crisis that began in 2007[1] have been dealt with at length and by a number of authors (Atwood 2008; Foster and Magdoff 2009; Kuttner 2008; Lewis 2010; Marglin 2008; McLean and Nocera 2010; Patterson 2010; Roubini and Mihm 2010; Shiller 2008; Tett 2009; Wolf 2014). Sorting through these and other answers to the question of "causes" would require another book, one different from this one. As we see the crisis as still ongoing, it may well be too early to write a definitive account, as new developments require new analysis. While we acknowledge that solving the problem of the crisis depends upon having a clear understanding of its causes, at present, other authors have more to contribute to the debate over this analysis than we do.

Many of these authors ask after the long-run implications of the crisis, which of course are deeply shaped by the causes. Some even wonder if they might be terminal for an economic system bent so strongly to the reproduction of capital; a few make this question their primary focus (e.g., see Harvey 2014; Wallerstein et al. 2013). In 2011, in the middle of the ongoing Great Recession, sociologists Craig Calhoun and Georgi Derluguian edited a series of three books, collecting up-to-date social science on the reasons for the crisis and on its potential outcome. The first of the books, titled *Business as Usual: The Roots of the Global Financial Meltdown*, analyzed the profound origins of the crisis and identified some of its most likely (and dire) consequences (Calhoun and Derluguian 2011). The title of the second, following collection asked, *Does Capitalism Have a Future?* (Wallerstein et al. 2013). (The topic was also addressed in several articles in the *Financial Times* newspaper.) The authors of several articles in the second book argued that any form of survival would mean radical change given the deep roots of the crisis. Among them, only Randall Collins was pessimistic overall about the likelihood of capitalism's survival, arguing two points (Collins 2013). He gives a technological determinist assessment of the dis-employing implications of digital technology mediation, and he reads current capitalism's ecological flaws as so deep as to be "fatal."

David Harvey also uses the term "fatal" to describe some of the current contradictions of capital (Harvey 2014). Even those who argue that capitalism will likely survive acknowledge that the price will be heavy and probably result in a much-reduced standard of living for most along with demanding, draconian social controls. What these writers share is a view that any future capitalism is likely to be marked by a sharp deterioration from the current standards of living. Michael Mann, for example, envisions a social structure in which two thirds of the population survives in marginality, while one third faces a dim future (Mann 2013). Even if humans were still able to pay low prices for goods produced globally, it would be largely through automated labor processes.

We tend to agree with Harvey about the specific fate of capital, but our main point is the bleakness of any compromise. There is a shared consensus among scholars that social formations bent to the reproduction of capital can probably only survive via anti-human means. Taken together, the books on crisis (whether social, environmental, or economic) identify several substantial "flaws" in the current SFR system organized to the reproduction of capital. Capitalism may or may not be doomed, but as dehumanizing change would doubtless be required, we question if one should try to save it. The flaws are such that, while some form of capital may survive, achieving a better future probably depends on radically lessening capital's influence on SFR dynamics. This in turn means identifying and building alternatives that are radically capable of bending capital reproduction toward a different dynamic. In any case, as "business as usual" is unlikely to be an option, shouldn't we strive for something better, beyond capital and its system? If so, how, then, can the necessary alternative path be created?

At the time we are writing, eight years after the crisis began, economic commentary has abandoned the Great Moderation idea. Consider a representative piece by *Financial Times* writer Edward Luce, entitled "Too big to resist: Wall Street's comeback" (Luce 2014). Luce is writing in the immediate aftermath of one of several crises of US governance where a shutdown of the State was narrowly avoided by the last-minute passage of a new budget. The budget legislation, however, increased by a factor of more than ten the ability of individuals to contribute legally to US political campaigns, effectively ending any limitations on opportunities for the wealthy to influence elections directly. The legislation also overturned a main plank of the banking reform intended to lessen the chances of a crisis. This part of the Dodd–Frank reform had prohibited a practice that was at the center of the crisis of 2007, one that allowed very large banks to use the insured deposits of individuals to speculate on exotic (and computer-enabled) financial instruments. As these deposits were government-insured, during the crisis, the US taxpayer had to make up the deposits lost in the speculation.

At the time when Luce was writing, investment in another new financial instrument, the collateralized *loan* obligation, was already greater than the evil twin it replaced, the collateralized *debt* obligations that were at the center of the 2007 crisis. What is most remarkable is that by 2014, while there were fewer banks (about six) in a position to speculate with depositors' funds, these banks had enough power to hijack for their own purposes what was arguably the most essential piece of legislation that Congress could pass. Luce wonders if it is wise that the lobbyists for the Citigroup were the ones who wrote the relevant clause in the bill that was recently passed "word for word." He goes on to warn about "two glaring deficiencies that will come back to haunt Washington *when* the next crisis strikes." One is that the banks that were deemed "too big to fail" in the crisis were even bigger by late 2014. The other is that Wall Street culture had not changed, there being, for example, no ethical code in evidence among the large financial houses. Most chilling was his contention that *"[a]t some point there will be another Wall Street crisis . . .,"* and that, as "[g]reed is once more in the ascendant[,] [n]o law can stop the next bomb from detonating . . ." (Luce 2014, 9, emphasis added).

We share the frustration and fear for the future that pervades Luce's analysis, which cries out for "a better way." Financialization has greatly increased the likely frequency and severity of the inevitable future crises. Estimates of the portion of the economy now dominated by the production and sale of financial instruments, driven by speculation rather than by use values, range as high as 80% (Tett 2009). The relative globalization of capital markets carried the crisis of 2007 quickly to many other nations. International capital markets had become strongly connected, but regulation by national bodies alone meant these markets were beyond control. This crisis deeply affected what economists are forced to call the "real," as opposed to the financial, economy. It was the globalizing financialization of entire economies that exacerbated the underlying economic problem and made the crisis into a general one, and not just an economic or financial crisis, but also a social one.

Moreover, more financialization isn't even the largest problem capitalism faces. While all human social formations are subject to the vagaries of change in weather, the current capitalist ones are the first to greatly accelerate their severity through fostering rapid climate change (Harvey 2014). To see how this has become problematic, consider how all human social formations create symbolic entities to coordinate a response to cope with threats. Under the right circumstances, these entities can themselves become more sources of crisis than solutions. Ours are not the first social formations to generate symbolically induced crises (e.g., mass starvation due to the failure of agriculture, the financialization aspects of the 2007+ crisis, etc.). Ours are, however, the first to do so on such a grand, systematically expanded scale such that they threaten the very conditions of all human existence. That is to say, ours is the first to be vulnerable because it is so heavily mediated by an artificial, culture-induced crisis with a direct impact on our environment (Klein 2014).

In the previous chapter, we discussed the many efforts of contemporary scholars to find a precise label for the current economic moment, ones that give proper recognition to the prominent digital mediation of commodity production. Scholars have offered alternate terms to characterize a highly DT-mediated social formation. Morini and Fumagalli (2010), for example, speak of "bio-capitalism." The term refers to "the commoditization of life," that is, the penetration of the commodity form in private spheres previously untouched. This is what in classic Marxism is called "the reproduction of the worker" carried out in the home. Services once provided by businesses, such as booking airline travel, checking groceries, or pumping gas have become the task of the consumer, reducing business costs and reducing the workforce. Corporate entities are reproducing capital through appropriating the profit derived from what people post on Facebook or make into YouTube videos. The acts of living and fun become sources of profit.

We give considerable prominence to such mediating roles of DTs in contemporary SFR. We also pay attention to pro-capital interventions into reproduction dynamics, such as financialization, interventions that are not reducible to digital innovation. Financialization was a consequence of a deliberate program. In *The Knowledge Landscapes of Cyberspace* (Hakken 2003), Hakken critiqued attempts to account for the current SFR dynamics in terms of labor, capital, and knowledge theories of value. His critique also gave causative attention to the highly aggressive form of capitalism associated with neo-liberalism, Hutton's turbo-capitalism. In line with the perspectives of Immanuel Wallerstein, the rise of such aggressive forms is better understood as an indication of the reproductive difficulties faced by capitalist social formations (Wallerstein et al. 2013).

Indeed, were we to have to choose a name for the current moment of SFR, we would choose something like "life world turbo-capitalism." Besides its stylistic infelicities, we would prefer to avoid such naming practices. This is partly because capitalism is a dynamic social formation type, rapidly changing. Its development is very uneven in place and time, so what is characteristic of one time/place is unlikely to be characteristic of most others. We generally avoid trying to identify the best name for the moment because we want to attend to mid- and long-term, rather than short-term, futures. Whatever the unique social properties of the current moment in SFR, understanding them on their own will not provide the basis for the development of the very different, alternative SFR project that we see as necessary. There is sufficient reason to conclude that any social formation that remains dominated by the reproductive dynamic of capital is highly likely to create increased inequality, more misery, and continued conflict. The ability of current social formations to reproduce themselves has been so compromised that new forms of social formation reproduction must be found and institutionalized. In a phrase, we can do better, and we need to take up *now* the identification of what should happen next.

COMPUTING PRACTICES SUGGESTIVE OF ALTERNATIVE SFR DYNAMICS

From a theoretical point of view, as we describe in Chapter 2, social reproduction is dependent upon cultural reproduction. Our social relations depend upon the communication and acceptance of the cultural constructs through which our actions are coordinated—the very ones that now carry such existential threats. Human social arrangements are created, not given. If we want different social arrangements, we need to change our cultural constructs, including rearranging their hierarchical relationships. Today, this means identifying and pursuing different values, those other than endless accumulation. A premise of our work is that it will be easier to convince humans to strive for new values if clear, existing examples of what might be achieved can be demonstrated to already exist, especially if the examples seem to be important, even if not dominant presences, in SFR. If social practices informed by the constructs we want to move to the top of the value hierarchy already exist, then the task is to articulate the values that are implicit in those practices so we can displace markets. Changing social reproduction via new relations of cultural reproduction will be easier with constructs that are already familiar than it would be to change them via completely new constructs.

To be clear, we see nothing inevitable about the eventual hegemony of such alternative values. We are not proposing to replace the various forms of "negative" technological determinism with a "positive" technological determinism. Social commentator Jeremy Rifkin has prophesied the inevitable end of capitalism (Rifkin 2014), based on the tendency of digital production to drive the production cost of the second and all ensuing widgets to zero. In his technological determinist reading, the rescue of the social formation will come automatically from technologies already in use. Unfortunately, this is not how positive change in SFR generally develops, because those with power use it to serve their own interests.

What should be the basis of an initiative to "do better?" In this section, we discuss certain computing practices that are suggestive of a viable alternative project. These computing patterns will not bring about a different SFR dynamic on their own. They can, however, be analyzed, encouraged, and expanded to provide a basis for strategic interventions. A major consequence of the existence of the patterns is their potential to be used to open a discussion of how alternative ways to compute suggest different ways to live. Our aim in discussing them is to encourage a particular approach to the "how to compute" choices we face. We can choose to let the imperatives of capital reproduction dominate how we compute. Alternatively, we can take advantage of the potentials revealed in these practices to help foster a discourse on what should happen beyond capital, which can, in turn, help us move beyond capital deliberately.

Our goal is to identify values to provide the basis for new, different forms of social formation reproduction. By no means do we wish to suggest that computing is the primary, let alone the only, possible basis for alternatives. Rather, we start with computing practices because they now mediate SFR, and they will not be done away with. Indeed, there is every reason to think that digital mediation will grow. New, different values are more likely to be accepted if they complement, not contradict, characteristic digital mediations.

Many scholars such as Tapscott and Williams (2010) use the term "virtual" to include all of the various organizing forms identified by Robert Travica (Travica 1998) and the potential relations described by Vincenzo D'Andrea and colleagues (Kokash, Heuvel, and D'Andrea 2006). Like Tapscott and Williams, they talk about virtual organization as if it were a Weberian ideal type, something never actualized in a pure form but so nearly emergent as to be treated as profoundly "real." Indeed, the term "virtual" has been used to cover so many different phenomena that it is drained of analytical value. Instead, we will focus on selected, digitally mediated, and organizationally related social patterns that suggest emergent phenomena. They therefore have the potential to have a profound influence on how we design DT interventions to achieve fundamental changes in SFR dynamics.

1. Digital Technologies Can Be Used to Informate, Rather than Automate

In her 1988 book *In the Age of the Smart Machine*, Shoshana Zuboff reports on field studies of early computerization in facilities producing large volumes of physical commodities (e.g., paper). Zuboff describes the potential "to informate" as a primary affordance of DT use:

> What is it, then, that distinguishes information technology from earlier generations of machine technology? As information technology is used to reproduce, extend, and improve upon the process of substituting machines for human agency, it simultaneously accomplishes something quite different. The devices that automate by translating information into action also register data about those automated activities, thus generating new streams of information. For example, computer-based, numerically controlled machine tools or microprocessor-based sensing devices not only apply programmed instructions to equipment but also convert the current state of equipment, product, or process into data. Scanner devices in supermarkets automate the checkout process and simultaneously generate data that can be used for inventory control, warehousing, scheduling of deliveries, and market analysis. The same systems that make it possible to automate office transactions also create a vast overview of an organization's operations, with many levels of data coordinated and accessible for a variety of analytical efforts. (Zuboff 1988)

What happens to the information generated? When the labor process is organized according to a Taylorist "representation" or "automation" model, this information is either ignored or channeled exclusively to upper management, who in turn may or may not use it to exercise even greater control over the work process. Conversely, when computing is used, in Zuboff's language, to "informate," it generates as much information as possible and then shares the information as widely as possible throughout the organization. When informating is accompanied by extending the authority to act on the information, generally and down the hierarchy, computing increases production. Zuboff also observed that, when this authority extension did not also happen, this partial informating just increased frustration.

Zuboff thus identified two basic DT strategies that organizations could use in the mid-1980s. A prime feature of the representational approach is that it increases options for automating and thus further marginalizing humans at work. The second informating strategy meant using computing to maximize the information generated and disseminating it as widely as possible to those who might use it or be affected by changes in the state of production. However, informating would only work if authority, as well as information, were increasingly dispersed as the organizing adapted to new conditions. Despite Zuboff's advocacy for informating, organizations often failed to adopt it or refused to do so.

2. "Free" Forms of Free/Libre and Open-Source Software Development Can Matter

Free software is often grouped with open-source software as free/libre and open-source software (F/LOSS). Both forms of software reveal the software's underlying source code, and they both differ from proprietary software, where the source code remains hidden—in many cases, it would be illegal to reverse engineer the software to identify the code. Scholars like Stephen Weber (Weber 2005) attribute the success of both free software (FS) and open-source software (OSS) to their distinctive social characteristics.

Free software allows anybody who wants to use the source code to do so and even to modify it, but *only* if they extend the same provision to everyone else. The licensing regime (i.e., the GPL or "general public license") means FS is free "like free speech" (Stallman et al. 2002). In contrast, open-source software permits the use of the source code in ensuing *proprietary code*, so it is then not always freely available for use. Free software is Richard Stallman's preferred form of F/LOSS project (Stallman et al. 2002; Weber 2005). Unlike much OSS, in FS projects, employment relationships are rare, although sometimes present. Anyone who wants to can join a project, although aspects of access to parts where they can participate are dependent first upon demonstration of project-relevant competence. Participants join the project, work on various aspects of it as shown by their skills, and choose roles within it on the basis of personal preference. The influence of large FS projects demonstrates the viability of the form.

Free software projects are based upon a form of sociality that does not make sense from a narrow perspective of a *homo economicus*, where the aim is to use markets to maximize personal marginal utilities. Free projects find a way to create orderly development out of volunteered action. An emerging set of ethnographic studies of free software (Bosio et al. 2014; Coleman 2012; Golub 2010; Kelty 2008) and studies of similar free projects, like Wikipedia (Reagle 2010), are demonstrating the variety of dynamics that can emerge in such activities. One problem that may arise in FS projects follows from not being able to plan on the satisfactory completion of parts of a project because of the voluntary nature of the work. Organizational entrepreneurs have tried to leverage FS dynamics by organizing them in not-for-profit organizations (Hippel 2005, 2006).[2]

FS projects, and some open source ones, create and use software developed within a unique organizing modality. While most of this software is not developed explicitly to support virtual organizing, the computing-mediated virtual relationships inherent in FS projects do have dynamics distinct from those of the organizational structures of classical organizational theory. Of particular interest is that advocates of FS generally draw attention to its social relationships as the source of its dynamics and outcomes. Recognition of the key place of social dynamics in FS suggests that merely mediating existing organizational processes with new machines does not bring about transformational organizing. Rather, the dynamics of such projects are significantly affected by social as well as technical factors (Davenport and Pearlson 1998; Hippel 2005; Hippel and Krogh 2003; Markus, Manville, and Agres 2000; Turoff and Hiltz 2009). The patterns manifested in "classic" Taylorist organizations and central to organizational sociology chronicles involve groups in a robust, formal sense (Tolbert and Hall 2008). Such organizations have well-defined membership and boundaries and a clear, often hierarchical system of behavior control, objectives, and predefined roles, such as employees and jobs. In contrast, the computing-mediated virtual relationship complexes manifest in FS projects, like the other computer-mediated activities discussed below, seem able to achieve the benefits of formal organization (coordination of human action) without features like rigidity, sunk costs, etc. They achieve "organization" without being "organizations" in the typical, classic sense. Free software projects are the most developed of the new, computer-mediated forms of organizing, taking place largely outside the ambit of capital reproduction. We note, however, that like many other aspects of computing, they are unfortunately male-dominated and at times, are male-exclusive activities (Weber 2005).

What is perhaps most distinctive of FS as opposed to OSS projects is FS's overt efforts to distance itself from the institutions of private property, especially those retroactively glossed under the umbrella of "intellectual property." Instead of using copyright to prevent duplication, even reverse-engineered efforts to understand how a program works, FS projects copyright via "copyleft." This is the form of licensing that guarantees the user the right to copy, understand, and even change the software, based only on the user's extending the same rights to everyone else. FS thus demonstrates how it is possible to circumvent the property institutions at the heart of capital reproduction.

3. Wiki's and Similar Activities Can Create Powerful New Social Forms

Wikipedia is an online encyclopedia that is collectively edited and supported via a unique not-for-profit model (Reagle 2010). The Wikipedia project has been the model for numerous other projects that address the problem of information overload by finding ways to move discussion collaboratively toward separating the things known from mere information. While it is about "content" rather than software, it is similar to FS projects in its effort to create alternative social dynamics, which also generally follow from the voluntary character of participation, involvement based on interest, and control based on demonstrated personal competence. Consider, for example, how editing takes place on Wikipedia. Any editor who wishes to do so may edit any entry they choose, which is then subject to anyone else's editing. Editors can and do participate in a meta-discourse in which they can argue for the correctness of their edits before an audience of others equally empowered to edit. In general, the result is that the text of any given entry roughly reflects the current consensus of those concerned about the issue given the entry's name. Of course, there are examples of conflicting edits that are not headed to consensus, in which case Wikipedia editors can step in and freeze the editing process, noting that the entry does not constitute a consensus view. The large proportion of un-frozen to frozen entries is a demonstration of how often this peer production approach to expertise can be successful.

This is not to say that there are no issues with Wikipedia and its approach. Identifying authorship and editing can be difficult. Writers and editors appear to be anonymous and many editors can contribute to an article, so from an academic perspective, the authority of authorship is not always clear. Students and scholars who wish to use information from Wikipedia often need additional sources to verify any claims. Disagreements about pages can result in frequent changes to the content of pages based on the perspective of the editor. For example, early in 2015, there arose a controversy among female gamers where female gamers were being threatened and harassed. The Gamergate controversy became a Wikipedia issue, resulting in the sanctioning by the Wikipedia arbitration committee of a number of editors, primarily feminists, according to *The Guardian* writer Alex Hern (Hern 2015). Hern argued that Wikipedia is the seventh biggest site on the Internet and that 10% or less of the editors were thought to be women. There is a potential to change these dynamics. Wikipedia and many of the other similar peer-produced compendia demonstrate that the new social dynamics of information creation manifested in informating and in free software projects can also be generated in the domain of knowledge. Wikis can democratize social interaction while also creating more room for individual initiative and self-determination.

4. People and Operators Can Participate in Design

While there are many ways in which the term "participatory design" (PD) is used, it refers most directly to a particular approach to the creation, development, implementation, support, and maintenance of computing systems, including hardware, software, and DT social organization (Simonsen and Robertson 2012). The approach involves those who will use or operate the eventual digital system in many or all of the phases of the design process, and their interventions are often evident in the final system. PD was developed first in the Nordic countries, but has since spread to other parts of the world. Scandinavian-inspired PD is based on the premise that those who will be affected by a digital mediation have a democratic right to participate actively in decisions about the mediation. Scandinavian PD has found that user involvement in design produces a system that: 1) runs better, 2) fits better into the specific organizing practices into which it is to be introduced, and 3) is more likely to draw the support and endorsement of those who ultimately run or use it. Moreover, participation in one sphere of life (initially work, later home, community, etc.) is expected to lead to more active participation in other spheres, for example, politics, trade unions, and other social organizations (Simonsen and Robertson 2012).

While initially deployed in for-profit employment contexts, PD is also in not-for-profit and community contexts, and it crosses national boundaries (Greenbaum and Madsen 1993). PD shares with FS and Wiki-type projects a strong commitment to voluntary and "based on interest" participation. The successful practice of PD in digital realms has complemented, been informed by, and been incorporated into the participatory practices of other sorts, from urban planning to organizational development.

Of the greatest interest to us are the many types of expertise that PD projects draw upon. This includes not only the code-writing talent manifested in FS projects, or the knowledge of content central to Wiki-ing, but also the expertise of those using and deploying digital design. PD challenges conventional notions of design, such as the idea that there is a distinct "design" moment in each project. One form of this idea is the "over the wall" or "waterfall" metaphors that assume that design, development, implementation, support, and maintenance happen sequentially (Grudin 1991). While these moments are separable conceptually, in practice, they often overlap and happen in unpredictable times and ways. Further, the multiple sources of input and inspiration contradict the notion that design is best created by an individual, either an "inspired" figure, or the technology expert. Instead, the key skill for a designer in a PD project is to facilitate the participation of users, maximizing their influence on project decisions. The digital PD approach highlights how each type of project participant—designer, user, facilitator, or adaptor of the operation of the system—has relevant knowledge that is important to share with all the others and to bring to the final design.

In digital work PD is strongly social rather than merely technical, and its success highlights how necessary the social is to effective in-use computing. To encourage broad and deep participation, PD projects are marked by a commitment to democracy while also demonstrating its benefits. While it is possible to conduct PD within the confines of a for-profit organization, this adds additional constraints.

5. Computing Can Be Organized Around a "Service" Orientation

Service orientation (SO) is another computing-based organizing practice suggestive of very different SFR dynamics (Bosio et al. 2014). The SO idea aimed to take advantage of DTs' capacities to make organizing more flexible. Efforts to promote SO grew out of the discussion of how computing enabled "virtual" organization in a variety of forms, such as the "network," "organic," "virtual," and "ad hoc" forms described by Robert Travica (Travica 1998). The last form, ad hoc, is a minimalist organizing structure, limited to only what is necessary to complete a specific task. After that, the organizing disappears. The possibility to do ad hoc organizing led Vincenzo D'Andrea and others to articulate an idea of organizing SO, with only a minimal formal structure. The idea was most developed with regard to "software as a service." Software is an ideal arena to construct minimalist organizing, as it is only marginally material and thus highly transportable at minimal cost. Additionally, it is very easy to circulate, has a low marginal cost of reproduction, is easily stored and communicated, takes advantage of a widely available infrastructure of connected machines, and so on (e.g., Bosio et al. 2014). All these properties make software ideal for creating an ecology of ad hoc organization. Imagine if each computing person or small group of people could be their "own" organization, working independently rather than being the employees of a large organization. On one project, individual or partnership A might approach individual B for help on a project, and B would connect A with C. C would provide the software service that A needed; B would provide oversight of the transaction. Once the project was completed, the "organization" would cease to exist. At another time, B might approach C, who would arrange for A to "serve" B, monitor the project, and so on.

The emergence of such an SO organizing ecology would radically reduce the need for organizational infrastructures of buildings, labor-management relations, supervisors, machines, ancillary staff, etc. This would be an ecology of small brokers, providers, and customers. Some short-term, narrow, ad hoc relations would evolve into ongoing relationships with a more robust supporting infrastructure, what Travica calls "organic" virtual organizing, but this would only happen when it makes sense through multiple projects. This ecology would increase individual autonomy, as it would be possible to find work without becoming a wage "slave," and work relations and longer-term relationships would be entered into voluntarily, out of desire. It would also greatly reduce organization overhead.

Of course, such an ecology could only be rare and marginal in economies like the current economies of today's nations, which are dominated by large, typically corporate organizations. As long as SFR is bent to the need to reproduce capital, promotion of SO might easily lead to even more workers on short-term contracts, with no commitment for future employment, that is, precarious workers. SO would only work effectively and humanely in a radically different political economy, one where hierarchy no longer led to increased power, where organizing power would be distributed. Additionally, SO would probably also require the provision of a basic income, one connected with a minimum wage, if workers were to be able to take advantage of SO opportunities to choose where, with whom, and how to work.

Despite its potential, the suggested SO ecology has never really emerged. What has emerged instead is a different home for software, not with the worker/owner but in the "cloud." Cloud models make software available for rent rather than through ownership, in the cloud per gigabyte, from some widely accessible repositories. Being able to access software from a cloud only when needed might seem to increase flexibility. However, in comparison to SO, cloud architectures tend to increase the dependence of smaller on larger organizations. This is because the latter, through controlling the cloud, attain quasi-monopolies on software. Their power vis-à-vis a user is even greater if much of the user's data are also stored in the same cloud. Indeed, it is not unreasonable to see "clouding," as a movement back toward the "dumb" terminal instead of the PC, as a preemptive strike against SO, a means to reinforce the power of big organizations and to protect their rent-derived profits.

Nonetheless, the development of service-oriented computing demonstrated how extensive computing's affordances of flexibility could be. Equally important, SO shows that within the right social conditions, such as basic guaranteed income and the elimination of social forms favoring large organizations, computing makes possible very different work relations. In conjunction with informating, "free" organization, wiki-ing, and participatory design, SO computing demonstrates that the huge costs of organization—from buildings to equipment to labor to management to exploitation to profits—are not necessary or even "rational" for extending SFR.

6. Creative Commons and Similar Arrangements Can Promote Broader Access to and Use of the Means of Cultural Reproduction

The computing affordances we have addressed thus far are mostly manifested at the level of organization, of interactions among real people in real-life spaces. We now discuss some affordances that are manifested at the larger level of social formations as wholes. As discussed in Chapter 2, we use the term "cultural reproduction" to refer to the process of creating and spreading a social formation's ideas about and constructs of human action. The now-popular notion of the "meme" is a good example of an innovative idea/construct that emerged through cultural reproduction. The means of cultural reproduction are the various devices and procedures that allow for the creation of and change in these ideas and constructs, even the expanding of or the replacing of one set with another. Education, skills training, work, and self-expression are all important arenas where people use such means to reproduce culture (Hakken 1987).

With digital mediation, access to these means of cultural reproduction is changed, both extending them and putting them at risk. Lawrence Lessig has attended to problems of cultural reproduction, most directly in his book, *Remix: Making Art and Commerce Thrive in the Hybrid Economy* (Lessig 2014). Here, Lessig's theoretical position is consonant with the theory of SFR that we presented in Chapter 2. For Lessig, the central elements of culture generally take a symbolic form, in laws, words, concepts, and understandings, and also like us, he posits a general need for the active reproduction of such elements. He argues that any society's capacity to reproduce itself depends upon there being considerable opportunity for those concerned about the culture's surviving and thriving to have access to the performance of its central elements. This means, "talking the talk," but it also means having many forms of access and considerable scope for playing with the elements.

In *Remix*, Lessig also points out that computing provides a wide range of new means of cultural reproduction, everything from spell checkers to paint programs. Computing makes it easier to put existing culture in more malleable forms. In these regards, computing increases the means of cultural reproduction and their potential power. However, at the same time, the current "intellectual property" (IP) institutionalizations of computing also decrease access to these means of cultural reproduction. To make this case, Lessig draws attention to how software comes in two forms: "read only," which can be "read" by a computer but not changed, and "read and write," which can be both read and changed, or rewritten. Lessig extends this differentiation to the more general dynamics of DT'ed cultures. Some are "read-only" cultures; i.e., ones in which things like copyright and patents mean artists are severely limited in their opportunities to innovate and change cultural elements. Such limitation is accomplished through a strong intellectual property regime. Other social formations have "read and write" cultures that allow reproducers to remix extensively via the use of the new digital means of cultural reproduction. We agree with Lessig, that this situation means that read-only societies are at reproductive risk. Software innovation itself is one of the critical elements in the capacity for cultural reproduction of a digital society, and therefore the SFR. Lessig worries that making most of the cultural reproduction software "read only"—as by "defending" it behind an IP wall of proprietary software—puts the social formation at risk.

We agree with Lessig about the prominence artists and creators generally have in cultural reproduction through providing new expressions that lead to new forms of SFR. To play this role, artists must have access to the existing forms of cultural expression, as well as the space to "mess" with them. These capacities are generally necessary, as SFR changes the conditions under which culture must reproduce itself, with the new means of cultural reproduction needing to be found to meet changed conditions. It is especially important that culture mavens are able to remix or "mix, rip, and burn" new forms of expression that are still recognizable as belonging to the culture. Alternative cultural performances provide the means for apprehending the meaning of the new conditions. Without them, people lose the means to interpret and to create what is new.

To address this risk, Lessig developed the "Creative Commons" (CC) licensing regime. CC contains a range of different licenses, one of which allows a creator to make her work available to anyone to use or change, as they will, as long as that right continues to be extended to others. This form does for copyright what the GPL does for FS: "copyleft." Lessig is not against all limits on access to the means of cultural reproduction. He acknowledges the need for rewards sufficient to encourage the continued creation of innovations like new software, but as a "wounded veteran of the copyright wars," he argues for creative alternatives to proprietization. One he suggests would be a small tax on the download of each software program or, more generally, any cultural creation that is digitally available (Lessig 2014). The proceeds from the tax would be redistributed to each creator in proportion to the use made of their creations. An alternative procedure for rewarding creativity like this one would face important problems of measurement, such as what things count as "creative" and how to measure it: by line of code or song, or by each finished piece? Would a poem count a much as a novel? These questions of proper reward to foster continued innovation are relevant to many of the alternative forms we discuss here, which is one reason why we devote Chapter 8 to metrics.

As computing becomes an ever-widening mediator of SFR, its centrality to cultural reproduction grows proportionally, and so too does the need to address its general role in SFR. The correlates of digital technology use in regard to cultural reproduction are two-sided. On the one hand, the means of use and their capabilities are expanded, while on the other, access to use and the cultural materials to which they need to be applied are greatly impeded, largely by proprietization and IP. Like Lessig, we attend to the contradictions in the current situation, and thus to the need for more robust forms of and for cultural reproduction, forms that enable the pursuit of values other than those of IP, which is bent to the reproduction of capital. For an alternative SFR dynamic to emerge, the pursuit of such alternative values must be supported via different institutions, which is the focus of Chapter 7.

7. Cyber-Activism Can Open Information and Foster Change in SFR

The Internet does afford many forms of cyber-activism, collective action, and intervention in cyberspace to promote positive social change. The initiatives we have in mind run from those of cyber-hactivists like Anonymous to local groups organizing unpublicized acts of public witness, like flash mobs. Although there is reason to believe that its causal role may have been overstated, there is little doubt that the use of social media forms like Twitter were important to the Arab Spring. Now we have a clearer sense of the motivations and actions of Anonymous because of Gabriella Coleman's ethnography, *Hacker, Hoaxer, Whistleblower, Spy: The Many Faces of Anonymous*. Ethnographies like this, and documentaries like Laura Poitras's *Citizenfour*, about NSA whistleblower Edward Snowden, enhance our understanding of cyber-activism (Poitras 2014).

One common cyber-activist practice is to use DTs to share information that otherwise would remain hidden. Another is to inform public debate by using DTs to direct public attention to important cultural materials that might otherwise be ignored. As neo-classical economics acknowledges, for markets to work well, all market participants need access to the relevant information. Given that universal access to information is rare, one might expect economists to support information-sharing social movements. Instead, however, they generally just presume universal access to information. As pointed out in Chapter 3, the risk models of the quants similarly abstracted from, rather than including, information relevant to long-tail problems, as investment bankers systematically misinformed clients about the value of new financial instruments before the crisis (Wolf 2014).

Unequal access to information is an important digital divide, and cyber-activists have developed several means to address this (Coleman 2014). However significant their provision of additional information, cyber-activists know they have to do much more. By entering into the debate on DT-related public issues, cyber-activism also opens the possibility of using digital communications media to organize directly for social change. (In Chapter 9, we discuss cyber-activism's potential role in moving SFR beyond capital.)

There are, of course, dangers in cyber-activism. One is that activists will tend to substitute action in cyberspace for action in real life when both are necessary. Nor is cyber-activism always a social good. It can compromise security and privacy, both of individuals and collectivities. The publications of internal Sony emails in 2014 seems to have had little redeeming social value—embarrassing the corporation may have more in common with pranking than with promoting the public good. (Although, as Coleman argues with regard to Anonymous, pranking and making jokes can serve legitimate community-building purposes.) Edward Snowden and the editors of *The Guardian* made a considerable effort to share information responsibly, to maximize useful information while lessening the chances of inadvertent disclosures of identities and risky actions, although some problems arose anyway. The quality journalistic vetting of *The Guardian* was more effective and responsible than the earlier huge document dump of Wikileaks. The activities of governments and businesses can and do co-opt cyber-activism for their own purposes.

If we are correct in our assumption that computing will continue to be an important mediator of SFR, cyber-movements for social change will also grow in importance. Cyber-activism is necessary if we are to realize two of the Internet's most important possibilities: first, creating a world where everyone has equal access to information, not only about markets but also to other values, such as peace and cooperation; and second, creating a world where activists can mobilize even broader constituencies. At the same time, cyber-activism necessitates a new approach to the more general question of personal/group privacy/security.[3]

8. Peer-to-Peer Computing Can Support Common-ing

One of the distinctive affordances of computing is toward lateral communication, and lateral communication importantly affords the building of relationships among those similarly situated. Computing based on such relationships is called peer-to-peer computing; Wikipedia and free software projects are perhaps the most well-known examples.

As described above, in the classic Taylorist organization, information is normally both siloed (i.e., kept in separate, division-related channels) and vertically directed (i.e., flowing up from the bottom, while control flows down). Digital mediation can open up communication across silos and foster two-way or multi-way communication. In an organization, the extent of lateralization achieved depends upon whether "informating" is the digital goal and how actual systems are engineered to reflect this intention. An email system can make it easier and more likely that one person will communicate directly with people in other silos and at all levels. It can also increase the likelihood that communication will be person-to-person and not broadcast, like radio (Sproull and Kiesler 1992).

Of particular interest to us are the social formation-wide affordances of peer-to-peer computing. They are similar to those we have described above for organizing, but of note is the way in which they prioritize connection over co-location. The term typically used to describe a topologically (rather than topographically) connected group of co-peers is "community," and a great deal has been written about community in cyberspace (e.g., Rheingold 2000; Renninger and Shumar 2002; Turkle 2011). The "communities" evoked by social networking tend to be rather thin, but peer-to-peer communities often develop thick social connections among their participants. This can be seen, for example, in free software projects, which not only draw participants from all over the world, but which make geographic distance all but irrelevant. Peer-to-peer computing takes many forms, but importantly, it tends to foster interest in developing and maintaining "common pool" computing resources (Hess and Ostrom 2011). As suggested by the term itself, common pool resources are useful things that are collectively owned, shared, and managed by a social group. Open source code is a clear example of a common pool resource, in that anyone can use it to code but it still needs to be cared for. If for example, there is too much "forking" or changing code in ways that make it less usable, its value to the community of users, and to computing in general, is degraded. As with service-oriented computing, software lends itself to common pooling, as the cost of the next copy is virtually zero. In theory then, the resource is inexhaustible and thus of potentially infinite utility if properly cared for.

Elinor Ostrom describes common pooling by communities as a basic form of social organization, one alternative to the state on the one hand, and markets on the other (Hess and Ostrom 2011). Peer-to-peer computing experience has encouraged a revival of interest in developing new commons in other aspects of social life. People in cities like Trento, Italy, form networks around buying clubs, to get fresh produce directly from the producer. Network communication enables coordination about where and when the exchange is to take place. "Ithaca bucks," a form of local currency in Ithaca, New York, fosters similar exchanges. By doing a service such as lawn mowing for someone in the network, a person gets X notional Ithaca bucks; these can be used to pay another person for a service needed, e.g., babysitting. The "service orientation" discussed above (#6) depends on as well as affords digitally mediated lateral communication.

"Community" is, of course, a term with a widely stretched meaning. Sellers of products, including computing ones, often talk about their "community of users," when they really just mean "customers." Peer-to-peer computing is sometimes grouped with things like Airbnb, Lending Tree, Uber, and other examples of the so-called "sharing economy." Different from commons, the businesses of the "sharing economy" reinforce the bending of SFR to the reproduction of capital. The effect of commons peer-to-peer computing is instead to distance the resource or resources, whether a service or farmed food, from the influence of the market. In commons, peer-to-peer relations tend to become relationships, and relationships are more mobilize-able for activism. These are not the affordances leveraged in the sharing economy. The business Lending Tree connects people desiring loans to people willing to give them, Uber those desiring rides to those wanting them, etc. Unlike peer-to-peer or commons computing, there is a corporation behind the interaction and managing it to make a profit.

Peer-to-peer computing is like the "mixer" an event that affords direct connections among those in the network before the big plenary session at a professional meeting. In contrast, the plenary is broadcast, usually from those at or near the top to those lower down, like much pre-computing organizational communication, like paper memos. A difference between Web 1.0 and 2.0 is the latter's greater potential for interaction, which can foster real peer-to-peer relating and relationship building. Potentials for multiplying lateral communication channels and increasing peer-to-peer connecting are two reasons why organizations choose to use "open" means to create a shared sense of mission rather than closed, formal ones. The importance of loose, informal communications was recognized early in the history of the Internet. At the beginning, when it was the ARPAnet, the people responsible for sending defense department research pre-prints to other nodes realized that they could also send personal messages, even recruit others on the network to engage in common tasks. Fortunately, those in charge decided not to try to stamp out such "irregular communication," instead encouraging it, creating an initial form of sharing (Campbell-Kelly, Aspray, and Ensmenger 2013). Peer-to-peer computing is highly suggestive of things that can be done to increase greatly the common good.

9. Governance Can Become More Widely Dispersed

"Governance" is a term political scientists use for all the means through which a social formation makes, or decides not to make, decisions. Governance involves formal state institutions, such as legislatures and courts, but it also includes things like design decisions that are made in hierarchical corporations or by professional groups. Michel Foucault developed the additional notion of "governmentality" to describe the process by which people are made amenable to the dominant governance institutions in their country (Burchell, Gordon, and Miller 1991). A true democracy subjects the institutions of government to popular control. It not only makes decisions by "majority rule," it also brings discussions and decisions into a public sphere open to all, and it achieves governance through actual citizen involvement in decision-making, not merely the appearance thereof.

Many of the computing affordances already described in this chapter, such as Wiki-ing, demonstrate how computing can support more dispersed decision-making. Political scientists tend to think that problems of governance are directly related to scale (Stasavage 2011). In a small New England town, the annual meeting is often the place to make decisions. This is a form of direct democracy. As social formations get bigger, direct democracy has generally been replaced by representative, indirect democracy, where people are elected to represent us in a legislative body. One of the early hopes of Internet advocates was that the Internet could become a means of extending direct democracy so decisions could be made by direct plebiscites rather than in deliberative bodies. In Italy, there have been some experiences in determining party or candidate positions or party demands via such means, but broader efforts have been less successful at fostering informed governance (De Cindio and Stortone 2013).

The problem of scale in governance remains one of the major challenges to greater globalization (Stasavage 2011). Still, other digitally mediated initiatives demonstrate that decision-making can be raised in scale and still be democratic. One is the Internet Society (IS), a non-profit body that has taken on the task of creating an open global Internet where as much information as possible is made available to as many people as possible. A primary IS mechanism is to establish open digital standards through open debate within ad hoc task forces. The IS group as a whole decides that a standard is needed for something, say, an Internet protocol. Often in face-to-face sessions but also via the Internet, interested individuals make suggestions about what the standard should be and why. Membership in the task force is open to anyone, including individual IS members and representatives of IS member organizations. These latter can be states, voluntary organizations, or businesses. Through such means, the IS has managed to provide the Internet with proper standards that have kept it functioning. As in an FS project, an appropriate mix of democracy and meritocracy is achieved by listening to everyone until a consensus emerges.

The success of IS task forces is arguably aided by the fact that much of what makes one possible standard better than another is technical, such as its degree of fit with an installed hardware base. Yet in most situations, multiple standards are viable. Thus, the aim of task force debate is not to identify *the one best way*, as it would be under Taylorism, but instead to find a solution that is optimal for multiple, often competing, goals. This means that everyone is heard but some voices carry more weight than others, because of demonstrated subject matter competence or because of greater social influence (Hanseth and Lundberg 2001).

Decision-making practices are important forms of cultural reproduction. As with the cultural reproduction discussed in the section on commons previously, computing's correlates are contradictory. On the one hand, decision-making is harder because of its support for both increased complexity and upscaling. On the other hand, clear decision-making offers means and forms for coping with these problems. Digitally mediated and face-to-face (hybrid) practices have arisen, like those of the IS task forces, that are able to reach consensus about complicated issues. The success of such dispersed digital decision-making practices is a major argument used by those who want to keep the Internet out of the control of nations as much as possible. Many states do wish to exercise control over both the computing of those within their boundaries, as well as over what those outside can learn about those within (Goldsmith and Wu 2008). For example, China has demonstrated that it is possible to control the Internet and make it responsive to state desires and regulations. The experience of the Internet Society indicates that openness and technical sufficiency are not necessarily in competition; it also provides examples of decision-making procedures that demonstrate this to be the case. We believe this experience has much broader implications for governance in the digitally mediated future.

TO THE CRITIQUE OF THE HEGEMONY IN CULTURAL REPRODUCTION OF THE VALUE "VALUE"

The experiences we have cited show that forms of computing exist that are suggestive of very different SFR dynamics, as these forms can and do operate at some distance from the reproduction of capital. We have described them in a way that highlights their potential for encouraging alternative reproductive dynamics that are similar to each other. In the rest of the book, we will argue that the values implicit in these practices can be shaped into a values structure that would foster SFR dynamics that are very different from those tied closely to the reproduction of capital. It is the purpose of Chapters 6 through 8 to flesh out some possibilities of a general alternative in terms of different values, as well as the institutions and measures that might support them.

Before we can move on to this task, we want to be more explicit about how we view the place of values in SFR and why we think a project to move beyond capital should focus so centrally on values. Put simply, we think it necessary to begin with a critique of the powerful place of "value" in capitalist SFR, a place that blocks the way to alternative projects. The remainder of this chapter presents the first part of our critique of the value "value"—that is, a critique of the specific value, "value." In the next chapter, we present the second part of our critique, the problems of SFR bent to only one value as opposed to a broader set of values. There, we focus on the ethnological uniqueness of single-value SFR, contrasting the current hegemony of *value* discourse with other cultures, where the discourse is typically over *values*. As SFR moves toward the more typical human condition, the value "value" will not disappear, but take a place as just one of a broader set of many values.

COMPUTING AND THE EXPANSION OF CAPITAL'S REPRODUCTIVE AMBIT

We want to begin our critique by returning to another of our previous scholarly efforts focused on computing to account for the origins of this hegemony. *Computing Myths, Class Realities*, Hakken's and Andrews' (1993) contextual study of the introduction of DTs in Sheffield, England, examined the various social correlates of diverse computing initiatives (Hakken and Andrews 1993). In searching for what could be said in general, we concluded that the best predictor of high-quality social correlates of digital mediation was the breadth of the workspace groups that an initiative mobilized and whose interest it served. The broader the mobilization of interests, the greater was the likelihood that the mediation would achieve its goals, whereas narrower mobilization often led to conflict. This result was confirmed by Hakken in a study of DTs in the US (see Hakken 1999). In the second decade of the 1980s, even in "Labour's Home" in the north of England, the private owners and controllers of the means of production were able to reduce the influence of others and take narrow control of the technology/employment nexus. This elite was able to minimize worker control and make workers the ones who negatively felt digitization's effects. Consequently, much computerization produced conflict, as evident in aspects of the Miners' Strike of 1986. The political interventions most supportive of this increased capital hegemony over cultural reproduction, Thatcherism in

Britain and Reaganism in the US, were very visible examples of the increased use of state power to accommodate the expanding reproductive ambit of transnational capital. The uses of state power generally meant the promotion of DT uses bent to capital reproduction, which is why the affordances of computing highlighted in the previous section of this chapter were neither visible nor realized.

In *Cyborgs@Cyberspace?*, Hakken described a slightly later (1990s vs. 1980s) but similarly prodigious expansion of the influence of capital over SFR, this time in the Nordic countries (Hakken 1999). One example of this expansion is the decision by the Wallenberg group of companies to abandon national-level bargaining. This change in practice reduced worker power and led in turn to a declining influence of Nordic working life legislation over the way DTs were actually used, as well as less enforcement of the legislation. Both contexts, England and Scandinavia, demonstrated that the job-enriching tendencies inherent in DT use (e.g., informating) were so highly mediated by the reproductive dynamics of capital that they had little independent effect. In *The Knowledge Landscapes of Cyberspace*, Hakken critiqued owner hegemony over values discourse (Hakken 2003). This was his attempt to take seriously a specific, new computing/social change discourse prominent in the 1990s, one that largely disappeared in the wake of the dot-com bust of 2000. One central aspect of this discourse was the claim that computing would make the world's knowledge available to everyone. Other related organizational discourses then current included the claim that knowledge was an organization's most important resource; therefore, management of knowledge resources should be at the top of any organization's concerns. These ideas came together in a slogan about the DT'ed world becoming a "knowledge society," one based on the notion that knowledge, understood to be the ultimate source of value, could be managed. If this were so, Hakken argued, it should be possible to articulate a knowledge theory of value, which should in turn replace the previously dominant, competing, 19th-century labor and the 20th-century capital theories of value. What would a knowledge theory of value look like? What features of SFR dynamics does it explain better than the capital and labor theories?

One thing that a knowledge theory would need to account for was the continually growing influence of capital reproduction over general SFR. While important throughout the history of employment social formations, capital reproduction's influence on general SFR was in 2000 greater than at any other time. Since then, it has become even greater. The increased centrality of transnational, corporate capital to most social formations was and remains the most distinctive aspect of current SFR, even though it is seldom talked about and is often masked by tangential discourses, like those about "globalization." In the example of the firms controlled by the Wallenberg family, they had used national-level bargaining to purchase social peace since the 1920s. In ending national-level bargaining practices, the Wallenberg companies reoriented directly to a world market, thereby undermining the Swedish workforce. They remain the most powerful capitalist force in Sweden.

This expanding influence of capital over SFR was indexed vividly by the emergence of the transnational firm ABB, particularly its chameleon-like attempt to be "the best corporate citizen wherever we happen to be." This was a different face for what some anachronistically insist on still calling "Swedish" capital. Danish and Finnish social formations similarly accommodated to a more globally exercised ambit of capital. Despite the potential for relative autonomy provided by nationally owned oil, even Norwegian enterprises and state institutions increasingly adapted themselves to the demands of capitalist institutions. Most of the money in the oil-derived Norwegian sovereign wealth fund was invested internationally in corporate stocks and bonds. As the loci of decision-making shifted to more assertive supra-national corporations, there was a contraction in the ability of Nordic nation-state structures, including state-sponsored participatory design institutions, to promote economic democracy.

The growing influence of capital contrasted with the decline of trade union power and the narrowing range of options available to influential working people's politics (e.g. Labour, Social Democratic or, in the US, the Democratic Party). Ideologies that inhibited working-class influence also gained wider influence outside of Scandinavia and Europe. Hakken identified how local government projects in the Upper Mohawk Valley in New York, like those in England and in Scandinavia, were unable to have much influence directly over how technologies got institutionalized (Hakken 2003).

TURBO-CAPITALISM, NOT KNOWLEDGE, AS DOMINANT

Structural theories of cyberspace, like many of the mis-framings examined in Chapter 3, largely ignored or downplayed the growing influence of capital reproduction on SFR. Instead, they insisted that something else (e.g., knowledge) had become the generative source of change in social reproductive dynamics. In contrast, Hakken concluded that it made no sense to trace the growing influence of capital on SFR to new the knowledge dynamics induced by the use of DTs. In setting up our critique of value, we want to return to Will Hutton's argument that turbo-capitalism, not knowledge, was the motor of SFR dynamics (Hutton and Giddens 2000). Hutton argues that, while commoditization was an "ugly word," it identified the way capitalism makes commercial exchange ubiquitous in the form of intellectual property. He argues that increasingly, the control of an idea is more important than the substance of what the idea contributes to production. He agrees with Lessig that intellectual property rights are at the center of what is different and central to what "makes capitalism tick." The rest of capitalism—private property, exploitation of workers, etc.—"remain remarkably the same" (2000, 25).

Hutton links the question of intellectual property to the widening market, arguing that the collapse in the Asian markets in late 1997 furthered the hegemony of US capital. This put US capital in the ascendency and thus raises questions about globalization. For Hutton, a key part of globalization ". . . is about opening up the world to American interest in particular and Western capitalism in general. . . . [U]nderneath the glitz there remains the exercise of raw power . . ." (2000, 41).

Along with rejecting the idea that new technologies were the primary force for change, he also doubts the causative importance of globalization. For him, the dominant influence remains capital, still a nation/region-linkable form, but in a newly aggressive form. Capital's increasingly active role developed because capitalist systems *don't*, in fact, tend toward a neo-classical equilibrium. Rather,

> [i]ts rationality lies in its inherent capacity to accommodate risk, to experiment over investment for the future, and to be creative about new forms of production and consumption . . .
>
> (Hutton 2000, 19)

In the relentless pursuit of its reproduction, turbo-capital was especially generative of *in*stability. The Great Recession of 2007 supports his assertion, that instability was a primary result of the extension of capital over SFR (see also Harvey 2014).

Other casualties of the accelerated instability of turbo-capitalism were the institutions of social democracy, including the so-called welfare state. Hutton sees that deregulation produced bubble economies. He argues that the Giddens's knowledge theory discussed at the beginning of this chapter encouraged a "naive trust in markets," one that provided ideological cover for greater capital power, producing the very injustices they claimed to be correcting. Reforms such as the structural reform of labor markets or welfare systems are "standalone recommendations" that are aimed at making wage costs lower and work less secure for workers, eventually resulting in the weakening of any system of social protections (2000).

For Hutton, phenomena like globalization are not caused by an emergent political economy of knowledge before which all must fall, but by destabilizing changes in the dynamic of capital reproduction. Technology change, the increasingly global reach of the corporation, and increased competition—all are quite real. However, they do not follow from any particular inevitable dynamic or laws native to knowledge technology. Rather, they follow from deliberate policy interventions, including the weakening of nation-based trade unions, in order to control labor. These interventions also weaken the capacity of geography-tied capital to enhance the conditions of its reproduction, for example, through tariffs. Forceful performance of knowledge mantras do impact social reproduction, but not because they reflect structural "truths." Rather, they are an ideological influence in policy discussions, ones that diverts attention from the increasing ambit of capital and therefore from any attempt to mitigate its undesirable consequences.

In Marxist terminology, readings like Hutton's stress the "social relations" of production, rather than the "technical relations" of production of interest to Giddens. Hutton and Giddens were writing at the end of the 1990s, a time of renewed, unprecedented capital dominance in the US, Britain, and indeed the Nordic countries, more powerful than it was in the 1920s. The time frame is associated with several global shifts, including dissolution of the Soviet Union and the assertion of renewed or new capitalist cultural legitimations (e.g., intellectual property, neo-liberalism) in the face of the challenges.

Turbo-capitalism did take advantage of the DT-enabled reorganizations of the labor process, such as matrix organizational structures[4] and collective forms of discipline, vs. the old Taylorist hierarchy. Yet while DTs added options for reorganizing the labor process, they were not the driving force behind the organization chosen (Braverman and Sweezy 1975). Perhaps DTs' primary role was ideological. It is in the *notion* that such reorganization was necessitated "ineluctably" by technology, that DTs' influence comes to appear to be structural. While DTs clearly were used to justify the re-imposition of a strong capital regime, they did not *have* to be used in this way. The rapid disappearance of knowledge society talk after the dot-com crash of 2000 suggests that this knowledge DT talk was not driven by an internal dynamic, but by ideology.

A CULTURAL THEORY OF CONTEMPORARY VALUE CONTRADICTIONS AND CULTURAL CONTRADICTIONS OF CAPITAL MYTHOLOGIES

Hutton's analysis explains capital reproduction's expanded influence over SFR. Unlike Giddens, he does so without extending it mythically, not hiding aggressive capital in knowledge clothing or deploying other metaphors that divert critique. We want to reformulate his analysis in more anthropological terms to allow us to specify what differentiates the reproductive dynamics of contemporary employment social formations from previous ones. This perspective also suggests some new challenges to capital accumulation.

Anthropologists use "myth" to describe the stories that humans tell themselves to account for cultural dynamics (White 1959). Because human social formations must reproduce socially, the development of myth is a necessary component of cultural and therefore of social formation reproduction. To an anthropologist, the political economics developed to account for the rise of the employment social formation constitutes the early mythologies of capitalism. It was not money, markets, production of goods for sale, nor even forms of mass production that were the distinctive feature of the new "employment" type of social formation that came to prominence in the 18th century. All of these existed in previous social formations. What was new was the extension of the commodity form (mediation by markets) into two new arenas of social practice. First, human labor became labor power (the capacity to do work). Second, profit—the difference between the value of what workers produced and the value of the costs of production—became capital. Once the institutions of labor and capital markets came into existence, one could buy and sell work in the form of labor power, and thus transform surplus value (profit) into capital (Marx 1967).

To become widespread, mythologies must provide persuasive, if not necessarily accurate, accounts of the dynamics of social reproduction. These accounts must be convincing enough to be regularly repeated. At the heart of the reproduction of capital from the start was a problem for creating a convincing myth—that between the explanation of value and where it was understood to come from, namely labor. Sellers had to convince potential buyers that the things they wanted to sell were worth the asking price. A labor theory of value followed. On the other hand, producers had to convince workers to produce these things at pay rates that, after accounting for sunk capital costs, were lower than the sale price. In the emerging industrial world of the 19th century, the owners of capital were able to do this because they had a monopoly over access to means of production, and former farmers and servants without access to commons had little alternative but to accept the wages offered. A mythology had to be created that acknowledged the value of labor but not how the work was extorted from the workers.

In the social formations where the institutions of labor and capital first developed (and now in developing nations), the initial markets were largely in luxury goods. As the commodity form penetrated more aspects of social reproduction, workers became important as consumers as well as workers. This enabled them to extended their collective means to influence general social reproduction, labor markets, and states. Capital markets require stability. This was provided by states that, for example, promoted sufficiently transparent banking and meaningful exchange rates (Smith 2014). If states failed to provide sufficient transparency in such matters, there were problems for planning, as in the Soviet Union. States also periodically served as crucial sources of investment, particularly in infrastructure, e.g., in canals or in the Internet. When organized, workers can exert influence over states. To the extent that workers were able to exert influence, the contradiction at the heart of the labor theory of value became more blatant, and its value as a justifying myth correspondingly declined.

The 19th century capital theories of value that displaced labor theories mythically resolved this problem. In these narratives, value arose not from ripping off workers, but from value generating potential inherent in capital. Freed from being moored in the real worth of things produced, the mythically powerful entity, capital, also became more malleable. From this malleability, new contradictions spring regularly. If public entities can lower interest rates to stave off recession, why not keep rates low longer so that small business can stay afloat, too? If public monies can be used to guarantee the profit level of military contractors, why can't they also fund worker cooperatives? If government monies can rescue savings and loans, banks, and insurance companies, why not also rescue communities? If interest rates for banks can be less than 1%, why are students paying much higher rates for student loans? Such questions indicate how these extended myths of capital reproduction are difficult to control. Its continuing actual dependence upon labor to produce value turned into profit then makes capital increasingly difficult to reproduce in the real world. It can only do so by bringing more and more domains of existence within its ambit, as is being attempted in education. The gap increases between the cultural reproductive potential of mythic "capital" and the reproductive demands of social formations sometimes called "late" capitalist are threatening the reproduction of entire social formations (Mandel 1999).[5]

KNOWLEDGE THEORIES OF VALUE AND THE FUTURE OF SOCIAL FORMATION REPRODUCTION

It is in the context of this history, particularly the declining persuasiveness of capital theories of value, that the knowledge value theory of Giddens and those described in Chapter 3 arose. If a knowledge theory of value were applied to policy, what would be the result? Could it extend the reproductive ambit of employment social formations into the future? The obstacles to be overcome would be formidable. The commodity form continues to expand its long march through the institutions of all social formations, colonizing new arenas like education. Turbo-capitalism eliminates or severely weakens institutions with any independent ability to influence social formation reproduction—such as educational institutions, governments, religions, families, and voluntary organizations/not-for-profits. At the same time, powerful independent capitals become harder to control, making SFR increasingly disorderly and crises more likely, as described in Chapter 3. Our capacities to extend social formation reproduction depend upon reversing the dominance of capital, and ultimately displacing it. A knowledge theory of value provides little analysis and few means to achieve these objectives (Hakken 2003).

In contrast, the beginning of computerization in Sheffield, England was the scene of a different approach (Hakken and Andrews 1993). This was not another theorized source of value, but instead the replacement of value in the context of other values. When computers arrived in Sheffield, the most important determinant of what happened was the actual technology actor network created, not the technical properties of the chosen machines, abstract labor/management relations, or the iron laws of the market. What mattered were the perceptions of the technology, the goals striven for, and the actual actions of the particular people in the organization. While the dominant social relations clearly marginalized some perceptions, goals, and actions, and economics and mechanics certain others, there was still a broad range of interpretive flexibility in the actual performance of DT actor networks. Value creation (i.e., capital) was only one of several values relevant to the outcome.

The conceptual problem before us is not to come up with another theory of the source of value, but instead to switch the focus away from the almost exclusive concern with where value comes from. Would replacing a theory of value with a theory of values necessarily mean ending capitalism? Will Hutton concurs with Meghnad Desai (Desai 2004) that it will not. He cogently argues that globalization favors shareholders or stockholders. This form of capital, then, challenges a different form, what he calls "stakeholder capitalism." This variant is more favorable to workers and tries to behave more ethically. It has been less successful than turbo-capitalism, "[b]ut that doesn't mean that the principle of stakeholder capitalism is wrong; it means rather that some of the means of achieving it have to be updated and modernised . . ." (2000, 31).

For Hutton, "stakeholder capitalism" is a form of capitalism where the reproduction of things other than capital is of concern, where capital reproduction doesn't run roughshod over everything else. Instead, it is disciplined in a manner that equally benefits all social stakeholders. Because turbo-capitalism is neither a technologically driven inevitability nor an unstoppable structural imperative, there remains considerable opportunity for dethroning "value," as well as a pressing need for the governance of the global economy. In 2000, Hutton saw the question that remained as, ". . . to what extent we can modify capitalism so that it can live with other values like quality and social justice . . ." (2000, 19). He points out that every form of capitalism must have a legal framework in order to carry out business. And laws, whether they are about banking or contracts or other aspects of business, are based on choices. Those choices shape the kind of capitalism that emerges. He further contends that laws "can be biased significantly to favour interest other than property owners and private shareholders" (2000, 34–35).

In Hutton's analysis, it remains possible to re-domesticate capitalism, perhaps to use knowledge technologies to construct ideological critiques of pure shareholder capitalism and thus of the reproductive influence of capital. We do not share Hutton's optimism about pushing the turbo-capitalist genie back into the bottle. In theoretical terms, interpretive flexibility with regard to the political economics of DTs does not mean, "Anything goes." Both turbo-capitalism and post-capitalism are terms that cover a wide range of specific, possible social formations of the future, and the dynamics of future SFR will not be determined by choosing among neo-classical capital mythologies, political-economic technological determinism, or chaos.

We can be subtle about causation without abandoning it altogether. DTs are better viewed as terrains of contestation than as ineluctable, independent forces. Technologies do have politics, but like all politics, they are not simple, but instead manifest multiple, contradictory tendencies. Their role in particular situations depends upon how multiple constructions play out through conflict and how contexts influence each other. Capitalism is an inherently anarchic political economy, and the "new economy" a mirage. But contradictory forces and conflicting constructions mean the future is yet to be shaped. Moments of underdetermination can be moments of opportunity. Before the opportunities that can be drawn out of the computing affordances described in this chapter can be seized, the centrality of value-centered capital reproduction must be displaced. We think this can be done through re-basing SFR on values (plural). Why and how to do this, we will take up in the next chapter.

NOTES

1. There is some disagreement as to when the crisis began. Those who tend to label it a financial crisis are inclined to pick 2008, with the collapse of Lehman Brothers and the events that led rapidly, in the US, to the federal Troubled Asset Relief Program. Those of us who see it in broader terms, as having many additional social and economic elements, tend to date it from 2007, when US homeowners, especially those with sub-prime mortgages, found themselves "under water"—with mortgages of greater value than that of the home so mortgaged. The narrower, later-dated view is associated with the idea that the crisis is over, while the earlier date indicates a sense that it is still with us.
2. Wheeler is the Vice President for Information Technology of Indiana University. The Sakai and Kwali projects that he heads determine what new features to add to the software at democratically run annual conferences. They provide free software to anyone or "any-org" wanting to use it. Some users, however, join the project board of directors. When they do so, they agree to bring with them an employed workforce that can be directed to work on and complete aspects of the software that have been identified as desirable. Through assuming responsibility for the development of a particular feature, board members, who in the case of Sakai and Kwali tend to be universities, introduce a greater degree of predictability into the project. This is only one of the diverse forms of "virtuality" exemplified by F/LOSS projects. In 2014, Wheeler shifted academic course support from Sakai to another open source project, Canvas.
3. A notion of privacy depends upon the ability to distinguish a public from a private sphere (Nippert-Eng 2010). While privacy remains an important basis for individual and collective action, digital technology use tends to undermine shared understandings of the boundary between public and private. Privacy remains important, but it is not clear to us how it is best protected in cyberspace.
4. Near the end of the 20th century, organizational theorists were exploring the options that might be taken if one rejected extreme, Taylorist efforts to control the work process and also Weberian notions of bureaucracy. Matrix structures were one of their more interesting ideas. Rather than the external control of managers, control was to be based on the internal force of worker motivation. The bureaucratic hierarchy was replaced by a "matrix" of workers, each of whom chose what projects to work on, and thus there were no job definitions or rigid reporting rules. Gideon Kunda (Kunda 2006) has the best description

of an actual matrix structure in operation, at the Digital Equipment Corporation in the 1980s.

5. A number of radical political economists have followed Ernest Mandel in referring to the current era as "late capitalism." This terminology is intended to suggest that contradictions like these are so overwhelming that capitalism's state is one of senility at best. We do not choose this terminology because, despite the anemic recovery, the last decade has demonstrated capitalism's resiliency, in both symbolic and political-economic domains. While its robust survival in the long-term remains doubtful, its demise does not appear to be imminent.

REFERENCES

Atwood, Margaret. 2008. *Payback: Debt and the Shadow Side of Wealth*. Fourth Impression edition. Berkeley, CA: House of Anansi Press.

Bosio, Enrico, Tiziana Girardi, Daniela Stefanescu, Vincenzo D'Andrea, and Maurizio Teli. 2014. "Understanding Online Deliberation: The Dis-Alignment Between Designers and Users." Paper presented at The Internet Policy and Politics Conference. Oxford, England.

Braverman, Harry, and Paul M. Sweezy. 1975. *Labor and Monopoly Capital: The Degradation of Work in the Twentieth Century*. Third edition. New York: Monthly Review Press.

Burchell, Graham, Colin Gordon, and Peter Miller, eds. 1991. *The Foucault Effect: Studies in Governmentality*. First edition. Chicago: University of Chicago Press.

Calhoun, Craig J., and Georgi M. Derluguian. 2011. *Business as Usual: The Roots of the Global Financial Meltdown*. New York University Press.

Campbell-Kelly, M., William Aspray, and Nathan Ensmenger. 2013. *Computer: A History of the Information Machine (The Sloan Technology Series) by Campbell-Kelly, Martin, Aspray, William, Ensmenger, Nathan, (2013) Paperback*. Boulder, CO: Westview Press.

Coleman, E. Gabriella. 2012. *Coding Freedom: The Ethics and Aesthetics of Hacking*. Princeton: Princeton University Press.

———. 2014. *Hacker, Hoaxer, Whistleblower, Spy: The Many Faces of Anonymous*. First edition. London: Verso.

Collins, Randall. 2013. "The End of Middle Class Work: No More Escapes." In *Does Capitalism Have a Future?*, 37–70. New York, NY: Oxford University Press.

Comaroff, Jean, and John L. Comaroff, eds. 2001. *Millennial Capitalism and the Culture of Neoliberalism*. Durham, NC: Duke University Press Books.

Davenport, Thomas H., and Keri Pearlson. 1998. "Two Cheers for the Virtual Office." *Sloan Management Review* 39: 51–66.

De Cindio, Fiorella, and Stefano Stortone. 2013. "Experimenting LiquidFeedback for Online Deliberation in Civic Contexts." In *Electronic Participation*, edited by Maria A. Wimmer, Efthimios Tambouris, and Ann Macintosh, 147–58. Lecture Notes in Computer Science 8075. Berlin: Springer. http://link.springer.com/chapter/10.1007/978-3-642-40346-0_13.

Foster, John Bellamy, and Fred Magdoff. 2009. *The Great Financial Crisis: Causes and Consequences*. New York: Monthly Review Press.

Desai, Meghnad. 2004. *Marx's Revenge: The Resurgence of Capitalism and the Death of Statist Socialism*. London: Verso.

Goldsmith, Jack, and Tim Wu. 2008. *Who Controls the Internet?: Illusions of a Borderless World*. First edition. New York: Oxford University Press.

Golub, Alex. 2010. "Being in the World (of Warcraft): Raiding, Realism, and Knowledge Production in a Massively Multiplayer Online Game." *Anthropological Quarterly* 83 (1): 17–45. doi:10.1353/anq.0.0110.

Greenbaum, Joan, and Kim Madsen. 1993. "Small Changes: Starting a Participatory Process by Giving Participants a Voice." In *Participatory Design: Principles and Practices*, edited by Douglas Shuler and Aki Namioka, 289–98. Mahwah NJ: Lawrence Erlbaum.

Grudin, Jonathan. 1991. "Interactive Systems: Bridging the Gaps Between Developers and Users." *Computer* 24 (4): 59–69.

Hakken, David. 1987. "Reproduction in Complex Social Formations." *Dialectical Anthropology* 12 (2): 193–204. doi:10.1007/BF00263324.

———. 1999. *Cyborgs@Cyberspace?: An Ethnographer Looks to the Future*. New York: Routledge.

———. 2003. *The Knowledge Landscapes of Cyberspace*. New York, NY: Routledge.

Hakken, David, and Barbara Andrews. 1993. *Computing Myths, Class Realities: An Ethnography of Technology and Working People in Sheffield, England*. Boulder: Westview Press.

Hanseth, Ole, and Nina Lundberg. 2001. "Designing Work Oriented Infrastructures." *Computer Supported Cooperative Work (CSCW)* 10 (3–4): 347–72. doi:10.1023/A:1012727708439.

Harvey, David. 2014. *Seventeen Contradictions and the End of Capitalism*. First edition. Oxford: Oxford University Press.

Hern, Alex. 2015. "Wikipedia Votes to Ban Some Editors from Gender-Related Articles." *The Guardian*. January 23. http://www.theguardian.com/technology/2015/jan/23/wikipedia-bans-editors-from-gender-related-articles-amid-gamergate-controversy.

Hess, Charlotte, and Elinor Ostrom, eds. 2011. *Understanding Knowledge as a Commons: From Theory to Practice*. Cambridge, MA: MIT Press.

Hippel, Eric von. 2005. "Democratizing Innovation: The Evolving Phenomenon of User Innovation." *Journal Für Betriebswirtschaft* 55 (1): 63–78. doi:10.1007/s11301-004-0002-8.

———. 2006. *Democratizing Innovation*. Cambridge, MA: MIT Press.

Hippel, Eric von, and Georg von Krogh. 2003. "Open Source Software and the 'Private-Collective' Innovation Model: Issues for Organization Science." *Organization Science* 14 (2): 209–23. doi:10.1287/orsc.14.2.209.14992.

Hutton, Will, and Anthony Giddens, eds. 2000. *Global Capitalism*. New York: New Press.

Kelty, Christopher M. 2008. *Two Bits: The Cultural Significance of Free Software*. Durham: Duke University Press Books.

Klein, Naomi. 2014. *This Changes Everything: Capitalism vs. The Climate*. New York: Simon & Schuster.

Kokash, Natallia, Willem-Jan van den Heuvel, and Vincenzo D'Andrea. 2006. "Leveraging Web Services Discovery with Customizable Hybrid Matching." In *Service-Oriented Computing—ICSOC 2006*, edited by Asit Dan and Winfried Lamersdorf, 522–28. Lecture Notes in Computer Science 4294. Berlin: Springer. http://link.springer.com/chapter/10.1007/11948148_50.

Kunda, Gideon. 2006. *Engineering Culture: Control and Commitment in a High-Tech Corporation*. Revised edition. Philadelphia, PA: Temple University Press.

Kuttner, Robert. 2008. *The Squandering of America: How the Failure of Our Politics Undermines Our Prosperity*. New York: Vintage.

Lessig, Lawrence. 2014. *Remix Making Art and Commerce Thrive in the Hybrid Economy*. New York: Epic Publishing.

Lewis, Michael. 2010. *Liar's Poker*. New York: W. W. Norton & Company.

Luce, Edward. 2014. "Too Big to Resist: Wall Street's Comeback." *Financial Times*, December 14, 9.

Mandel, Ernest. 1999. *Late Capitalism*. Second edition. London: Verso.

Mann, Michael. 2013. "The End May Be Nigh But for Whom?" In *Does Capitalism Have a Future?*, 71–98. New York: Oxford University Press.

Marglin, Stephen A. 2008. *The Dismal Science: How Thinking Like an Economist Undermines Community*. Cambridge, MA: Harvard University Press.

Markus, M. Lynne, Brook Manville, and Carole E. Agres. 2000. "What Makes a Virtual Organization Work?" *Sloan Management Review* 42 (1): 13–26.

Marx, Karl. 1967. *Capital: A Critical Analysis of Capitalist Production: The Process of Capitalist Production*. Edited by Friedrich Engels. New York: International Publishers.

McLean, Bethany, and Joe Nocera. 2010. *All the Devils Are Here: The Hidden History of the Financial Crisis*. New York: Portfolio Hardcover.

Morini, Cristina, and Andrea Fumagalli. 2010. "Life Put to Work: Towards a Life Theory of Value." *Ephemera: Theory & Politics in Organization* 10 (3/4): 234–52.

Nippert-Eng, Christena E. 2010. *Islands of Privacy*. Chicago: University of Chicago Press.

Patterson, Scott. 2010. *The Quants: How a New Breed of Math Whizzes Conquered Wall Street and Nearly Destroyed It*. New York, NY: Crown Business.

Piketty, Thomas. 2014. *Capital in the Twenty-First Century*. Third edition. Cambridge, MA: Belknap Press.

Poitras, Laura. 2014. "Citizenfour." Produced in Berlin: Praxis Films, 2014.

Reagle, Joseph Michael. 2010. *Good Faith Collaboration: The Culture of Wikipedia*. Cambridge, MA: MIT Press.

Renninger, K. Ann, and Wesley Shumar, eds. 2002. *Building Virtual Communities: Learning and Change in Cyberspace*. First edition. London: Cambridge University Press.

Rheingold, Howard. 2000. *The Virtual Community: Homesteading on the Electronic Frontier*. Revised edition. Cambridge, MA: MIT Press.

Rifkin, Jeremy. 2014. *The Zero Marginal Cost Society: The Internet of Things, the Collaborative Commons, and the Eclipse of Capitalism*. New York: Palgrave Macmillan.

Roubini, Nouriel, and Stephen Mihm. 2010. *Crisis Economics: A Crash Course in the Future of Finance*. New York, NY: Penguin.

Schumpeter, Joseph A. 2008. *Capitalism, Socialism, and Democracy*. Third Edition. New York: Harper Perennial Modern Classics.

Shiller, Robert J. 2008. *The Subprime Solution: How Today's Global Financial Crisis Happened, and What to Do about It*. Princeton, N. J: Princeton University Press.

Simonsen, Jesper, and Toni Robertson, eds. 2012. *Routledge International Handbook of Participatory Design*. First edition. New York: Routledge.

Smith, Adam. 1863. *An Inquiry into the Nature and Causes of the Wealth of Nations*. London, UK: Adam and Charles Black.

Sproull, Lee, and Sara Kiesler. 1992. *Connections: New Ways of Working in the Networked Organization*. Cambridge, MA: MIT Press.

Stallman, Richard M, Lawrence Lessig, Joshua Gay, and Laurence Lessig. 2002. *Free Software, Free Society: Selected Essays of Richard M. Stallman*. Boston, MA: Free Software Foundation.

Stasavage, David. 2011. *States of Credit: Size, Power, and the Development of European Polities*. Princeton, NJ: Princeton University Press.

Tapscott, Don, and Anthony D. Williams. 2010. *Wikinomics: How Mass Collaboration Changes Everything*. Expanded edition. New York: Portfolio.

Tett, Gillian. 2009. *Fool's Gold: How the Bold Dream of a Small Tribe at J.P. Morgan Was Corrupted by Wall Street Greed and Unleashed a Catastrophe*. Reprint edition. New York: Free Press.

Tolbert, Pamela S., and Richard H. Hall. 2008. *Organizations: Structures, Processes and Outcomes*. Tenth edition. Upper Saddle River, NJ: Pearson.

Travica, Bob. 1998. *New Organizational Designs: Information Aspects*. Stamford, CT: Ablex Publishing Corporation.

Turkle, Sherry. 2011. *Alone Together: Why We Expect More from Technology and Less from Each Other.* New York: Basic Books.

Turoff, Murray, and Starr Roxanne Hiltz. 2009. "The Future of Professional Communities of Practice." In *Designing E-Business Systems. Markets, Services, and Networks*, edited by Christof Weinhardt, Stefan Luckner, and Jochen Stößer, 144–58. Lecture Notes in Business Information Processing 22. Berlin: Springer. http://link.springer.com/chapter/10.1007/978-3-642-01256-3_13.

Wallerstein, Immanuel, Randall Collins, Michael Mann, Georgi Derluguian, and Craig Calhoun. 2013. *Does Capitalism Have a Future?*. First edition. Oxford: Oxford University Press.

Weber, Steven. 2005. *The Success of Open Source.* Cambridge, MA: Harvard University Press.

Weisskopf, Thomas E. 1979. "Marxian Crisis Theory and the Rate of Profit in the Postwar U.S. Economy." *Cambridge Journal of Economics* 3 (4): 341–78.

White, Leslie A. 1959. *The Concept of Culture. American Anthropologist* 61 (2): 227–251.

Wolf, Martin. 2014. *The Shifts and the Shocks: What We've Learned-and Have Still to Learn-from the Financial Crisis.* New York: Penguin Press.

Zuboff, Shoshana. 1988. *In the Age of the Smart Machine: The Future of Work and Power.* New York: Basic Books.

5 An Ethnological Theory of Values

INTRODUCTION

In the preceding chapters, we discussed how computing has become central to social formation reproduction (SFR), as well as the problems in a range of existing social theories that prevent them from properly representing the computing/SFR connection. We also wrote about why we think contemporary social formations are at risk of being unable to extend their reproduction and what needs to happen to overcome this risk. In Chapter 4, we identified several computing practices that suggest a way forward. In the remainder of the book, we outline a possible program of computing-afforded social changes to reestablish social reproductive capacity through committing to a new set of values.

A major block to the ability of contemporary social formations to commit to a new set of values is the preoccupation with one value, that of "value." Complicating our task of explicating this preoccupation is another, more general expository problem, one deriving from the multiple meanings of the term "value." One meaning is that described by David Graeber (Graeber 2001), where "a value" is something socially defined as what is beautiful or important, and is typically then one of many such values. The other meaning is that explicated later in this chapter identified by David Harvey (Harvey 2007). In this meaning, "value" is used to identify the results of creating a commodity. This "value in general" is the meaning whose measurement dominates current human interaction, and this concept of "value" has hegemony in contemporary discourse. Rather than using a new word for one or the other meaning, as well as the different social processes involved in each, we are not inventing anything. When it is important to be clear that we are talking about the Graeber meaning, we try to use the plural, to speak of "values," and the term "valuation," and on occasion even "valuesing" to refer to the process of creating/advocating for something to be "valued" or "valuable." When it is important to be clear that we are talking about the second meaning, we sometimes resort to the odd expression—the value "value" or we speak of "ratio value."

To face the crisis in SFR, it will be necessary to find a new set of values, and develop associated institutions and measures. In this chapter, we present an account of what it will take to move forward, in the form of a theory of values and value. The chapter builds on recent anthropological work that lays the conceptual foundation for an alternative program. We approach value(s)[1] in the context of what anthropologists call "ethnology," the study of the general development of social formation types. Central to our ethnology of value(s) are distinctions among nominal, ordinal, and ratio notions of values and valuation, which we see as three different, basic—that is cross-culturally discernable—types of values. We borrow these labels from statistics. We point out that social formations able to extend their reproduction manifest a rough balance among these three value types. Current social formations suffer from the hegemony of ratio over nominal and ordinal valuation. The overwhelming dominance of ratio valuing is at the core of the current risk to SFR. We also need to be able to overcome the current preoccupation with one value, namely, ratio value. This problem is at the core problem of the *imbalance among value types*. We can't just replace one value type with another; there must be a general rebalancing among value types if reproductive capacity is to be restored. However, this rebalancing won't take place if humans stay committed to pursuing ratio value alone rather than pursuing it among other values. Achieving such a rebalancing depends upon expanding SFR focus beyond the pursuit of individual utility functions, which in turn means relying on human sociability and humans' capacities for liberation.

Another of our basic convictions is that values, institutions, and measures are human cultural constructions. Humans have the collective capacity to develop and carry out projects for changing and creating new sets of values. This conviction is central to what makes our project utopian, as we argued in Chapter 1. We want to show how a future-oriented approach can guide the discovery and construction of an alternative valuation regime on which to build a viable future. We also see creation of a proper understanding of the computing/social change connection as central to understanding current valuation processes, and visa versa. Even though the value affordances of computing discussed in Chapter 4 have promise for renewed reproductive capacity, merely showing that they can be connected to the pursuit of new or renewed values is not enough. In addition to ethnology, we draw upon other theories, some of which we discussed in Chapter 2, including Autonomous Marxism. We focus especially on its theoretical and political key points to justify our belief that rethinking values is both desirable and possible. A conceptual enlargement must take place before advantage can be taken of the new set of values implicit in digital mediation. In subsequent chapters, we will explore several elements that could enable the new/renewed values implicit in computing forms to be at the center of a new, rebalanced system of value(s). We will argue that these values need to be accompanied by new organizational and measurement practices. The articulation of one possible alternative set of values, institutions, and measures is the preoccupation the book's remaining chapters. This chapter's goal is to explicate an approach to the process of finding value's foci, one necessary for the broader program we articulate later.

Before outlining this theory of valuation—really, values-ation—we remind the reader of our rationale for thinking that the domain of digital technologies (DTs) is a basis for extending SFR via new values. First, the idea that DTs are generative of social change has been an accepted part of DT rhetoric since the early days of computing itself (Iacono and Kling 1988). Second, change advocates treat computing as an ideal driver of radical social change, pushing for more of it (Friedman 2006; Toffler 1980). Third, as DT-centered corporations (e.g., Apple, Microsoft, Google, Facebook) have achieved market dominance through inscribing their products into technological infrastructures, computing logic has become essential to capital accumulation and reproduction—the primary determinants of SFR dynamics at the moment. DTs are central to how corporations extract profits from humans' capacity to create social relations, and this centrality will have to change if SFR dynamics are to be extended (van Dijck 2013). Fourth, new practices suggestive of alternative futures, such as those oriented to the common, are greatly afforded by computing. Computing practices like those discussed in the previous chapter provide empirical proof that computing can support different values, such as differently valued distributions of things to roles like production and consumption. In the remainder of the book, we aim to show how these new forms of valuation have the capacity to address current SFR problems.

KNOWLEDGE, VALUATION, AND THEORIZING VALUE

Additionally, the factors cited above also manifest themselves in problems for SFR. For example, computing advocacy has been an important source of the widespread information overload that has become a feature of everyday life. While building on the sense of change associated with computing, new valuations will also counterbalance the information overload downside of computing. Digital technologies are contributing most to the information diffusion aspect of the data-information-knowledge-wisdom (DIKW) cycle. Although we may well feel like we are drowning in information, the increased amount is not our most serious problem. A kind of paralysis sets in when we have a great deal of information but don't know what it means. This experience results in the disengaged, blasé outlook described by Georg Simmel, when a human being is overwhelmed and the reaction to new stimuli is weak and underdeveloped (Simmel 2014). Both as individuals and in our social formations, we have to deal with huge leaps in the amount of information we have, in spite of not being about to figure out what the information is *worth*.

When we look at knowledge as a situated practice, as Lucy Suchman does, what emerges is that a key failure of contemporary computing is not attending sufficiently to the moment of connection between information and knowledge in the DIKW cycle (Suchman 1987). People in their everyday lives frame some information as knowledge; that is, as information whose meaning is known. Making knowledge involves ordering information and finding ways to evaluate it. In other words, *knowing is valuation.* Consequently, understanding how people value and how general values are inscribed into everyday life is an essential part of confronting the too-much-information society. We need to understand the institutions in which valuation practices take form, how they might be changed, and the means through which such institutions are and could be evaluated. As the knowledge valuation problem is both intellectual and practical, we need to theorize valuation both in general terms and in relation to computing.

Before we can advocate effectively for different future values, we need to attend to current valuation, namely problems in the relations between the specific value of value and value in general. We need to account for how, as manifested in phenomenon like the rise of money, a general sense of value displaced in cultural reproduction the sets of multiple values that had been central before to SFR. In short, we need a more transcultural, developmental ethnology of values and value, or valuation.

THE ETHNOLOGY OF VALUES AND DIGITAL MEDIATION

David Graeber is one of several anthropologists who answered Arjun Appadurai's call for renewed efforts to account for the diverse ways that cultures, in their practices, come to treat some culturally constructed things as important, while others are not so treated (Appadurai 1996; Graeber 2011). In addition to Graeber, others have taken up the issue, for example, Stephen Gudeman (Gudeman 2001), and Bill Maurer and Gabriele Schwab (Maurer and Schwab 2006).[2] Taken together, these scholars' efforts have reinvigorated the anthropological discourse on value and values. They have developed notions to illuminate the process across wide swathes of human cultures, perhaps even all. As important steps toward the ethnology of value and values, this work enables us to place changes in contemporary valuation in the context of prior changes.

The renewed discourse on values to which Graeber and his colleagues have contributed has arisen at the same time as the spread in use of digital technologies. We think these two events are linked. The link is sometimes made directly, as in the idea that non-instrumental online interactivity (often called "playbor," or play plus labor) changes political economy by arguably displacing traditional labor (Scholz 2012). DTs and change in values can also be connected indirectly through wider change processes, such as financialized "globalization," as argued by Saskia Sassen (Sassen 2001). Ideas about change in valuing are an important part of a powerful late twentieth and early twenty-first century trope that there is a *causal connection* between computing and social change. Our ethnological agenda includes extracting what the new anthropology of values suggests about what and how cyberians value. Cyberians are those whose social formation reproduction is substantially mediated by computing (Escobar et al. 1994).

One indication that there is a crisis of valuation is evidenced in the recent disagreements among social theorists. For example, Christian Fuchs (2012) has debated with Adam Arvidsson and Eleanor Colleoni (Arvidsson and Colleoni 2012) over how value is created and circulated in a digitized social formation: is it by labor, or by affect? Such debate on valuation is a manifestation of the broader ongoing discussion about the relationship between computing and socio-cultural change. The persistence of these discussions acknowledges that this relationship is important. However, often it lapses into one-directional claims that any change in values is caused by computing; these claims need deconstruction. An example is the idea that a specific form of computing "changes everything," as in Tapscott and Williams's effusive commentary on peer production (Tapscott and Williams 2010).

Such claims typically ignore the important social and cultural antecedents that shape particular forms of computing, a blindness that greatly encourages technological determinism. The starting point for science, technology, and society (STS) is that societies, cultures, and technologies co-construct each other. Acting on this premise, one of the aims of social informatics has included specifying what can be said with confidence about computing and socio-cultural change (Hakken 1999). Social informatics can contribute to and elucidate a base of empirical scholarship on the relationship between particular forms of computing and particular socio-cultural changes. This scholarship has been hampered by a predilection for technological determinism regarding the computing/social change nexus. Discourse on the extent and forms of the connection of computing to value and values have also been hampered by the lack of clarity about what value and values actually mean. This is an important source of our interest in David Graeber's work. In theorizing a distinct theory of valuation, Graeber distances himself from what is normally *presumed* in the discourses of formal economics. Academic discourses on change in values/value production can, like popular talk, get quickly mired in nostrums, hype, or misleading metaphors.

GRAEBER ON VALUE AND VALUES

Graeber describes his intent as being to contribute to anthropological theories of value. These theories, Graeber asserts, should aim to account generally (ethnologically) for how cultures ". . . define what is beautiful, or worthwhile, or important" (Graeber 2001, ix). Thus, an understanding of value and values is part of a wider process of valuation, that is, the social practices through which something becomes valued (see the journal *Valuation Studies*, http://valuationstudies.liu.se). Our aim here is more specific: instead of a generating a new, general theory of valuing, we want to develop, in the light of existing theory, the following:

- First, a specific critique of valuing among contemporary human beings whose social formations are substantially computered[3] in order to articulate;
- Second, an approach different from current valuation, one related to but encompassing current valuing and that is appropriate for a sustainable future.

We want to build on the important framework Graeber has developed, analyzing answers to specific value questions in a manner similar to the way he accounts for diverse cultural systems of valuation. Like Graeber, we also want a theory of contemporary valuation that can serve activism. While a theory of value supportive of activism is something we value personally, we also want a better theory of value, because the contemporary crisis in SFR is linked to a crisis of valuation. Current notions of what is valuable and how to achieve it undermine more than they support the reproductive requirements of the social formations through which we become human and renew our humanity. *A new theory of values is needed, in other words, because of substantial evidence that the current valuation practices no longer work well enough.* If we are right, a new understanding of valuation is a necessary component of developing an alternative to the current, crisis-ridden dynamics of SFR.

Graeber's focus, like ours, is on practices—that is, on what people do—because practices say a great deal about what our "real" values are, at least as much as what we say. Again, we are interested in the ultimate implications of these practices for the reproductive dynamics of current and future social formations.[4] Graeber goes on to frame a theory of valuation as something that should help us ". . . see how meaning, one might say, turns into desire" (2001, ix). This connects to Shaowen Bardzell's premise that "Utopian thinking is a form of labor, guided by hope" (Bardzell 2014). Desire and hope inform both the activity of thinking about the future and the articulation of the values we want to put into practice.

OTHER ASPECTS OF A "GRAEBERIAN" ETHNOLOGY OF VALUES

Another important dimension to Graeber's re-theorization of value is the unified focus on both consumption and production—or, in a phrase, the combining of Mauss's focus on the exchange of gifts with Marx's focus on production (Mauss and Halls 1954; Marx 1967). In doing so, Graeber echoes contemporary authors like Alvin Toffler, who problematize boundaries between production and consumption (Toffler 1980; see also Ritzer,

Dean, and Jurgenson 2012 in relation to digital technologies). Graeber also directs our attention to the importance of *where* in space the transformation of meaning into desire takes place. Similarly, Giovanni Arrighi, in *Adam Smith in Beijing: Lineages of the Twenty-First Century*, underlines the importance of current shifts in the geography of how values are pursued and realized (Arrighi 2009). David Harvey has directed attention to how the location of a new productive enterprise affects the structure of value realization (Harvey 2014).

Matters additional to production/consumption and geography are also relevant to the comparative study of valuation. To draw this out, we focus on three other aspects of how humans value:

1. Cultural constructs, generally but especially those about the valuable, tend to be arbitrary. They are not connected in any necessary way to physical or biological "natures." As Graeber documents, humans can and have valued a very wide variety of things/notions;
2. Human valuations develop in path-dependent trajectories; that is, what is valuable today depends at least somewhat on what was valuable previously. Once a particular valuation is chosen, this choice has implications for those valuations that follow. This path dependence is often obvious in what humans say about what they value;
3. It is often the case that values develop dialectically. New values are in one of several semiotic ways related to old ones, elaborating upon or even contrasting directly with the old values. Marx developed his form of the labor theory of value partly as an elaboration of the ideas of predecessors like Ricardo. Nineteenth-century capital theories of value developed in opposition to eighteenth-century labor theories of value. Then, as described in Chapter 4, knowledge theories of value grew in response to the contradictions that accumulated as humans tried to act on capital theories of value.

Neither path dependence nor dialectical reference implies teleology; i.e., a valuation system based on capital is not necessarily "better" than one based on labor. One should not examine conceptions of value with the expectation that tracing their developmental trajectory will indicate the path to a better place or space. The path taken is typically a response to the conditions under which values were previously pursued, so context is important to values' developmental trajectory. As Graeber also shows, articulating what a group actually values is necessarily a critical activity, revealed through the frequent contradictions between how they act and how they speak. Critique is also necessary to identify and argue for meaningful alternative valuations. In order to bring to bear Graeber's insights, let along Arrighi's commentary on the re-rise of China, we need to locate contemporary ways of valuation within their relevant trajectories. Being able to describe what has changed as well as providing an account for why it has changed are both necessary to the project of promoting a fundamental alteration in how we think of values and valuing.

A TYPOLOGY OF VALUATION PRACTICES: NOMINAL, ORDINAL, AND RATIO VALUING

What kind of thing is a value such that its character can change fundamentally? How does this change both reflect and alter the way the social formation around it is reproduced? Intimately connected to the capacity to impose a cultural order on the world—that is, to culture—is the tendency to identify things that are worthwhile or meaningful. We suggest that ethnologically relevant distinctions can be drawn among the types of valued "things," or valuables.

One can identify and distinguish from each other *the various things cherished in any particular culture.* We call these things *"nominal"* or basic, ordinary, individual valuables. Nominal values share the quality of being valued, but nothing further can be derived from this condition about the relationship among values.

Nominal values can, in turn, be distinguished from *ordinal values, those that are related to each other in a hierarchy.* Ordinal values exist when a people's actions and words suggest that one valued thing is held to be more or less valuable than another valued thing. Wampum among the Iroquois, and honey to the Mbuti "pygmies" are examples of such "greater than/lesser than" ordinal valuables. That is, as it becomes possible in a social formation to identify where one value fits in relation to at least some other values, we can speak of these values as becoming ordinal, or of valuables being "ranked."

In turn, ordinal values can be distinguished from *the class of valuables not only ranked as more valuable than others, but whose degree of difference can be measured.* Such values, those equilibrated in relation to each other, are *ratio* (or interval) values.[5] They involve similarly more valued things whose degree of being valued can be measured in relation to an interval scale and thus can be compared (see Graeber 2011).

Ethnologically speaking, nominal and ordinal valuing seems to be widespread, arguably of universal importance in human social formations. Graeber's account of values in *Debt* is an extended demonstration of this point. However, ratio values are important in only some social formations. For example, those social formations in which valuing institutions of the ratio type have reached a modicum of developmental complexity typically have something that functions as "money," a value in terms of which the ratio of multiple things to each other can be articulated. Ratio value is measured in terms of things like currencies or other units for economic transactions accounting.[6] It is in such social formations that one finds talk of "value" in the abstract, as a singular thing, as opposed to specific, concrete values. Over time, the value called "value" can become hegemonic and displace other values.

IMPLICATIONS OF THE RISE OF RATIO VALUING FOR SOCIAL FORMATION REPRODUCTION

Societies in which a singular, ratio notion of value is hegemonic over other values are different from those in which it is not. To recognize the implications of this difference, we need a sense of how ratio valuing became hegemonic.[7] A full account would suggest bridging between Graeber and the work of economic anthropologists, such as Marshall Sahlins's *Stone Age Economics* (Sahlins 2013). We have in mind something less ambitious, but to us, more important: we want to link our contemporary muddles over digital technologies and social change to the emergence of the hegemony of ratio valuing.

The extent of reducing many values to just one varies across social formations. The wide extent of the hegemony of ratio valuing in contemporary social formations is indexed by a number of things, including the prevalence of nostrums like, "Everything has its price." Sometimes, valuing *per se* mediates only a small portion of the aspects of a social formation's reproduction, and sometimes a very large portion, but never everything (at least, not so far). Introductory economics courses illustrate the lumpiness, the incompleteness, of ratio valuing by pointing out how humans in current "developed" social formations value clean air. However, it is also difficult, even in such social formations, to equilibrate—to compare in terms of a ratio—the value of clean air to, say, a piece of chicken from a supermarket. In general, air is a nominal value, while the chicken's value is more likely to be established in ratio terms. Nonetheless, it seems reasonable to posit a continuum of the different extents to which social formations are mediated by ratio valuing. A social formation in which individuals and/or their families, clans, or tribes produce most of what they consume would be on one end of such a continuum, the less ratio value end, whereas social formations in which most people get what they need by buying it with wages or salaries would be closer to the ratio-hegemonic end. The deeper in the past the emergence of a social formation, the less likely it is to be located toward the ratio-hegemony end. This is because ratio-valuing institutions are a later innovation, built on a foundation of nominal and ordinal institutions, which have continued to be manifested for a long time.

With this values continuum, we can draw attention to a major mediator of the computing/social change connection, namely, the exaggerated extent to which computing's connection to SFR is mediated by ratio valuing. The more hegemonic ratio valuing, and thus the less present vestiges of nominal or ordinal valuing institutions, the greater the likelihood that computing practices will also be bent to ratio valuing. The values afforded by the selected, alternative-fostering forms of computing identified in Chapter 4 are not ratio values. They would be difficult to bend to the ratio valuing essential to reproducing capital, and they are unlikely to become hegemonic on their own. For the affordances of alternative computing forms to flourish, the hegemony of ratio valuing processes would need to be reduced. To enable the new values implicit in computing to have a greater impact on SFR, it will be necessary to decrease ratio value mediation.

The reader might raise the following objection: in the face of such ratio valuing hegemony, how can any affordances like the ones cited in Chapter 4 be developed? One part of the answer is simply that any one-kind-of-valuing hegemony can't become totally dominant. Social formation reproduction requires other kinds of valuing, even if they are only marked by silence. The shifts in kinds of valuing need to be understood from a deep ethnological perspective. For example, what follows historically from increasingly valuesing in ratio terms? Marx's argument in *Capital* for the importance of the commodification of labor can be rephrased in our terms, as stressing how the mediation by ratio valuing of the capacity to do work is a key development in social formation type (Marx 1967).

For Marx, this mediation is the feature that distinguishes "capitalist" from other social formations, including those with large markets in things but not a market in labor, as in peasant societies. Moreover, as Graeber shows, bringing human life into the ratio system of equivalence is often accompanied by extreme violence. This is just one of the reasons why shaping SFR to the reproduction of capital has been so often disruptive. A social formation in which labor power is a commodity would be nearer to the ratio-hegemony end, more thoroughly mediated by ratio valuing. It thereby reduces people to only one aspect of their being—the capacity to work—than one where labor is less commodified. Equally important for Marx, the surplus value out of which profit can arise depends on the *absence* of the commoditization of the reproduction of the worker's capacity to work, something carried out in the non-commodified home.

This analysis can be summarized in the following propositions:

- All social formations deploy/have deployed nominal values; that is, they have values/valuables/and engage in "valuesing."
- Most, probably all, social formations, deploy/have deployed ordinal values, too; that is, some valuables are/are perceived to be more important than are others, and may, in our language, be more centrally implicated in social formation reproduction.
- *Some* social formations deploy/have deployed ratio valuing. That is, a selection of things are "connected" in ways that make it possible to specify the degree of "equate-able-ness" of this selection of things—or measurability among them on an interval scale.
- In many social formations with much ratio valuing, the capacity to do work is itself brought into these measurable, equating systems. These are social formations in which labor, or the human capacity to do work, has been commodified.

Marx went a step further, arguing that under the commodification of work, the creation of many of the things valued via ratios is controlled by a small, elite proportion of the population, so ratio valuing disadvantages the rest. To survive, this remainder must select how to get a sufficiency of the things needed to reproduce themselves and their families on a day-to-day basis from an array that is historically more limited than previously. This is, for example, the situation of peasants after enclosure of a commons. Is making ratio-ing of all valuesing possible? Even though it becomes necessary to "get a living" in order to "have a life," arenas of sociality escape making everything into ratio values.

FURTHER STEPS TOWARD AN ETHNOLOGY OF CONTEMPORARY VALUATION

Even though the ratio-hegemonized social formations described above are only a small portion of all the human social formations that have ever existed, they have come to dominate SFR dynamics in the last couple hundred years. Although it is not yet true in contemporary social formations that "everything has its price," many more things do. As David Harvey has pointed out, the last thirty years of neo-liberalism or the Washington consensus have been characterized by the expansion of pricing. Things not priced before, such as things available as a common good, like water, become subjected to pricing mechanisms, like bottled water. When more things get commodified, access to these things decrease for many people. Harvey calls this "accumulation by dispossession" (Harvey 2014). Commodity-oriented notions, as when people talk about "human capital" and "social capital" as if humans or social relations could be commoditized, start to colonize language.

In other words, ratio valuing becomes the overwhelming mediator of SFR. In order to argue that computing in general changes social life fundamentally (or any particular form, such as "Web 2.0" or "social computing"), one would have to show how using computers causes radical changes in the dynamics characteristic of current SFR, such as undercutting the predominance of ratio valuing. Instead, as the dynamics of SFR often exert a direct influence on computing, and computing has become more central to cultural and social reproduction, many forms of computing have become centrally implicated in the processes of commodification.

How is computing connected causally to changes in how social formations valuate?

Arvidsson and Colleoni promote the idea that valuation is currently changing. They argue for a transition from value being determined by labor toward value being determined by reputation. In this view, capital accumulation/reproduction is driven by forms of negotiation connected to brand reputation (Arvidsson and Colleoni 2012). In contrast, Fuchs stresses continuity, arguing that value is still being determined by labor, albeit labor enhanced. Continuity can be accomplished through what Dallas Smythe calls "audience as commodity," where the time audiences spend is converted by labor into value (Fuchs 2012). To identify any such changes *and* to determine if their implications for society in general are profound, it is necessary to begin with a specific understanding of ratio valuing dynamics *before* the mediation of substantial aspects of social life by computing.

We want to articulate an account of valuation before the current moment using the concepts of Karl Marx's general theory of value. This general theory is less well known than his more specific use, exchange, and surplus theories of value (Harvey 2010). In focusing on this general theory, we follow those who adopt at least a quasi-Marxist vocabulary in arguing for computing-related SFR change. For example, those writers who attempt to measure a "rate of exploitation" in playbor activities use such language (Scholz 2012). Using these concepts also makes sense given the renewed attention Marx's work has gained in the social studies of computing (e.g., Fuchs and Mosco 2012).

Many people living in societies where ratio valuing is important, including social scholars, are familiar with Marx's notion of "use value," which refers to the (nominal) utility of something to a person. They can distinguish use value from "exchange value," how much in money one could get by selling something; this is typically measured as a ratio value. Marx also theorized a significant third aspect of value, "value in general." As argued by David Harvey (Harvey 2010), we don't understand Marx's general theory of value until we understand the relationships among all three of these values (as well as ultimately a fourth, "surplus value," which we will put aside for the moment). This three-sided account of valuation—use value, exchange value, and general value—is very helpful to understanding the dynamics of ratio valuing.

THE RISE OF VALUING IN GENERAL

Harvey begins his account of Marx's general theory of value by stressing how important it is to understand how Marx's expository style grounds theorizing in everyday, ongoing practices. By connecting the emergence of and changes in ratio valuing to the historically changing institutions of work, Marx is able to provide developmental, relational accounts of both the history of ratio valuing and of commoditization. As more labor and things get translated into money, the rationale for any change in how work is done becomes seen in more strictly monetary terms, while other needs get relegated to the shadows. "Material" accounts (a good thing for Marx) describe human processes via connecting "cultural constructs" to the physical experiences of things, explaining both in terms of their relationship to each other. In a material account, we explicate the connection of the names of things to their physical properties, which enables us to talk more meaningfully about relationships things, like "efficiency."

Similarly, by linking use values to socially defined needs, we can link economics to changing histories of societies and institutions. For Marx, under the "modern" conditions of production, when use values are made under conditions where labor has been made a commodity, we enter the terrain of political economy. It is under the conditions of general commoditization that ratio value starts to be measured and can be measured, both widely and clearly. Only under these conditions does value attain a general material equivalent, which for him is "socially necessary average labor time." This is the average time necessary to create a unit of general value under the standard prevailing conditions.

The existence of a general material equivalent makes it possible to measure value in money terms. This is for us a key point, as it is exactly this measuring that allows us to account for "value" in the ratio sense. Value in general becomes a part of normally functioning human society, because all commodities have the use of human labor power in common and value is the crystallization of this common element. Indeed, the value "value" comes to stand in for valuation in general. For labor to become measurable, a form of money is necessary. For labor to become *commonly measured*, it must be made into a *commodity*. When this happens, specific forms of work become abstracted into a general form, what Marx refers to as the emergence in history of "the law of value."[8] However, because of a general tendency to conceive of relations that are really social among people as relations among things (the famous "fetishization" of commodities), contemporary human beings don't see value as such, let alone a "law of value" as centrally relating people to each other. Instead, contemporary humans tend to think of value as a property inherent in things themselves, as separate from rather than mediated by social connections.

THE AGE OF VALUE

With Marx, we see the regime of value as affording and being afforded by the emergence of a whole set of social relations, especially social institutions like laws that protect private property.[9] For any "law of value" to operate, certain preconditions are needed, especially the widespread adoption of some specific ideas, like a notion of things being "equate-able," which comes down to "having comparable monetary value."[10] Once value takes on such forms, it becomes possible to organize society around what is perceived to be its self-expansion, as when value in the form of capital is invested in the creation of commodities using wage labor.

When labor power as a commodity trades at less than the value it can produce, it becomes possible to make a profit through employing workers.

That is, it becomes possible to invest a given amount of capital into the creation of commodities that can be sold at a higher value than the cost of their creation. This is surplus value, and the source of profit. Subtracting the initial capital invested from the value of the goods or services sold leaves the amount of extra or "surplus" value (profit). As one can only sell what others want to use, "use value" is connected directly to—indeed, is a pre-condition of—both value in general and surplus value. Since surplus value is only created by capital invested (or "in motion"), the value of a given capital declines in relation to others if it is not invested. In order for a social formation to be capitalist or have a capitalist political economy, its capital must generally be in constant motion.

To be a capitalist for Marx is to do what one must, namely, invest one's wealth in order to make more wealth. This is not a matter of personal choice, but a role compelled by the organization of society. Indeed, for Marx, the rise of a social formation organized around profit through investment in the creation of commodities was a social inevitability as soon as a given level of exchange and competition was reached. Competition operates as effectively as an external coercive law once it is widespread. This has the effect of accelerating the speed at which profit must be realized if the capital is to survive, leading to accelerating accumulation, investment in technological change, and geographic spread. It is Harvey's emphasis on this latter in *Seventeen Contradictions and the End of Capitalism* that is an important contribution to political economy (Harvey 2014).

Also spread more widely is an increased likelihood of crisis. This dynamic is a main locus of the Marxist critique of capitalism, that it is a social "system" prone to ever-increasing crises. One can even measure the likelihood of crisis. The ratio of the surplus value realized in a given production process to the value of the capital invested is what Marx chose to call the "rate of exploitation," similar to the rate of profit. Indeed, as the opportunity to exploit or make a profit arises from the equation that the value of what labor can produce is greater than what it costs, and the cost of labor is related to the necessary labor time that is socially determined, it follows that the extent of social inequality is effectively measured by the rate of exploitation. Since the higher the rate of exploitation, the greater the likelihood that workers will not be able to reproduce themselves, a higher rate of exploitation is one indicator of potential crisis.

The development of the institutions of wage labor, like the other institutional aspects of capitalism, is both historically driven by and dependent upon the pre-existence of unequal social power. For Marx, it is this inequality in wealth that enables inequality in value. That is, one social group is thereby initially able to grasp a monopoly of ownership over means of production, forcing others to sell their capacity to do work at a rate lower than the value the work creates. These economic relationships of value are class relationships, ones of basic social inequality with historical roots but manifesting in newly evolving forms.

Harvey's explication of the basic Marxist value categories enables us to see that "value," as opposed to "values," derives its primary meaning in its relation to the specific social conditions associated with capitalism as an SFR regime. The ethnology of valuation locates all values, including the value "value" in a conceptual and time-specific manner through the demonstration of particular historical trajectories. This ethnology of value provides an empirically based set of theoretical constructs on which to base our alternative valuation project.

ADDITIONAL THEORETICAL STEPS NECESSARY BEFORE ALTERNATIVE VALUES CAN BE ADOPTED

As indicated in our introductory chapter, our alternative project involves rebalancing the relative influence of nominal, ordinal, and ratio valuing. We see this as a major part of any project of imagining an alternative value(s) regime. While the narrow focus on value explains important aspects of crises in SFR, it does not tell us how to go about reducing the dominance of ratio valuing in current SFR. Before we can do this, we need to be able to look at how values discourses got reduced to a single-value discourse.

Marx's argument in "The Fragment on Machines" in *The Grundrisse* provides a good starting point (Marx 1993). In this work, Marx underlines how the expansion in the use of machines in the labor process is accompanied by a generalized diffusion of knowledge as a productive force. Both production and knowledge become more and more socialized. Marx conceptualized the new knowledge as inscribed in machines, but recent Marxism has argued instead for thinking of such knowledge as distributed *among* the machines and the workers (Virno 2001). The commodification of labor results in the commodification of the knowledge needed for production. In this instance, the workers, the machines, and the knowledge all begin to be analyzed for their ratio value. This is an example of how diverse valuables can be subjugated to ratio valuing. It is also important that the forms of the commodification of things, like machines and knowledge, are based fundamentally on the commodification of a social relationship, that between the people selling labor and the person or corporation owning the means of production. As Marx pointed out, such social relations among humans underlie the apparent relations between things—the fetish of commodities. Our task is to understand how ratio valuing became imbricated in the reproduction of social relations among people (Callon 2001). Once we have an adequate theory of how this happened, we can turn to the task of articulating alternative theories of values, institutions, and measures to replace them.

ON VALUE AND CREATING SOCIAL RELATIONS
AMONG PEOPLE AND THINGS

Actor–Network Theory (ANT) from the STS field provides an analytical language to explicate the imbrications in social relations of value and valuation practices. Value reproduction is always extended and never simple. Using both historical and geographical comparisons to combine ANT with Graeber's perspective enables us to identify the role of innovative actions in increasing the domain of ratio value(s)ing.

A more explicit ANT-like version of Graeber helps clarify how value permeates cultural constructs, including language and the construction of knowledge discussed in previous chapters. In looking at both human and non-human actors, ANT helps reveal how value is made material, and how value is implicated in objects. To specify what we mean by making value material, we will draw upon two aspects of ANT. First, ANT analysis provides an empirical approach to the problem of the different modes of knowledge production—that is, the collective definition of what is true. This analysis highlights how material objects are central to such processes. Second, using Nancy Munn's conceptualization of the role of "things of value," we see that entities can transform the invisible potential of people into the concrete. Munn's approach stresses how value is the result of the work needed to realize this invisible social potential of material things, of making the invisible visible (Munn 1992). We think Graeber's anthropological theory of value, ANT's materialism, and Munn's concepts can be fruitfully combined.

Actor–Network Theory is useful for understanding the conditions, practices, and processes through which facts, whether scientific or technological, are produced (Latour and Woolgar 2013). In ANT, "facts" are fragments of knowledge that are tied together by the discourses of scientific and technological disciplines. These discourses bring a sense of cohesion to the questions, methods, and techniques selected, as well as answers. Together, they form a discourse "bandwagon" that makes certain views acceptable and taken as reliable (Fujimura 1988). In the way that it focuses on the construction of techno-scientific facts, ANT provides tools to investigate the practices by which scientific constructs are performed, concretized, and reproduced. ANT investigations like those of de Laet and Mol (2000) and Bruni (2005) result in a robust materialism. Material objects are seen to participate more fully in the flux of social life (Callon and Latour 1992). They are not theoretically external to it, either as passive objects of human action or as exogenous forces structuring human actions. Objects are part of social life and, like any other participants, can be both powerful enough to *affect* the behavior of other (both human and non-human) participants and also weak enough *to be affected by* the behavior of other (human and non-human) participants.

The empirical question that many ANT case studies try to answer is what conditions make a participant powerful enough to change the way facts are constructed? In answering this question, ANT studies also show how material objects carry cultural meanings and moral prescriptions (e.g., Callon 1986). They show how objects can define the set of possible worlds compatible with the objects themselves by way of their use by other participants (Akrich 1992). While an object has its own values, these values unfold in the relationships between the object and other objects, values, and human beings populating social life. This orientation provides a useful lens through which to identify how values are translated and made visible in material objects. Callon and Muniesa (Callon and Muniesa 2005) refer to valuation as calculation, an activity that involves a capacity distributed among the thing evaluated, the agencies making the calculation, and the infrastructures supporting such an effort. In their analysis, contemporary market functioning is full of calculative devices, of socio-technical arrangements built in order to make calculation widespread. Callon and Muniesa use as an example the case of supermarkets. The supermarket chain is organized to provide goods with prices, but also to allow a calculation by the buyer on the basis of her attachment to a specific good. Within the supermarket is a whole set of socio-technical arrangements that translate how things are calculated.

Nancy Munn's work points to how activity itself is the process through which the invisible potential of a person (or thing) becomes concretely visible—that is, how value emerges from social activity (Munn 1992). Material objects are part of the process of transformation, because value is socially attributed to human action via the social mediation of material objects. Consider the example of weapon appropriation in ancient warfare. In individual fighting during face-to-face battles, the person killed was often relieved of his sword, shield, etc. The object won was particularly valued by its connection to famous warriors, as represented in peculiar hilts, not just as a sword. The status of the winner as a warrior was increased by the possession of the sword. The sword mediated between the values of the defeated warrior, the time the sword was won, and the time it was displayed. When displaying the sword, the warrior also made visible his potential power, whether he used it or not. Munn's focus is on the nature of human actions that gain value through the mediation of objects. Through the circulation of things of value, humans extend their ability to influence others in space and time.

Put differently, things of value are objects that extend the ability of people to mobilize others. Bruno Latour calls them "immutable mobiles," these valued things that circulate (Foster 2008; Latour 1987). Common to both Munn and Latour is a focus on how the distributions of mobilized time, energy, and intelligence act as the underlying equilibrating elements among artifacts (or products). Things of value—immutable mobiles—enable an assessment of the importance of what people do to create social relations. In ANT language, things of value are a particular kind of technology, the kind through which it is possible to establish new forms of economic and linguistic relations—even, in some cases, to make these forms durable (Latour 1990). The ANT-Munn empirical tasks thereby becomes twofold: first, to describe the forms of social relations connected to the dominance of particular things of value, and second, to figure out what makes the given social relations have this quality if these relations are durable.

OTHER WAYS IN WHICH VALUE PERMEATES SOCIAL RELATIONS VIA THINGS: BEING VALUABLE

R.J. Foster (Foster 2008) leverages Munn's analysis by focusing on brands. Specifically, he is concerned with the way that brands solidify ratio valuing's permeation of cultural constructs, including the language of daily life. Foster's analysis focuses on connections between brands, use value, and exchange value, as well as broader concepts, like "fame." In his reading, it is clear how ordinal valuesing—that is, when some values have higher status than others—is made subservient to the accumulation of money, the ratio valuing typical of current societies. The particular personal and affective relationship between the person (buyer) and objects-differently-ranked-in-value-turned-into-commodities is leveraged for the purpose of constant accumulation.

In the seminal work of Terence Turner (1984), things valued turn into "concrete media of the circulation" of value. Graeber cites Turner's idea when discussing things of value (Graeber 2001, 85), or valuables, arguing:

- Valuables reflect value according to the three different logical principles: being present or absent, being ordered, or establishing proportionality. This is similar to our distinctions among nominal, ordinal, and ratio value(s)ing.
- The valuable becomes a medium of value, a material object in which value itself is realized and displayed and performed before a wider audience, as in the sword example above.
- Valuables are goals in themselves, becoming fetishized objects, like money in capitalistic societies.

Valuables are the material objects that act both as mediators among different possible values and as devices capable of measuring value in general. From initially being goals in themselves, i.e., valued things, some valuables emerge as the stable translation point for other practices, able to mobilize human and non-human actors—not only in their production but also in their preservation, realization, and accumulation. Put simply, *valuables are the things around which social formations organize themselves, the things human beings desire, and the impetus to humans selecting one or another course of action.*

Graeber argues that things of value "reconcil(e) social structure and individual desire" (Graeber 2001, 76). They provide specific ways for individuals to make manifest the goals they have through their pursuit of those goals. Framed in ANT terms, we see things of value as the material fragments through which we can bring together cultural discourses on both values and value. Through assembling many different discourses on valuables, we can relate both the subjectivities of individuals and the collectives they are part of, as there are different collective articulations to the current modes of the production of value in relation to things. Discourses on value constructed *through* things of value are also used to justify and promote practices that preserve and allow distinct, valuable things to be reproduced. In critiquing such discourses, we make visible the relations among humans that stand behind the relations among visible things. The black boxes of fetishized things of value need to be opened. They are not only phenomena to be explained in themselves (ethnographically) but also things that, once explained ethnologically, enable humans in our social collectives to re-frame and thereby reappropriate them.

David Harvey has explicated how the main process of accumulation—in particular, money—via expropriation can change using this process. The dominant form, which he calls "accumulation by dispossession" (2003), is a process based on force and violence, where justice and commonality are marginalized as a criteria, justifying the accumulation of wealth. In Harvey's description, the accumulation of capital no longer happens mainly through profit coming from production and the market. Rather, it is happening through the inclusion in the process of capital accumulation of social dynamics that previously weren't subsumed by capital itself. For example, the extension of the intellectual property regime and the privatization of public goods are part of this direction, as is the creation of a new domain of capital accumulation through the financial market. This process is one of dispossession in that, as in the case of public goods or intellectual property, it is a process of enclosure. It is the subtraction of goods from collective possession in order to privatize them. Some scholars (e.g., Morini and Fumagalli 2010) go even further, arguing that virtually all of life is becoming subordinated to the reproduction of capital via value—i.e., money-type ratio valuing.

Our theory of contemporary "valuation reduced to valuing" must not only deal with the new forms of accumulation described by Harvey. It needs to explicate how deeply accumulation distorts knowledge, goods, personas, fame, or many other aspects of life. As pointed out by philosopher Michael Sandel (Sandel 2012), the accumulation of value becomes inscribed politically. Having realized how this has come to be, we humans now can choose either to promote a flourishing new values balance or continue to accept an expropriation-based, single-value imbalance. If we choose to strive for a new values balance, we have to dethrone the process of the accumulation of social wealth (including forms other than capital). We also have to reinstate the ways things of value can be accumulated without being transformed violently into expropriation. The problem is to identify new, more desirable practices of valuation and also find just ways to carry them out.

A PRELIMINARY LOOK AT REVALUATION PRACTICE: TRANSLATING BETWEEN THE VISIBLE AND THE INVISIBLE

Making social relationships visible is the key goal in moving toward an alternative, less crisis-prone SFR dynamic, one that can also support new values/valuables. This goal is anti-fetishistic, in that it aims to reinstate the relations among people hidden by relations among things. Theorizing valuation critically lays a basis for displacing the ratio valuing that currently mediates SFR. It points toward how valuation discourses might be moved back to more ordinal and nominal forms. Graeber shows that such a "re-valuesed" social formation might suggest more nuanced ways of thinking about values. This involves a very different social process, an "accumulation" of multiple, diverse kinds of social relationships. The exchange of wampum belts is the example chosen by Graeber to describe the political character of this dynamic (Graeber 2001). The process of the accumulation and circulation of wampum belts is complex, in that the Iroquois used the belts in two distinct ways. One was as a currency in the fur trade with the Europeans, where the Iroquois sold furs for wampum, or the raw materials needed to build the belts. The second was within the Iroquois social formation alone, where wampum was used as a peace instrument, a way to open a communication channel between two groups who had a conflict.

The second use is important to our understanding of valuation. The Iroquois were a matrilineal and matrilocal society, one built up out of re-invocable "personas." That is, names and functions were resurrected, and wampum was used to provide old names and functions to new people. In this way, wampum served to structure individual identities, and thereby the broader social organization, or politics. Whether accumulated via trade or a peace offering, wampum belts were kept hidden, made visible only when needed. The Iroquois League was organized as a federal society and characterized by a substantial role for woman as well as a strong egalitarianism. In such a context, when a conflict emerged (even violent ones—for example, murder), it was solved not through acts of revenge, but through the exchange of wampum belts, the sign of the will to make peace. In the exchanges, the wampum belts provided were not equated to each other (as in the case of money). Rather, each belt was reworked into new arrangements, where the particular peace proposed was inscribed into the belts offered. They were things of value *because* they were used to redefine the boundaries and concepts supporting the collective existence of the Iroquois as a society. Wampum belts were therefore explicitly unique as well as political.

Wampum had a dual existence—when accumulated and acquired through the fur trade, they were general and indistinguishable from each other. However, when transformed into something visible through the creative inscription of being reworked, they became specific, valuable things, each with their own identity and history, and therefore with more restricted potential patterns of exchange than those of more general valuables.

Another way to describe the dynamic of wampum in Iroquois SFR is to view it as an example of how ratio values can become ordinal values (and maybe even nominal values) and vice versa, and how these transformations are related to the relative visibility of the value and values in question. Shifts in valuation like those in which wampum was implicated are open to further theoretical reflection, but also to more empirical inquiry. Theoretically, any of the three conceptualizations of values can be attached to things, but the specific value of any object unfolds only in the relationships between the object and the other objects and human beings populating social life. This makes values a relational concept. Empirically, any shifting from valuables to value, or vice versa, opens a set of questions about the social relations inscribed in the form or forms of value present, the "mode of valuation," and about what makes the social relations durable or vulnerable.

In his analysis of wampum, Graeber highlights how valuation practices often involve issues of the visibility and invisibility of things of value. Drawing on Bourdieu (1984), Foucault (1977), and Edward Tylor (1871), among others, Graeber stresses the place of value with power ethnologically. Human beings engage in reflection as well as action. They not only do things; they also, often at the same time, think about what they have done and might do. That is, they distinguish among past, present, and future actions. These distinctions are relevant to different kinds of power. The first is the power to act directly on others (action). This is opposed to the second, the power to affect another's self-reflection, i.e., to act in new ways toward themselves (reflection).

Graeber shows how the accumulation of things of value always involves a movement between action, including both the invisible power of future action and the visible power of past actions, mediated through reflection. Studies of social interaction show how persuasive action, what Goffman called "impression management" (Goffman 1999), manifests in the ability of human beings to conceptualize themselves in the gazes of an imagined other (Mead 1934). The concepts of visibility and invisibility are social concepts. What is invisible is what an individual or a small group is able to hide from the wider collective they participate in, and what is visible is what is shown on purpose. This latter has the social effect of defining socially the status of either the individuals or the group.

An example can help clarify the complexity of the relationship between the different powers exercised by invisible and visible things of value. This is the present, almost common sense understanding of consumption processes described both by Thorstein Veblen as conspicuous consumption and by Georg Simmel in his analysis of fashion (Simmel, Frisby, and Featherstone 1997; Veblen 1912). Both in the analyses of Veblen and Simmel, the acquisition of expensive objects and their display is a visible way of signaling the capacity to spend the money needed to acquire such objects. Before the display of the object itself, the capacity to spend the money was invisible, an unseen potential to act. The transformation of the invisible into the visible has social consequences for the spender, such as being treated with more respect or gaining access to inaccessible subsets of society. This also makes it possible for the displayer to accumulate money, the invisible thing of value, in new ways. The interaction, the translation of valuables between invisibility and visibility, is the starting point for a rethinking of the political relationships surrounding value production and accumulation.

This dynamic—between the invisible that is a potential for future actions, and the visible that testifies to past actions—shows how the accumulation and display of things of value is a political act. It affords the construction of one type of social relationship instead of another. The political dimensions are consisted of how the boundaries between the visible and the invisible are traced and retraceable, as well as how the transformation of the invisible into the visible (and visa versa) takes place. It is a dynamic of power.

Inquiry into durability can open space for rethinking the relationship between particular modes of valuation and social relations based on concepts like "justice." A theory of value that is of use for activism would need to be able to be related to political concepts. If justice is the opposite of exploitation, one could afford justice by reducing the possibilities for accumulating things of value through depriving others. To afford justice would require study of how access to and accumulation of things of value currently take place and of the instabilities as well as stabilities of the current mode of valuation. Then we could identify possible triggers for the construction of new modes of valuation.

REBUILDING THE COMMON: ON FREEDOM, LOVE, AND STRUGGLE AS VALUES TO BE SUPPORTED

In certain regards, our upscaling world is becoming a more common, shared place, a world in which we all increasingly relate to the same environmental issues. While still a long way from real globality, the products that we sell and purchase travel more and more widely and are, on occasion, regulated by transnational agreements. Michael Hardt and Antonio Negri describe the contemporary world as one that is losing much of its "outside" as the physical and symbolic aspects of life are more and more universally shared (Hardt and Negri 2009). The world is now more often a place where actions in one location mobilize things (forms of knowledge, material products, technical solutions) relevant to an increasing number of other locations.

We want this book to demonstrate that values are an emergent possibility. Such emergence can point toward a world based on more values than ratio value, one that affords values such as justice and commonality. This is the kind of world toward which the values implicit in the computing practices of Chapter 4 can incline us, the valuation practices we should try to promote or revive into actual valuables. While Callon and Muniesa (2005) see contemporary economics as the science of constructing society through "market devices," we identify a path toward another economics, one including "common devices" that promote a just and common world rather than an expropriation-based one. To make this path more explicit, we draw on the perspectives of Hardt and Negri discussed in Chapter 2. The priority they give to multitudes, freedom, and love illuminate how human value inclinations compatible with social devices can be inclined toward collective liberation—a communal human as opposed to an economic human.

In an actual social formation, any of a number of factors might afford government by a "communal people" who exercise power through freedom, reason, and love. We suspect they would converge toward:

- The connection of love and political force through the nurturing of the common;
- An orientation toward the freedom of individuals connected by what Hardt and Negri call "the singularities" of horizontal forms of organization or associations;
- The ability to construct consensus among individuals;
- Ways of using love (or "desire," in Graeber's terms) that are oriented toward the institutionalization of its accumulation, rather than its subordination to value accumulation.

In their reading of "the common," Hardt and Negri include all the elements that connect free and loving singularities into a "multitude." ANT-like, the common includes the material resources of the planet and the cultural resources needed to sustain life in the common, social interactions, and production. For "common devices" to extend SFR, the social formation needs to be mediated by a range of valuables, ones that reflect the actual freedom and love of the singularities. By reinforcing both freedom and love through valuables, institutions might be created that afford positive change in the dynamics of SFR. Hardt and Negri's approach demands a more dense relation between values and value. To get this, we need theory, like Graeber's or the one we have developed in this chapter, to move to the next task, to identify existing efforts of the "multitude" to extend social formation reproduction, as we have found in computing. Once such values have been identified, we can begin a project to accumulate and preserve love and freedom, thereby sustaining the common.

CONCLUSIONS AND SUMMARY: TOWARD COMMON DEVICES?

In Chapter 4, we outlined aspects of the general crisis in SFR that are not being resolved. We believe it will not be resolved until a better analysis of the basis of the crisis is understood. We also identified computing practices with implicit values that might, if institutionalized, afford this extension. In this chapter, our task has been to present a theory of valuation that lays a foundation for future social formations to be able to extend their repro-ductive dynamics. This foundation rests on a theoretical understanding of where valuing as a general practice has come from, including its historic relationship with SFR dynamics. We argue for an ethnological approach that could prove useful to the reconceptualization of valuation practices and value theories, both generally and in relation to the digitized world. Our case for being ethnological is based in part on the "information over-load" that undermines the ability of humans to turn available information into knowledge. Our second task was to understand the possible basis for building more robust institutions that could transform new information into situated, usable knowledge. We suggest an ethnological generalization, that human beings learn what is worthwhile both through socialization and through the delegation of value to non-humans. We looked at how people come to value, and particularly how things are turned into things-of-value, i.e., the things that orient behavior.

We see an ethnological theory of valuation as a way to state our own understanding of valuation in some basic tenets. First, humans have val-ued many things in many ways, but they also change the way they value, and these changes follow trajectories of path-dependency. Second, we can identify three elementary forms of valuing, which we refer to as nomi-nal, ordinal, and ratio valuing. Third, we traced how ratio valuing has historically come to dominate the other forms, yet we pointed out how this domination is not total. Fourth, we showed how capitalism could be understood as the social formation type where work is subjected to ratio values, money becoming the general measure of what is shared among the different values.

All social formations value; in many, some valuables are more centrally implicated in social formation reproduction than others. Among the latter, ranked value often becomes the basis of equitable, ratio values, and in some basic human life activities are brought into the equivalence system where life itself is becoming a commodity. Drawing upon traditional Marxian accounts of value, these perspectives give a new sense to the distinctions among use value, exchange value, general value, and surplus value. The main conclusions we draw are that the hegemony of ratio valuing over valuation in general creates crisis, and that to extend SFR capacity in the future, we need to return to an better balance among nominal, interval, and ratio valuing.

The ratio valuing that permeates and often distorts human relations is not the only form of valuing. An awareness of the dynamics of different forms of valuing opens our eyes to visions of alternative social formations, and to the possibility of creating more and stronger affective relationships among persons and objects as social life is de-commodified. By focusing on a better balancing of ratio, ordinal, and nominal valuing, it is possible to imagine new sets of values, such as those necessary to the nurturing of commons.

We have drawn upon much recent theoretical work to support our analysis, including STS literature and ANT. ANT stresses how material objects translate and mediate social relations, including those of value(s). Additionally, Marxian perspectives on value can be fruitfully connected with recent anthropological theory. Anthropological thinking contributes to our ability to identify in work and in creative action the basis for value. If nominal values represent a kind of social relationship, ordinal values represent social relationships that are differentially relevant in other specific contexts, and ratio values stand for social relations based on an equilibration among value practices prone to exploitation in the context of social hierarchy.

We argue for focusing on material objects both as concrete media of circulation and valuing, and as indicators of social relations. In their mediation and translation of values, material objects integrate human beings. The case of wampum was used as an example of how change in valuing in different social domains is possible. Different valuation practices can both coexist and also be transformed from one kind of valuing to another. Our ethnology of value is of more than descriptive use. We can compare different valuation practices, and we can also promote the replacement of an existing value regime, promoting liberation instead of dispossession.

But is such a replacement possible? To help us answer this question, we embraced the ability of Autonomous Marxism to identify sustainable elements. These include what we called common devices, perspectives that convert the working class, freedom, and love, as conceptualized in contemporary social formations into more general subjects in social formation reproduction. Our quest for understanding value in digitized society therefore moves beyond comprehension of existing valuation practices toward overcoming them. Theoretically, this can happen through leveraging the values implicit in uses of digital technologies that promote new conditions that nurture the common.

In the following chapter, we make explicit the new values set hinted at in digital practices. In the subsequent chapters, we identify the kinds of institutions and measures that would make a social formation based on this new set sustainable. What we outline are possibilities, not probabilities, and they are certainly not inevitable. We aim at a program of what might be done to go beyond capital, as a way to persuade others to join in a debate over what should be the path chosen.

NOTES

1. With the spelling value(s), we refer to three concepts (values, the specific value "value," and the process of valuation). All are related to value in anthropological language: the cultural, the economic, and the linguistic. In this manner, we underline how their distinction and dis-alignment is a contemporary construction.

2. As will be evident in the remainder of this chapter, our work on value has drawn greatly on the work of David Graeber. While most of our references in this chapter are to his earlier book on value, we are equally indebted to his more recent book on debt (Graeber 2011); indeed, our goal in an important sense is to make more explicit the contemporary implications for the debt-as-value argument implicit in *Debt*.

   At the same time, we do not follow all of Graeber's theorizations. For example, (Graeber 2001) articulates several forms of value, including adding to "economic value" a "linguistic value" associated with linguistic performance; that is, the kind of activity that, by articulating what is good, appropriate, and desirable, makes meaningful differences between objects, thereby adding what we call ordinal and nominal as well as ratio value.

   In Graeber's reading, both economic value and linguistic value are "already" attributed to objects as they are created. This view is quite compatible with the materialism of STS approaches like ANT. However, while Graeber's multiple forms of value have some descriptive usefulness, we have concluded that there is little benefit to trying to articulate them with our primary concern, the theorization of nominal, ordinal, and ratio notions of value, so we have not incorporated them into our analysis here.

3. It is, of course, increasingly difficult to find humans for whom it is not at least indirectly the case that their lives are significantly mediated by DTs.

4. For a recent update on practice-based perspectives in organization studies, see, for example, Gessica Corradi (Corradi, Gherardi, and Verzelloni 2010).

5. Both terms are used in statistics as descriptors. In order for two numbers to be in a ratio, the size of the intervals between them must be the same; that is, the two terms must imply each other. We choose to use "ratio" to describe equitable relations, as we find it more descriptive.

6. The statistically minded reader will have recognized that we draw our three labels from this field, where these labels classify types of statistics. We call our third category "ratio" rather than "interval" because comparisons are *not* only made on scales with equal intervals, but because such scales usually have an anchoring end point. That is, it is possible to say that something has no, or "zero," value.

7. In this and the following section, we use "hegemonic" and "hegemony" to refer to an entity with strong influence over cultural reproduction, the symbols and concepts through which social processes are perceived. In contrast, we use the term "domination" to refer to an entity with strong influence over SFR. Marxists make a similar distinction between "superstructure" and "structure" or "infrastructure."

8. Marx, like other political economists, develops his accounts of social life in terms of governing principles expressed as "laws." However, his "laws" are different from say, the laws of physics, in that they describe and derive from specific aspects of the historical process, and are a product of history, rather than being trans-historical.

9. The connection between a particular property regime and particular operation of the law of value suggests, as we will argue below, that particular attention

should be given to the recent emergence of so-called "intellectual property" and its association with computing. This has already been noticed by Bollier (2007).

10. This suggests, more generally, that particular economic relations affect broader social terrains—how, for example, the things one does to improve one's skills and ability to think get transmogrified conceptually (i.e., fetishized) into "human capital."

REFERENCES

Akrich, M. 1992. "The De-Scription of Technical Objects." In *Shaping Technology, Building Society: Studies in Sociotechnical Change*, edited by W. Bijker and J. Law, 205–224. Cambridge, MA: MIT Press.

Appadurai, Arjun. 1996. *Modernity At Large: Cultural Dimensions of Globalization*. First edition. Minneapolis, MN: University of Minnesota Press.

Arrighi, Giovanni. 2009. *Adam Smith in Beijing: Lineages of the 21st Century*. London: Verso.

Arvidsson, Adam, and Eleanor Colleoni. 2012. "Value in Informational Capitalism and on the Internet." *The Information Society* 28 (3): 135–50. doi:10.1080/019 72243.2012.669449.

Bardzell, Shaowen. 2014. "Utopias of Participation: Design, Criticality and Emancipation." *ACM Digital Library*. http://dl.acm.org/citation.cfm?doid=2662155. 2662213.

Bollier, David. 2007. *The Rise of Collective Intelligence: Decentralized Co-Creation of Value as a New Paradigm of Commerce and Culture*. Aspen, CO: Aspen Institute.

Bourdieu, Pierre. 1984. *Distinction: A Social Critique of the Judgement of Taste*. Translated by Richard Nice. London: Harvard University Press.

Bruni, Attila. 2005. "Shadowing Software and Clinical Records: On the Ethnography of Non-Humans and Heterogeneous Contexts." *Organization* 12 (3): 357–78.

Callon, Michel. 1986. "Some Elements of a Sociology of Translation: Domestication of the Scallops and the Fishermen of Saint Brieuc Bay." In *Action and Belief: A New Sociology of Knowledge?*, edited by John Law, 196–233. London: Routledge and Kegan.

———. 2001. *Acting in an Uncertain World*. Cambridge, MA: MIT Press.

Callon, Michel, and Bruno Latour. 1992. "Don't Throw the Baby out with the Bath School! A Reply to Collins and Yearley." *Science as Practice and Culture* 343: 368.

Callon, Michel, and Fabian Muniesa. 2005. "Peripheral Vision Economic Markets as Calculative Collective Devices." *Organization Studies* 26 (8): 1229–50. doi:10. 1177/0170840605056393.

Corradi, Gessica, Silvia Gherardi, and Luca Verzelloni. 2010. "Through the Practice Lens: Where Is the Bandwagon of Practice-Based Studies Heading?" *Management Learning* 41 (3): 265–83. doi:10.1177/1350507609356938.

Escobar, Arturo, David Hess, Isabel Licha, Will Sibley, Marilyn Strathern, and Judith Sutz. 1994. "Welcome to Cyberia: Notes on the Anthropology of Cyberculture [and Comments and Reply]." *Current Anthropology* 35 (3): 211–31.

Foster, Robert J. 2008. *Coca-Globalization: Following Soft Drinks from New York to New Guinea*. New York: Palgrave Macmillan.

Foucault, Michel. 1977. *Discipline and Punish: The Birth of the Prison*. New York, NY: Pantheon.

Friedman, Thomas L. 2006. *The World Is Flat [Updated and Expanded]: A Brief History of the Twenty-First Century*. Expanded and Updated edition. New York: Farrar, Straus and Giroux.

Fuchs, Christian. 2012. "With or Without Marx? With or Without Capitalism? A Rejoinder to Adam Arvidsson and Eleanor Colleoni." *tripleC: Communication, Capitalism & Critique. Open Access Journal for a Global Sustainable Information Society* 10 (2): 633–45.

Fuchs, Christian, and Vincent Mosco. 2012. "Introduction: Marx Is Back—The Importance of Marxist Theory and Research for Critical Communication Studies Today." *tripleC: Communication, Capitalism & Critique. Open Access Journal for a Global Sustainable Information Society* 10 (2): 127–40.

Fujimura, Joan H. 1988. "The Molecular Biological Bandwagon in Cancer Research: Where Social Worlds Meet." *Social Problems* 35 (3): 261–83. doi:10.2307/800622.

Goffman, Erving. 1999. *The Presentation of Self in Everyday Life*. Gloucester, MA: Peter Smith Publisher.

Graeber, David. 2001. *Toward an Anthropological Theory of Value: The False Coin of Our Own Dreams*. First edition. New York: Palgrave Macmillan.

———. 2011. *Debt—Updated and Expanded: The First 5,000 Years*. Updated Exp edition. Brooklyn: Melville House.

Gudeman, Stephen. 2001. *The Anthropology of Economy: Community, Market, and Culture*. First edition. Malden, MA: Wiley-Blackwell.

Hakken, David. 1999. *Cyborgs@Cyberspace?: An Ethnographer Looks to the Future*. New York: Routledge.

Hardt, Michael, and Antonio Negri. 2009. *Commonwealth*. First edition. Cambridge, MA: Belknap Press.

Harvey, David. 2003. *The New Imperialism*. Oxford University Press.

———. 2007. *The Limits to Capital*. Updated edition. London: Verso.

———. 2010. *A Companion to Marx's Capital*. London, UK: Verso Books.

———. 2014. *Seventeen Contradictions and the End of Capitalism*. First edition. Oxford : Oxford University Press.

Iacono, C. Suzanne, and Rob Kling. 1988. "Computer Systems as Institutions: Social Dimensions of Computing in Organizations." *ICIS Proceedings*, no. Paper 32: 101–10.

Laet, Marianne de, and Annemarie Mol. 2000. "The Zimbabwe Bush Pump Mechanics of a Fluid Technology." *Social Studies of Science* 30 (2): 225–63. doi:10.1177/030631200030002002.

Latour, Bruno. 1987. *Science in Action: How to Follow Scientists and Engineers Through Society*. Cambridge, MA: Harvard University Press.

———. 1990. "Technology Is Society Made Durable." *The Sociological Review* 38 (S1): 103–31.

Latour, Bruno, and Steve Woolgar. 2013. *Laboratory Life: The Construction of Scientific Facts*. Princeton University Press.

Marx, Karl. 1967. *Capital: A Critical Analysis of Capitalist Production: The Process of Capitalist Production*. Edited by Friedrich Engels. New York: International.

———. 1993. *Grundrisse*. New York: Penguin.

Maurer, Bill, and Gabriele Schwab, eds. 2006. *Accelerating Possession: Global Futures of Property and Personhood*. New York: Columbia University Press.

Mauss, Marcel, and W. D. Halls. 1954. *The Gift: Forms and Functions of Exchange in Archaic Societies*. New York: W. W. Norton.

Mead, George H. 1934. *Mind, Self, and Society from the Standpoint of a Social Behaviorist*. Chicago: University of Chicago Press.

Morini, Cristina, and Andrea Fumagalli. 2010. "Life Put to Work: Towards a Life Theory of Value." *Ephemera: Theory & Politics in Organization* 10 (3/4): 234–52.

Munn, Nancy D. 1992. *The Fame of Gawa: A Symbolic Study of Value Transformation in a Massim (Papua New Guinea) Society*. Durham, NC: Duke University Press.

Ritzer, George, Paul Dean, and Nathan Jurgenson. 2012. "The Coming of Age of the Prosumer." *American Behavioral Scientist* 56 (4): 379–98. doi:10.1177/0002764211429368.

Sahlins, Marshall. 2013. *Stone Age Economics*. New York: Routledge.

Sandel, Michael J. 2012. *What Money Can't Buy: The Moral Limits of Markets*. New York: Farrar, Straus, and Giroux.

Sassen, Saskia. 2001. *The Global City: New York, London, Tokyo*. Second edition. Princeton, NJ: Princeton University Press.

Scholz, Trebor, ed. 2012. *Digital Labor: The Internet as Playground and Factory*. First edition. New York: Routledge.

Simmel, Georg. 1997. *Simmel on Culture: Selected Writings*. Edited by David Frisby and Mike Featherstone. Thousand Oaks, CA: SAGE.

Simmel, Georg. 2014. *Die Großstädte und das Geistesleben [The Metropolis and Mental Life]*. Seattle, WA: CreateSpace Independent Publishing Platform.

Simmel, Georg, David Frisby, and Mike Featherstone. 1997. *Simmel on Culture: Selected Writings*, edited by David Frisby and Mike Featherstone. Thousand Oaks, CA: SAGE.

Suchman, Lucy A. 1987. *Plans and Situated Actions: The Problem of Human-Machine Communication*. Second edition. : Cambridge University Press.

Tapscott, Don, and Anthony D. Williams. 2010. *Wikinomics: How Mass Collaboration Changes Everything*. Expanded edition. New York: Portfolio.

Toffler, Alvin. 1980. *The Third Wave*. First edition. New York: Morrow.

Turner, Terence. 1984. *Value, Production and Exploitation in Non-Capitalist Societies*. In Unpublished Essay Based on a Paper Presented at the 82nd Annual Meeting of the Association of American Anthropologists. To Appear in Critique of Pure Culture, Berg Press, New York.

Tylor, Edward Burnett. 1871. *Primitive Culture: Researches into the Development of Mythology, Philosophy, Religion, Art, and Custom*. London: J. Murray.

Van Dijck, José. 2013. *The Culture of Connectivity: A Critical History of Social Media*. Oxford University Press.

Veblen, Thorstein. 1912. *The Theory of the Leisure Class: An Economic Study of Institutions*. New York: B. W. Huebsch.

Virno, Paolo. 2001. *Grammatica della moltitudine: per una analisi delle forme di vita contemporanee [Grammar of the Multitude: For an Analysis Contemporary Forms of Life]*. Soveria Mannelii (Czn), Italy: Rubbettino Editore.

6 Theory Applied
Selecting and Fostering New Values

INTRODUCTION

In Chapter 4, we identified digital practices that establish the possibility of new dynamics of social formation reproduction (SFR). In Chapter 5, we identified capital as *the* thing that is valued, and "value" as the dominant way of understanding our relationships and interactions. Consequently, the "leveragability" of the alternative affordances is greatly diminished. For example, academic social science and general rhetoric become infused with terms like "social capital," "human capital," or "cultural capital"; the use of these *reductio* limits our capacity even to see beyond money calculation. While some scholars think they use the terms only as analogies, their use still leads listeners to confuse the analogy with reality. When turbo-capitalism makes our personal lives and social interactions measureable in currency, our social networks become "rational" extensions of economic engines. Our friendships, affiliations, commitments, education, etc. are reduced to serving capital reproduction, to the single dimension of "value." While the values of citizens coming together to discuss, to create communities, and to generate civic engagement are occasionally honored in their breach, because they are not ratio values, they are seldom honored in observance.

In Chapter 4, we argued that the existence of these digital practices demonstrates the initial feasibility of our project, to intervene in favor of an alternative SFR dynamic, one supporting the construction of a real alternative future, cyberspace. This feasibility follows from the premise that an intervention promoting new values is more likely to succeed if the values are consonant with phenomena already present in computing and likely to loom even larger in the future. Basing alternative futures on what is likely to be present provides a better start point than counting on practices evoked *ex nihilo*. To demonstrate feasibility further, we make explicit in this chapter a set of alternative values that we see as implicit in these practices. The values are divided into two groups: the first contains those with most relevance at the general social formation level, and the second contains those relevant to how people organize their direct, face-to-face social relations.

The following are the general values we extract from computing:

1. Sustainability
2. Increased and broadened access to the means of cultural reproduction
3. Flexibility in the scale of social formation reproduction
4. A broader understanding of "the economic"
5. A social constructivist perspective on technology
6. Democracy

The following are the specific values relevant to face-to-face (or screen-to-screen) interaction:

7. A processual approach or "processuality"
8. Informating as the basic goal of computing
9. A "free software" approach to "openness"
10. A service orientation
11. Participation

Our aim is to show how values implicit in the existing practices identified in Chapter 4 can be articulated into a new set of values consonant with the theory of valuation articulated in Chapter 5. A new set of values could support a substantially new way of life, one with social formation dynamics that extend prospects for viable SFR. We see stating these values explicitly and exploring them in detail as important steps in identifying a more promising social reproductive future. As we discuss each value, a cumulative case for how the candidate value(s) relate to the project of shifting SFR away from capital is made. We want to be clear that the values work together—they need each other. We also address the feasibility of dethroning ratio valuing, moving toward more nominal and ordinal valuing, and changing human relations to extend SFR. The chapter concludes with a discussion of the extent to which "commonness" is likely to be the shared characteristic of the elements of the new value set.

The remainder of this book fleshes out our feasibility case. Chapter 7 identifies possible initiatives to institutionalize these values, to make this kind of future a reality by supporting the values/valuesing discussed in this chapter. Chapter 8 goes on to discuss measures that could show if the intended institutionalizing was being successful.

CHALLENGES TO OUR VALUES PROJECT—GENERAL CHALLENGES

Before addressing each value, we want to address some possible challenges to our project. First, several of the "pro-cyberspace" phenomena discussed in Chapter 4 exist in a dialectical relationships with their opposite. For example, digital technology (DT) can broaden access to forms of cultural reproduction, at the same time that new forms of proprietization (like "digital property" and proprietary software) limit access. Similarly, while cloud computing can increase the range of software a user can access, it can also give corporation more control over access to information. Consequently, in addition to making explicit the "pro-cyberspace" values implicit in the practices, we also need to think about how these aspects of each dialectics would emerge, i.e., become dominant over the "anti-cyberspace" aspects.

Additionally, the chances for a new culture based on these emergent values depend upon the mutual compatibility of the values. In order to lead to something really new, they need to have substantial potential for synergy, for reinforcing each other; that is, the values *set* needs to be coherent. The degree of coherence can be understood in terms of the "post-modern" study of ethics. As explicated by Bernard Williams (Williams 1985), for example, the modernist ethical project of moral philosophers like Kant was a project to identify laws of ethical behavior that could be universally applied, and it has not worked. For Williams, the continued pursuit of ethical certitude results in moralism, an habitually aggressive, even surly, argumentativeness among those convinced of the rightness of their particular moral code. By fostering frequent ethical confrontations, moralism interferes with the capacity of a social formation to extend its reproduction.

In place of pursuing categorical imperatives, Williams draws out the implications of the empirical existence of "thick ethical constructs" in each social formation. Michael Sandel focuses on justice, a good example of a thick ethical construct in many cultures (Sandel 2012). Thick ethical constructs are ideas about proper behavior that have immediate appeal in the particular social formations where they are manifested. Their appeal derives from two factors: 1) that they "have echo," make sense, seem right; and 2) that they fit well with other, similarly echo-having constructs. "Justice," for example, fits well with "fairness," "appropriateness," and similar ethical ideas. Indeed, much of the echo can be seen as deriving from individual ideas fitting with others; that is, that there are complexes of reinforcing thick ethical constructs. For Williams, the existence of such thick ethical constructs causes each culture to foster an ethical discourse, a reflective and reflexive discussion about how those in the culture should behave. One can often perceive similarities in the thick ethical construct complexes of different cultures. Drawing out such similarities is a better, less fraught way to foster a cross-cultural discourse on ethics than trying to prove the universal validity of any single set of ethical ideas.

Despite our having evoked ethics, the focus of this chapter is not on ethics per se, although many of the values we focus on have aspects that could be developed ethically. Rather, what we wish to do is extend Williams's notions about how ethical ideas work to values in general. They give us a concrete idea of what we are aiming for—the identification *of thick values construct complexes*, ones composed of values that "have echo" because they "go together," "make sense together," and that at the same time constitute a basis for very different SFR dynamics.

CHALLENGES WE CHOOSE NOT TO FACE HERE

It is important to be clear about what we are *not* saying about the values we would like to encourage by way of computing-related practices. We will not perform the common but misleading trope that computing "changes everything" (Tapscott and Williams 2010). As we said at the beginning of the book, we object to such technological determinisms, both in principle and on the basis of empirical work. It is *not* our view that the mere existence of the phenomena cited above make inevitable the rise of new values based on them. Nor do we think that a viable future is the most likely consequence of their presence, so the reproductive dynamics of the future society can simply be extrapolated from them.

Our view is that achieving more successful SFR is contingent upon many factors. We focus on this contingency: that the specific dynamics encouraged by these practices, *or others like them*, are recognized, encouraged, and fashioned into making sense together, at the same time as their opposites are discouraged. Extending SFR depends on a deft intervention, and that is why we need to go beyond an analysis of the possible values themselves in order to identify institutions and corresponding measures that could be cultivated, as we will in the subsequent two chapters. Our task has both empirical and normative dimensions, but it is *not* the aim to derive the "oughts" of building cyberspace from the "is-es" of what goes on now.

To be more explicit about what we mean by saying "or others like them," we need to clarify our utopian aim. Central to Marxist theory of social revolution was the rejection of a specific kind of utopianism, that which concentrated on specifying *now* the characteristics of the desired future society and then developing a plan to achieve them. This approach was rejected because of its idealist character—to start living now in the expectation that living in a new way would de facto create a new reality (Engels 1972). Marxists argued instead that the basic forms of the new society would be fashioned in the struggle to bring it about, which meant that the forms of struggle were implicated in its success. Thus, our aim here is not to identify *the* complex of thick values on which the struggle for cyberspace must be based. The actual complex will be created in the activity and struggles to extend SFR. Our aim instead is to show that the values implicit in these forms of computing (and others we have not focused on) can be assembled into thick value concept complexes for a basis on which to build an alternative future. We also want to identify activities that are likely to be necessary to support values of these kinds. This, in our view, is what it means to show that a new future is really possible.

NEW VALUES EMERGENT IN SELECTED DIGITAL
TECHNOLOGY-SUPPORTED FORMS

The first group of values emergent in the selected forms of computing includes those relevant to general processes of social formation reproduction.

1. Sustainability

Like many ideas generated by social movements, in this case, the ecology movement, the meaning of "sustainability" has been diluted as its ambit has grown. Many would argue that it is now merely a catchphrase (Blevis 2007). From a reproductionist perspective, "sustainability" exists when the activities and practices necessary to deal successfully with threats to the physical and social perpetuation of life forms actually take place. We think of sustainability as a primary reason why SFR needs to be extended, i.e., that major interventions need to be made in SFR if the successful reproduction of the global ecosystem is to be achieved into the future.

It is in regard to sustainability that the difficulty of extending social formation reproduction is most obvious. The strongest reason for pessimism regarding the future of capitalist social formations is the contradiction between the reproduction of capital and dealing with ecological degradation. The profound implications of climate change for our common well-being is powerfully articulated in Naomi Klein's recent book *This Changes Everything* (Klein 2014). David Harvey includes climate change as the most fatal contradiction in his *Seventeen Contradictions and the Ending of Capitalism* (Harvey 2014). The Intergovernmental Panel on Climate Change, in its Fifth Assessment Report, states clearly that only a strict, immediate, worldwide mitigation plan has any hope of keeping planet temperature growth below 2°C (Pachauri and Meyer 2014).

The scientific evidence of damage to the planet grows daily, yet there is little sign of significant change toward ecological sustainability. Most of today's social formations ignore or put off what needs to be done to avoid further degradation. The problems of SFR being bent mostly to the reproduction of capital are evident in the risky, unsustainable environmental practices of current social formations. Many of their practices, such as the rapid depletion of nonrenewable resources, are material in a very literal sense. These material conditions are the baseline upon which existence is built. They have obvious consequences, such as locales having to protect themselves from the increased frequency and severity of extreme weather events. Some states have implemented piecemeal plans, coping with them rather than tackling the causes. The most degraded environments are the ones where the poorest or least enfranchised people live. Practices that lead to degrading environments are connected to what is most profitable. Efforts to demonstrate how a market orientation to value can solve this problem have been unscientific and unconvincing. If humans survive, future generations will find it difficult to understand how it was possible for twentieth- and twenty-first century social formations to avoid making the interventions necessary to stop obvious threats to the physical substrate on which SFR depends.

In digital practices, pursuing the value of sustainability would involve both replacing digital practices that add to the problem and using digital technologies to constructing solutions. The large energy requirements of digital devices are a direct contributor to global climate change. DTs have also afforded the scale increase of trade in goods and services, enabling forms of globalization, such as transportation, that contribute to climate change. Hardware is often designed using rare metals, extracted at high human and environmental costs. Facile cyberspace concepts and metaphors tend to delocalize human activity, diverting attention from the ways physical movement through spaces involves extra energy. A common trope among early studies of the social correlates of computing was that DT "decouples space from place," which identifies digitally mediated connections rather than face-to-face interactions (Hakken 1999). In our own professional experiences, try as we might to sustaining human connections via Skype, broadening our networks effectively has necessitated an increasing number of periodic, direct interactions. Given their centrality to SFR, DT use practices will necessarily be implicated if sustainability is to be achieved.[1]

At the same time, it is important to acknowledge the important real and potentially positive role that DTs can play in achieving sustainability. The use of DTs has contributed to an increased awareness of the sustainability issue in the current era. Late in her career, Elinor Ostrom turned to computer modeling to demonstrate the efficiency and effectiveness—and, thereby, the contribution to sustainability—of common-pool resource practices (Jensen et al. 2012). Digital technologies played an essential role in making the case for approaching sustainability problems in an inclusive manner. Being able to construct theoretical models of vast complexity affords conceiving of the universe as an interactive "system" in balance, as in e.g., Lovelock's Gaia hypothesis (Lovelock 1983). It is complex computer modeling that has enabled the Intergovernmental Panel on Climate Change to conceptualize the very challenges to sustainability, as well as affording the needed strategizing about what to do.

Yet even these roles are not straightforwardly positive. In the early academic study of climate dynamics, a small number of computerized models gained popularity. Once in place, it became difficult for climate scholars to find funding for their work if they did not use these standard models, despite their increasing limitations, e.g., in handling complexity. The computered models themselves became part of the problem, making it more difficult for non-experts to understand the causes of climate change. In many ways, computing simultaneously enables and disables coming to terms with climate change. The absence of a set of distinct computing practices that directly promote sustainability explains why we did not include such practices in Chapter 4. Our aim here is not to determine whether DTs are more part of the problem or of the solution, but to point out how DTs both demand and enable a more holistic—and therefore, a more sustainable—approach to the extended co-reproduction of the biosphere and sociosphere.

Using the idea of an interactive system in balance allow us to understand that the sustainability of a "system" is contingent. It is at risk of becoming permanently unsystematic, of being out of balance. The increased capacity to conceptualize models iteratively is key to conceiving of sustainability as necessarily involving extended reproduction, not simple replication. Adopting sustainability as a general social value allows for the essential development of the capacity to create and use such "mega" conceptions. It is also an important precondition for identifying the tactics and constructing the strategies that could be adopted to deal with mounting threats to sustainability. Adoption is by no means inevitable. Promoting ways to compute that enhance chances for sustainability, rather than mindlessly promoting consumption, is assuredly part of what needs to happen.

2. Increased and Broadened Access to the Means of Cultural Reproduction

In Chapter 4, we drew on the work of Lawrence Lessig to demonstrate several important contradictory aspects of the current condition of cultural reproduction (Lessig 2014). They include: the centrality of access, especially for artists, to the means of cultural reproduction; how these means are increasingly digital; and how institutions of so-called digital property interfere with such access and thus reduce opportunities to intervene in SFR. Similarly, cyber-talk often promotes *the possibility* of digitization to increase cultural reproduction activity, but *an inclination toward* it has yet to be shown. There are good empirical reasons to think that computing has broadened access to cultural materials, like forms of expression, through the use of new means of ripping, mixing, and communicating the results. The role of social networking software in the "Arab Spring" is a recent example of all three. The invention of new digital forms for cultural reproduction has clearly taken place at a high rate. Users have been able to access and download digital files of cultural materials despite a more or less continuous effort make it harder to do so, as by trying to contain use behind high walls of digital laws and punishing at least some of those caught violating them.

Lessig's initiatives have highlighted how the recent use of legal instruments to "protect intellectual property"—things like copyright and patents—has diverted action toward the goals of promoting the diffusion of culture, encouraging the circulation of cultural products, and fostering technological innovation. While copyright was first intended as a way to avoid an eternal monopoly on a single cultural product—books, initially—it is now used to preserve a monopoly on expression. Similarly, patents were intended to promote access to knowing how to do things, to make the inventions public, but are now used in regard to software to block access to knowledge. Lessig sees copyright and patents as institutions that enable rent seeking and discourage lively flows of cultural products. If we are to correct this trend, such uses of these instruments need to be discouraged.

One useful perspective on the history of the digital era has been to see it as turning on recurring manifestations of a fundamental ratio-valuing conflict. Napster versus the Recording Industry Association of America (RIAA) is one manifestation. On the one hand, there was the creation and use of new means of cultural representation that, even though commoditized as means to reproduce capital in the form of software, promoted the sharing of information about use (Napster). On the other hand, the existing social form (RIAA) aimed to restrict the use of new means and the channeling of their use through already existing commodity forms. This often takes the form of challenging the new means with litigation and expanded legislation, as the RIAA did. As can happen in market ratio forms of valuing, a real conflict exists between these two ways of reproducing capital, one of which is based on reappropriating old legal doctrines to protect existing forms, the other on exploring new means. The fact that value in the form of technology stocks now dominates the world's equity markets suggests that, at the very least, this struggle will continue for some time. This contradiction has indeed fostered digital innovation, performed in the automatic recitation of clichés like "Moore's Law".

Thus far, there has been both a high level of access to means of cultural reproduction and thus considerable cultural elaboration at the same time as there have been extensive efforts to inhibit the access and use of these means. Is there reason to expect that the contradiction will continue to have these manifestations? Future studies scholars are wary—with good reason—of straight-line projections of current innovation rates and rates of resistance into the future. If rates of cultural innovation/access were to falter substantially, the prospects for the emergence of a developed cyber culture would be diminished. Given the wide extent to which the reproduction of many social formations has become digitally mediated, such a faltering would put their continued reproduction at risk, as Lessig fears. While we make no case that an inclination toward increased innovation and access to the means of cultural reproduction are *dominant* characteristics of SFR, we do believe that such inclinations would be *likely to be supportive of* the successful emergence of cyberspace, and, like Lessig, we think they are necessary. This is why it makes sense to support developments that lead to greater access, and that behavior based on values supporting it would likely increase the chances of full cyberspace emergence. This is one of the several ways that the emergence of cyberspace is not technologically inevitable, but depends upon deliberate human intervention. The question then is, what kinds of interventions are likely to promote the continuation of the kind of social development where the value of increased access to the means of cultural reproduction is reinforced?

In Chapter 7, we present several programs that could institutionalize greater and wider access to these digital means. Any institutionalization of alternative procedures, say for rewarding design or software artistry, would also have to cope with substantial problems of measurement, such as how to determine which parts of a string of code was written by which individuals. We go on to deal at greater length with such measurement issues in Chapter 8. Increased capacities to mix, rip, and burn will need to be valued, and as software becomes a more important mediator of SFR, the need for access to source code will grow proportionally.

3. Flexibility in Relation to the Desirable Scale of Social Formation Reproduction

In Chapter 5, we argued that the current problems in extending reproduction derive from a narrow pursuit of value alone, in part because single-value pursuit narrows reproductive fitness. We want to extend this argument to the idea that independent pursuit of *any* individual values will not succeed in promoting cyberspace. Intervention ideas must be based on understandings of the relationships among all the elements of a complex set of thick value constructs.

The value of flexibility is particularly suggestive of how social reproduction could be oriented toward multiple values. This is valuing the wide range of options that follow from the multiple dynamics of scale that in Chapter 3 we argued are mislabeled as "globalization." This acknowledges only one ultimate dynamic while ignoring others. There continues to be good reason to doubt the validity of preoccupations with an inevitable globality, or to think it is a necessary outcome of digitization. There has been little or no slowing of the pace of digitization in the last few years. However, the social crisis that began in 2007 and manifested itself initially in overt economic forms was associated first with a slowing in the pace of globalization, then with a reversal toward greater localization. Accounting for this pause in scale increase necessitates analytical perspectives that are more explicit about the multiple dynamics at work, and to talk about these phenomena in more subtle ways.[2] Appreciation of their complexity has created room for a more nuanced discourse on scale dynamics—especially since the socio-financial crisis of the late 2000s. To reflect the many-stranded movements of SFR, rather than the one-sided discourses of globalization, "globalspeak" tropes have to be abandoned.

A basis for a more nuanced discussion of scale lies in the recognition of the fuzziness of what is conceptually necessary for globalization, a goal or end-state toward which it was presumably moving, what we can call "globality." Fuzziness about what globality would be was less obviously a problem as long as globalization seemed to be proceeding apace. The recent pause has forced a more pointed discussion of what globality would entail, such as all-important SFR occurring on a single, worldwide basis. Articulation of the empirical conception of globality and globalization means also attending to their dialectical partners, locality and localization, situations in which important SFR takes place in locales, on small scales. Thus, the dialectical partner of globalization—localization—involves the adaptation of things with larger scope to things that are smaller. An example would be the development of a local word processing program not only in a region, but that incorporates culturally significant premises.

Inserting a globalism/localism continuum into globo-talk further affords conceptualization of the reality of a range of intermediate forms. In recognition that the process framed as globalization has multiple possible strands, this continuum can also be broken down further. Different moments in the reproduction of a given social formation are typically at different points on the globalism/localism continuum. For example, while finance operates transnationally, most regulation is still national or even sub-national—e.g., a US state or German *Land*. There are multiple ways and other terms to summarize the collective condition of the strands of SFR, such as globalization/localization. Scholars think it important to articulate terms for "intermediate" processual forms. One is "glocalization," the localization of reproductive forms with initially broad, even very broad "global" purchase, forms that have changed in the process of adapting to diverse socio-geographic conditions. An example of deep glocalization would be changing the source code of Microsoft Excel so that the ontological and epistemological presumptions in the code more closely reflect Malaysian culture.

Another, less frequently articulated but still important intermediate process is "lobalization." This term refers to a reproductive pattern developed in relation to a local condition that turns out to have much wider, perhaps even global, relevance. Claudio Ciborra argues that it is lobalization rather than abstract system design that is responsible for many of the most acclaimed digital innovations (Ciborra 2002). He draws attention to the developmental history of the SABRE[tm] system for airline reservations, which originated as a solution to a problem that was unique to Eastern Airlines, but is still the basis of the worldwide reservation system. "Lobalization" is what would have happened if source code changes initiated in Malaysia would have lead to new, more culturally flexible database forms, with broader utility and therefore widely adopted throughout the world. Skype, developed for Swedish speakers and now used all over, is another example of lobality.

A Ciborra/lobal perspective helps us understand why so many efforts at strategic thinking fall short of their objectives—e.g., strategic planning in organizations, or strategic design in industrial design. Successful interventions are more likely to grow out of dealing flexibly with specific local problems rather than from *ab initio* grand design, for example, in digital technology design and use. The lobal perspective is also relevant to issues of economic and social development. It suggests, for example, that less developed countries should not get trapped into simply adopting each technological innovation promulgated by organizations in developed countries. A better approach might be to build local capacity and to use it for addressing pressing local issues, recognizing that a prime source of general innovation is clever solutions to local problems. Countries should consider supporting development of a higher level of local skill through addressing local issues with self-developed or modified free software, rather than the proprietary variety. When a powerful local solution arises, it can demonstrate the power of "lobal thinking," a slogan of the annual Feste d'Economia (Festival of Economics) in Trento, Italy.

From a value perspective, computing is compatible with a wide range of possible scale phenomena, some involving increasing scale, some maintaining existing scale, and some lowering scale. Rather than assuming that it normally affords upscaling toward some mythologized state of globality, we should see that DTs have no inherent upscaling trajectory. Rather, computing offers ways to organize flash mobs and reinforce relations of proximity as well as support for global networks of email correspondence. In cyberspace, we should be able collectively to select the scale implications we want rather than being forced only to upscale. Recognition of the manifold ways in which SFR can be influenced actually enables more space for cyberspace.

4. Broader Understandings of the "Economic"

Since economistic approaches focus on value rather than values, they inhibit the lobal thinking described above. That is, they presume the valued, rather than enquiring into what might be valued. To overcome narrow economism, we need to broaden our understanding of what is basic to the dynamics of social life. In late 2010 the venerable *Financial Times* (FT) felt compelled to run a series on whether there was a post-crisis future for capitalism (as discussed in MacNeil and O'Brien 2010). In Chapters 3 and 5, we point to how the world economic and social crises that began in 2007 prompted reflective consideration of general failures in economics, as well as other problems. Computing, and the computationalist perspective on which it is based, played a central role in the crisis, if not *the* central role.

Much of the reflection by the FT addressed the discipline of economics itself. Of particular note is the retrospective view of his career in economics by Harvard economist Stephen Marglin, in a book entitled *The Dismal Science: How Thinking Like an Economist Undermines Community* (Marglin 2008). As suggested by the title, Marglin focuses on the way that regnant, neo-classical economics ties "the economic" tightly to "the market." This distorting perspective interferes with the reproduction of other essential aspects of the social i.e., how ratio valuing displaces other forms of valuation. This interference has particularly a negative effect for Marglin on what he calls "the community." Acknowledging the plasticity of the concept, he identifies its distinctive feature as providing ". . . a kind of social glue, binding people together in relationships that give form and flavor to life." Community also depends ". . . on constraints and obligations that transcend the calculation of individual utility"(Marglin 2008, 20).

The elevation of scarcity forms to causal status is the core of neo-classical economic models—the calculation of utility preference curves by individuals. These models have been at the center of the dominant form of economics in the developed world since the early 20th century. In Marglin's words, we have to "[t]ake . . . experience seriously" (Marglin 2008, 20). This means extending behavioral models beyond "*homo economicus*," recognizing that the "economic person" provides a poor model of how individuals actually behave regarding resources, even the scarce ones that are the sole focus of mainstream economics.

There are many possible examples of the failure of economic models to inform practices, food providing just one. According to the Food and Agriculture Organization of the United Nations, in 2014, almost 30% of the world population ate more food than was needed for diet (*Food and Nutrition in Numbers 2014*, 2014). The percentage was only 20% in Oceania, but 44% in developed countries. These statistics partly suggest that a capitalist allocation of resources does not work evenly. The malfunctioning of allocation is even more visible in the observation that about 11% of the world population is generally undernourished (which goes from <5% in the developed countries to 20% in Africa). The health implications are obesity in one part of the world and malnourishment in another.

Equally relevant to the broadening that Marglin calls for is the scholarship of Elinor Ostrom, the first female winner of the Nobel Prize in Economics in 2009. Ostrom built her career on emphasizing the importance to social life of what she called "common pool resources" (Ostrom 1990). These are means of living governed by human social relationships alone, without state or market. Ostrom paid particular attention to the institutions pivotal to social wealth commons, arguing for both their technical superiority under certain circumstances to state and market, as well as to their essential role in social formation dynamics and the reproduction of social formations that maintain vitality. Commons' institutionalized practices protect resources from the tragedy of overexploitation while also making them widely available. An example is a commons that protects fishing resources from overexploitation by inhibiting its use by those outside of a community, while at the same time maximizing equal access for those within it (Ostrom 1990).

Toward the end of her career, Ostrom gave particular attention to computing as a common pool resource, including, but not limited to, free/libre and open-source software. With Charlotte Hess (Hess and Ostrom 2011), she drew attention the variety of small and large social practices out of which such institutions are composed. The flowering of new, digital common pool resources, from the Internet to Wikipedia, was in her view an important characteristic of our current era. Acknowledging the importance of pooling common resources points away from an exclusive dependence on markets to extend SFR. Ostrom's attention to common pool resource institutions combines well with Marglin's attention to community. This combination fosters broader visions of a social infrastructure that reframes market, state, and community relations. The broader view affords a project of de-emphasizing ratio and re-emphasizing nominal and interval notions of values/valuing. Of course, not all correlates of digital technology point at a Marglin/Ostrom alternative. We need additional interventions that promote broader notions of what is basic to society, ones that undermine perspectives too long accepted as "obvious" in mainstream economics.

5. Social Constructivist Perspectives on Technology

An emergent, DT-associated general value is closely connected to a newer form of scholarship. Although its conceptual ambit is broader, the rise of social constructivist perspectives on technology is closely correlated with DT mediation (Hakken 1999). Social constructivism (SC) develops out of the critique of problematic ways that technologies are typically talked about (Bijker et al. 2012). Technologies are often treated as being autonomous and largely composed of a collection of machines, arising from the disinterested, abstract cogitations of scientists and engineers. In this technological determinist view, technology has a profound influence on SFR, while the effects of SFR on it are ignored. By contrast, in social constructivist analyses, technologies are understood to be like other social entities, subject to SFR rather than autonomous from it. In Technology Actor–Network Theory, a technology is understood as constituted by a network of people, machines, and organized relationships. It is a network, moreover, that emerges from the very social process of recruitment and alliance building, rather than isolated cerebration (Hakken 2003). The social and the technological are understood to co-construct each other. The various forms of technological SC emerged initially in the academic field first called science, technology, and society, or science and technology studies.

There is reason to be concerned that some early forms of SC may have overemphasized the causative role of the social, merely replacing technological with social determinism (Latour 2005). While SC is a necessary antidote to technological determinism, even SC can reinforce conceptions of technology and society as being more distinct than they actually are. Any analytical act that separates the technological from the social obscures how they are interrelated aspects of the same whole. Even the popular notion of "the socio-technical" reinforces a sense that they are more additive than unitary (Bijker and Law 1994). Social formation reproduction is similarly a complex whole. Constructivist approaches remind us not to background or ignore one component over another. The task for the future is to turn this analytical view into one of a set of values, in order to construct a form of sociality sufficient to the needs of a digitally saturated SFR, that is, to make a humane cyberspace.

6. Democracy

Broadly speaking, democracy can be defined as "the practice or principles of social equality" (Stevenson 2010). This conception of an egalitarian social order is central to the elements of our new value set, both the general social values already discussed and the more face-to-face organizational ones that follow. Participatory design, for example, can only be practiced by a team of people who acknowledge the equal importance of the involvement of all the others. Each person is then able to participate fully, but when hierarchies and inequalities intervene, the prospects for participation wane. Understanding power relations and the political is key to effective participation, as Tone Bratteteig and Ina Wagner have discussed in their recent work on *Disentangling Participation* (Bratteteig and Wagner 2014). Broadened access to the means of cultural reproduction implies the principle of social equality.

A democratic approach is necessary if we are to take advantage of the DT affordances discussed in Chapter 3. The Internet holds out the promise of new kinds of social equality, egalitarianisms that are new forms of democracy, as well as new types of democratic participation. Online, we should be able to choose how we represent ourselves, what we show or don't show to the world, as the contributions of a person can be looked at without the lens of race or class or gender. Of course, this depends upon access to the Internet. As discourse in the public sphere expands with Internet access, people are able to access other parts of the world, and viewpoints can connect across space and time (Habermas 1991). Decision-making can be enabled because information is shared widely. A BBC poll in 2010 of people in 26 countries found that 79% saw access to the Internet as a fundamental right (WebObserver. net—Global I BBC World Service Poll 2010). In the US, the FCC has now classified the Internet as a public utility (Brodkin 2015). As use of the Internet becomes more ubiquitous, its potential importance to democracy becomes more apparent.

Scholars such as Seyla Benhabib have long noted how democratic participation depends on personal privacy (Benhabib 1996). It should not be surprising that a major challenge to the expanding democratic vision of the Internet comes from Internet service providers that are bent to the reproduction of capital. Shoshana Zuboff has recently pointed out that Google, the provider of the dominant web search engine, arguably offers the greatest challenge (Zuboff 2014). As the major search engine, Google controls how most users find information on the web. Its algorithms are secret—its preferences and workings unknown and invisible. Zuboff has emphasized that, at the same time that the NSA and Google invade our privacy, they ". . . assert a right to privacy with respect to their surveillance tactics and then exercise their choice to keep those tactics secret" (Zuboff 2014). When Google entered into an agreement with the NSA in 2010, the data generated by the Internet became part of international surveillance and a larger question about where the public domain begins and ends.

Google, of course, is not the only actor in this equation. Facebook, phone providers, cloud providers, and others have supplied data to the government. They in turn look for ways to mine data, to turn it to profit. What President Dwight Eisenhower famously called into question as the "military industrial complex" has become both more complex and more secretive. As became evident in the 2013 revelations of Edward Snowden, we might know even less about this alliance and its reach into our daily lives and communications (Greenwald 2014). Without the work of media outlets like *The Guardian*, we would hardly know about these intrusions. The role of the state in undermining Internet democracy has been made clear in revelations about the NSA and GCHQ (Government Communication Headquarters), which have put paid to the idea that what people communicate on their computers and smartphones is "private" (Harding 2014) What is public is what is put online—all of it. What is private, how it is kept, who keeps it, and who has access to it are different questions. The way we have thought of this equation has been turned on its head.

The capacity to mine our data is potentially so lucrative that it is difficult to imagine that these agencies will simply stop doing so. If democracy is to be a meaningful value, we will have to find ways to recover control of the information on the Internet. This, in turn, will mean coming to terms with the many forms of social inequality.

7. "Processuality," Or, a Processual Approach (to Organizing)

The values we have discussed thus far would be manifested mostly at the general level of social formation and general SFR. We turn now to values that are more relevant to the ways in which people organize actual, face-to-face social life. This first face-to-face value we have named the admittedly awkward neologism "processuality." We use the term to mean an orientation to the quality of experience, to organizing in a way that maximizes this experiential quality. Processual approaches to organizing interactions have recently been recognized as necessary to overcome the problems manifested in structural ones, those that put emphasis on the arrangement of roles rather than how the roles are experienced. The switch from emphasizing structure to emphasizing process has been slow. It is most easily seen in the change in how to conceive of the scientific object of the research field called "organization studies" (OS) (Hernes and Maitlis 2012). In the DT world, this is now often called "information systems" (Lee, Liebenau, and DeGross 2013).

Early in its history, the field was dominated by efforts to identify the proper structure of "the firm." This ideal type was a combination of the means that maximally extended management control—i.e., F.W. Taylor's "scientific management" (Taylor 2004)—with Max Weber's conception of the ideal type—the hierarchical bureaucracy (Weber and Gerth 1991). Over time in OS, this preoccupation with ideal structure has been displaced by a concern with process, that is, "organizing" rather than "the organization." Even structure is now often approached as being like a process, a change highlighted by the increased use of the term "structuration" (Giddens 2013). Giddens invented the term to stress the basic unity of structure and process and to embrace how organizations actually work. This switch to process grew out of recognition that the characteristics of large corporations, far from being ideal, often impede aspects like flexibility, dexterity, and speed of adapting.

One of the more salutary consequences of this change of focus to organizing from the ideal organization has been a growing recognition of what studies of social movements can suggest to OS, and visa versa (see Davis et al. 2005). Contemporary students quickly understand how the dominant forms of social media—e.g., Facebook—are more like social movements than bureaucracies. Facebook is less about creating a structure of proper roles and more about fostering relations and relationships (however hackneyed, e.g., "liking"). Focus on process is reinforced via extensive digital mediation, where the model centers attention on the flow of information rather than on hoarding information as a power resource, as in Claude Shannon's information to noise ratio (Shannon and Weaver 1949). DT use is associated with new organizing dynamics, driving OS to recognize multiple different ways to organize. An already-cited example is Robert Travica's distinctions among "networked," "organic," "ad hoc," and "virtual" as distinct, new forms of organizing (Travica 1998). They all share a rejection of bureaucracy and hierarchy, replacing them with affordances for flexibility and the dispersal of responsibility.

With regard to technology in general, there remains a tendency in OS to mistake possibility for reality, especially in discussion about organizational structurations. OS sometimes sounds as if it claims that DTs are saving organizing from contradictions, such as the contradiction between bureaucracy and motivation. This is evident in the often-repeated notion that digital mediation leads automatically to less hierarchical, more "flat" organizations. While certain affordances can be characteristic of DT use, there is nothing inevitable about their actual manifestations. As with the other values discussed in this chapter, for a processual organizing focus to become the central pillar of thinking about organization, it has to be *valued*. DT affordances for valuing process must be actively encouraged in order for new dynamics of organizational reproduction to emerge. Digital mediation creates new opportunities to reinforce a process perspective, but these opportunities must be seized and developed.

8. "Informating" as the Basic Goal of Computing

Another practice we have identified as possibly pre-figurative of alternative SFR is Zuboff's notion of "informating" (Zuboff 1988). This involves sharing DT-developed information as widely as possible to promote more "informed" behavior by organization members. Zuboff's demonstration of the viability of informating as a goal for organizational computing makes it a possible value for alternative SFR dynamics, especially given our desire to take full advantage of DTs' cyberspace affordances. "To informate" is a good answer to the question: what is the point of creating and apprehending all these data, then storing and manipulating them—i.e., turning them into information? The opposite strategy she identifies is to use computers mostly to automate and increase top management control over work. This also increases informational inequality and decreases an organization's abilities to adapt. Informating enables more effective *collective* control. Informating means fostering a different dynamic in organizing organization—to maximize information flow and use. One way to make sense of the current "data/information glut" is to see it as a consequence of digital mediation without informating, that is, mindlessly creating information without first being clear about who and what it is for.

While clearly an advocate of informating, Zuboff was nonetheless fully aware of the problems that emerge when an organization tried to graft this approach onto an existing hierarchical structure, or when organizational structures and processes lag behind digital mediation. One problem is the increased frustration of those who could see the implications of expanded information but lacked the authority to act on it. This may be the central issue of DTs in organization, whether its purpose is better control of the process of making paper or of creating more knowledge. Informating can only work well in organizations that disperse authority. Without developing adequate procedures for spreading authority to use the extra information, the likelihood is that DT mediation does not actually mean better-informed decisions.

Zuboff showed how choosing informating as a value is more likely to foster new practices than automating. Despite her discouragement about the failure of more organizations to adopt informating, Zuboff's demonstration of the viability of informating is an important pointer toward accomplishing a fuller cyberspace. Since her book was published, the study of organizations has begun to adopt basic changes, like the processuality that we have already discussed. Informating is not inevitable, but recent organizing experience suggests that choosing it often results in the adoption of new organizing forms, e.g., the "virtual" organization. Organizations can choose to informate, and when they do, they promote more general social realignments. We think it possible to foster movement to such general social dynamics through institutions and measures that value informating over automating.

9. A "Free Software" Approach to "Openness"

One of our more specific values is the free approach to making software (free software, or FS), something that emerged from the most visible computing-associated new social form, the set of patterns typically manifested in free/

libre software projects (Coleman 2012), and, to a lesser extent, in open source[3] ones (Weber 2005). Central to the "free" approach is the marginalization of the employment relation, which makes collaboration dependent upon personal preference and which itself becomes the chief determinant of what one does—which particular project to join, on which aspect of the project to work, and on what role or roles to take in the project. FS openness also affords a greater opportunity to create new roles. The many substantial FS products in use demonstrate that this approach works technically. They also demonstrate that coordination can be achieved through the emergence of collaborative roles rather than having to be imposed from above.

The core of this value is manifested in the FS approach to openness, that anybody can contribute, an attribute that free software projects share with similar projects like Wikipedia. The use of the term "open" evokes such social dynamics. Ethnographic studies of FS (Coleman 2012; Kelty 2008) and these of other open projects (Reagle 2010; Teli 2010) illuminate the multiple ways they create orderly development out of volunteered action and thus also the viability of non- or partial-market social relations, even within a market-dominated social formation.

What change in the aspects of SFR would follow from taking a free approach to openness? In what ways do these consequences depend upon the particular characteristics of this form? Being "open" is widely valued in current computer culture, not just in "open source" but also in "open data," but there are many, quite different forms of "openness" to choose from. Basic to the free approach is the avoidance of proprietary code. This allows code to be changed and therefore affords broader appropriation of it by those who want to use it. It also adds to the capacity to be "open" in the "mix, rip, and burn" way of using tools of cultural reproduction. Valuing "openness" in this very broad sense serves an additional purpose for us, in that it affords great flexibility in deciding what a collective wishes to do by freeing it from the need to make money. We say more about this in Chapter 7.

FS and similar projects, e.g., Wiki-based projects, are suggestive of the variety of alternative SFR dynamics that can be fostered, as well as what can follow in response to these alternatives. As pointed out in Chapter 4, one of the problems that can arise in FS projects is that the voluntary nature of the work can make it difficult to predict when the parts of a project will be satisfactorily completed. In our study of these projects, issues are generally resolved by focusing on developing the right social relationships. This is another way in which FS projects can foster new dynamics in the evolution of social relations.

10. A Service Orientation

The emergence of service orientation (SO) can create a flexible rather than a ridged, rational approach to organizing. Conceptualized as a value, an SO is an example of how approaching organization from process, informating, and openness might afford the emergence of an alternative model of how to do computing. This model also shifts the focus in thinking about organization away from ideal social structures and toward centering on the process of relationship building.

An SO might radically reduce the need for organizational infrastructure, especially the need for permanent structures of *inter*mediation between need and service provider. When ensconced as a value equal to or greater in importance than market, there would be a strong affordance toward networked ecologies and numerous ad hoc social relations developing into relation*ships*. Economies of scale could grow out of repeated positive experiences with known partners, resulting in more robust forms of organizing reproduction without organizational reproduction. Moreover, this model is extendable to other human activities. Consider, for example, the rise of the massive online open course, or "MOOC," in higher education. Setting aside for the moment the admittedly huge problems of certification, MOOCs have a potential to make it possible for an individual student to assemble educational experiences from multiple, highly desirable providers.

The computing industry at present is experiencing a pendulum swing back toward service, but not generally of an SO kind. Many organizations now define service in terms of getting their information stored in "the cloud" as opposed to buying additional memory for storing multiple copies on machines they own. In addition to lessening sunk costs, "clouded" information can, via the Internet, be easily accessed from multiple locations. While clouds could allow a growth in the kind of service computing we are imagining, as it exists now cloud computing works to keeps big organizations at the center of computing. For example, tablet users now must rent their copy of MS Word, paying annually to use the software. The growth of cloud computing can also be viewed as an effort to reinforce the central role of large organizations in social reproduction. Having data and the software stored on servers owned by large organizations makes both individuals and companies dependent upon their reproduction. Further, the widespread use of the cloud makes it easier for organizations and states to obtain and aggregate information on individuals and organizations.

The vision we propose of a radically decentralized SO economy is appealing in an era of privacy infringement. SO could make it easier for users to keep control over their data, sharing it only in each ad hoc relation rather than having it accessed centrally. SO is also a way that individual freedom could be further increased, possibly leading to the re-emergence of something like the anti-authoritarianism of Jeffersonian democracy. The fact is, despite these ad hoc relational affordances, only a small proportion of computing services are provided through SO networks. This suggests that current SFR does not embrace them. The eclipse of 1990s SO suggests that other developments would be necessary to make SO generally attractive. For example, extending a basic income to everyone would lessen concern that striking out on one's own would put one's livelihood at risk. Here, we are foregrounding an issue that we take up in Chapter 7, the extent to which the success of institutions to promote the kinds of computing uses we are envisioning depends upon the development of other, perhaps less computing-connected, institutions. The service orientation was demonstrated in an arena of practice, i.e., software, whose characteristics made it particularly appealing. There is no theoretical reason why it could not be extended to other arenas, as long as SFR was inclined toward it and away from large corporations. As so often in computing, deciding what we *should* do and being clear about our values (rather than fixating on what already exists) is the necessary first step to finding better solutions.

11. Participation

The last organizing value in our set is participation. The Nordic tradition of user participation in digital system design and development was intended to include all moments of system design, from beginning to end (Ehn 1989). It demonstrates the resonance between the creation of systems to handle organizational information and the distribution of involvement in their creation, or participatory design (PD) (Simonsen and Robertson 2012). The benefits to well-done participatory design are many. They suggest that the creation and implementation of digital systems are arguably good points at which to initiate broader programs of processuality, informating, freeness, and service orientation, extending them to non-digital organizing practices (Wagner, Bratteteig, and Stuedahl 2010).

Among the things demonstrated by Nordic PD is its dependence for success on involving the "right" people. Right does not mean those with formal credentials or those with the most experience. Nor is PD about management support, the direct involvement of management in PD being unnecessary and maybe even counterproductive. The right people for PD are curious about their work, want to make a difference, and are sensitive to the needs and desires of their workmates. Perhaps most importantly, they have an active imagination, which gives them the ability to see how things could be different and thus why it makes sense to go through the difficulties of trying to make them so. They are the ones most likely to see the value of thinking beyond capital, to join in creating a better world.

Moreover, participation is central to the pursuit of all the other values outlined in this chapter and thus to thinking "beyond capital." The benefits of taking a processual approach to "re-engineering the organization" depend upon achieving broad participation in making it happen (Hammer and Champy 2009). There is little benefit to be derived from informating in an organization if people from all areas and levels of the organization are not active in using the information created and shared. Leveraging the "free speech" -type freedom demonstrated in free software depends upon broad voluntary participation of developers and users. Attempting to organize along the lines of a service model depends upon computing people seizing the opportunities to operate on their own and developing trusting relationships with others who are so inclined. Similarly, the creation of a serious movement for sustainability requires the commitment of many different computing people. There is little point in increasing and broadening access to the means of cultural reproduction if there are only a few means to be taken up. The opportunities at various levels opened by computing will have little merit if they are not seized for lobal development. Broadening the conception of the economic creates opportunities for dignifying many kinds of work unmediated by capital reproduction, but this only works if those whose work is open participate in dignifying it. People doing this work must be ready to make use of the opportunity when a really new, alternative social formation base is to be constructed socially. Finally, our conception of democracy—a substantive, not a formal one—is participatory and active.

NEW VALUES AS THE BASIS FOR A SHIFT FROM RATIO VALUING TO FOSTERING NEW, HUMAN RELATIONSHIPS

These are the eleven values that we have extracted from our analysis of the alternative SFR affordances of selected forms of computing described in Chapter 4:
General Values:

1. Sustainability
2. Increased and broadened access to the means of cultural reproduction
3. Flexibility in the scale of social formation reproduction
4. A broader understanding of "the economic"
5. A social constructivist perspective on technology
6. Democracy

Values Specific to Organizing:

7. Processuality
8. Informating
9. A "free software" Approach to "openness"
10. A service orientation
11. Participation

In the previous sections of this chapter, we elaborated on how the practices that encourage each of these values individually afford alternative SFR dynamics, ones with better prospects for meeting the SFR challenges we currently face. There is little reason to think that, on their own, or brought about individually, any one of these values would have much impact on SFR, let alone overcome the momentum of current SFR dynamics or prevent SFR decline. For this to happen it will be necessary to develop an integrated complex of values, one like the complex listed above, but not necessarily the same ones. A well-thought-out values collectivity will have many interdependencies among its individual values. Moreover, it will have substantially greater prospects for fostering a viable alternative SFR dynamic than would values individually pursued, and of course, will also be harder to organize. Still, being "a well-thought-out collectivity" on its own is not enough. The collectivity of values will have to strongly afford a transition process to the new social formation.

Do the set of values we have identified collectively have enough transformative potential? Could they create the basis for alternative general dynamics more likely to extend social reproduction? We try to answer these questions in two parts, first by looking at how the general values interrelate and second by considering how the organizing group does as well. Again, we are *not making claims* that our value complex makes such an alternative dynamic inevitable, likely, or that it is even the best basis for such new dynamics. We are only suggesting that it *could* lay such a basis. Ultimately, our hope is that consideration of them contributes to a more general discussion of the ways to create a viable future, to build a cyberspace beyond capital.

MORE GENERAL VALUES AS ENABLERS OF NEW FORMS OF SOCIAL REPRODUCTION

As we set out our values path toward an alternative SFR dynamic, we frame our discussion in terms of the social reproductionist theory outlined in Chapter 2. We intend this theory to replace the now-dominant social theory, which we call "compu-technicism" or "technicism" for short (Hakken 1987). As a combination of technological determinism (Hackett 2008) and computationalism (Golumbia 2009), at its core is a naïve belief that the technical properties of the dominant technology, i.e., computing, determine the social consequences of its use. The corollaries are the grander belief that first, there is little role for choice with regard to technology, and second, that technology determines the broader course of social development. Technicist views focus on specific machines and envision history as something whose dynamics, including social change, are the product of the properties of artifacts. The same technicism generally exempts artifacts from enquiries regarding any social influences on them, presuming them to be exempt from any social influences.

In contrast, social reproductionist perspectives like ours emphasize how artifacts and social phenomena co-construct each other, so the technical is included within the social, and the social within the technical. In the social reproductionist perspective, artifacts do not articulate with the world independently, but do so instead through Technology Actor Networks (TANs) of artifacts, people, and organizing. Computers have no independent impact on social life, but they interact with the social through the agency of already-social TANs (Hakken 1999). Consider, for example, a situation where a form of computing is associated with a new or re-emphasized social dynamic, as in the way FS is associated with phenomena claiming to promote greater "openness." It is true that the FSs in use have affordances toward greater openness, but this is not part of the code itself. Rather, it is *the openness of the social processes* through which the code is developed (written or constructed), the open means through which it is accessed, and the openness with which the code is used that gives it this affordance, as in FS application projects.

The importance of the shift in analytical perspective from technicism to social reproductionism is key. First, the term technicism implies the unacknowledged but powerful analytical preference given to technological determinism, as in phrasings that describe computers as the greatest force for globalization (Friedman 2007). Because technological determinism treats technology as having an internal developmental dynamic, it undermines any inclination to take control of the future. Since things are the way they are, they are compelled to be so by the properties of technologies. Further, since the properties of technologies are themselves determined by "rational scientific truths," people can at most only chose whether or not to use a technology, and even this choice is increasingly not an option. For example, signing up for Obamacare in the US requires the application to be completed online even if aided by a navigator. Technology policy studies document how choice is often an illusion, as the important decisions have already been made (Winner 2010). The covert message is that the social correlates of a technology's use cannot be influenced: one can only "take it or leave it."

In social reproductionism, technological properties are manifested in social dynamics, and the social in the technology. The extent to which social correlates can be encouraged or discouraged is seen as much broader. Even the "path dependence" so often cited as set off by a technological choice becomes open to public intervention, as long as the interventions for choice happen early enough in the process, before irreversible dynamics have taken hold. The social constructivist aspect of social reproductionism is foundational to our project to create a viable future. We can both observe the ways the social manifests itself in technology uses, and we can influence which social correlates are actually manifested in technology use. In other words, technology use can itself be approached as a form of social construction. It makes sense to try to influence the correlates of particular uses of specific technologies. A project to foster alternative SFR dynamics will not be easy, but the choice we face is not between social construction and no social construction. Rather, our choice is between trying to influence social construction and letting technology develop in the manner most afforded by contemporary SFR dynamics. If we are critical of such dynamics, then choosing to influence them should follow.

The opportunities for intervention revealed through social constructivism are increased even more if we broaden our social understanding of what constitutes "the economic." In this broadened view, through a constructivist lens, the economic opens up to include more space for human action. When we describe market/ratio valuing as hegemonic, we are not saying that people make no nominal or ordinal value choices. Rather, when they do so, it doesn't seem to matter much, because that valued (other than "value") is not valued in action. We need to acknowledge this situation and bring it and its resource implications into the realm of public choice making.

Perhaps it is in regard to conscious choice making that the broadening in access to means of cultural reproduction is most important. Even though there is reason to be skeptical about what they actually accomplish, movements for "open data" and "open government" suggest that it might just be possible to give real access to important information for decision-making. In general terms, digital technologies also spread access to the cultural means to "rip, mix, and burn" old cultural forms into new ones. Broadenings in access to means of cultural reproduction are associated with periods of social innovation, of the sense of discovery of new ways to do old things and of new things to do. This broadening opens up space to compare stark ratio valuing with richer ordinal and nominal choices, to explore different options than those driven by the market, and to discover new ways to use the cultural-generative properties of computing. The broadening also increases the possibilities for non-elites to enter the process of choice making.

"Upscaling," or the constant push toward the bigger, is a fixation of the technicist take on globalization. Our alternative value approach focuses on *choosing the scale on which to operate*. Holding to this approach also enhances opportunities for making choices. When perceived as an inexorable process driven by digital technologies, "globalizationist" thinking severely limits the SFR imaginary. The financial crisis not only halted the internationalization of capital markets; it also tore off the cloak of inevitability and undercut illusions about the capacities of states and international organizations to keep the agents of capital from destroying the basis of their own wealth. Searching out local, glocal, and especially lobal projects would reinforce the sense that scale is a variable that can be controlled, that it is not a juggernaut overrunning everything in its path. We should chose a scale for action because it is most likely to foster the SFR dynamics we want, not mindlessly because "bigger is better."

Recognizing scale as a variable rather than a vector has implications for sustainability. While sustainability must be achieved at a global level, it is likely that many practices for a sustainable world will operate best at a local level, where the risks are often most evident. Put differently, we need to be able to find more sustainable practices at each level of scale, with no one level being more important than any other. At the core of each of these ways to value the social (and evaluate its dynamics) is a commitment to democracy, not in some vague, general sense, but as manifested in each general value. This society would be different, pursuing a number of different values seriously, not just market performance. The influence of these other values should place significant new pressures on SFR.

NEW ORGANIZING VALUES

In addition to the complex of general, macro-level values discussed above, we have articulated a parallel, able-to-be integrated set of organizing or "micro" -level values, also based on qualities emergent in the computing practices discussed in Chapter 4. No new SFR dynamic will arise from the articulation of general values alone, no matter how well institutionalized and measured. Values must also be based on changes at the person-to-person level, that of "organizing." To understand our use of this term, it needs to put in its linguistic context. The terms "the organization," "an organization," "organization," and "organizing" constitute a linguistically tight word complex. At the time of the structure-focused intervention of F.W. Taylor in the early 20th century, the most substantive form, "the organization," became the preferred way to evoke the complex. "The organization" came to refer in the first instance to an entity created to pursue private profit, particularly the limited liability firm or the corporation. A new academic field, organization science (a distinct form of organizational studies), emerged around the term, as well as derivative terms like "the organization man." The goal of the field, following Taylor, became to identify the structure appropriate to this presumed-to-exist ONE BEST WAY, which was always capitalized by Taylor (Taylor 2004). Using "*the* organization," not "*an* organization" or "*organizations*," reinforced the Taylorist agenda.

Our seventh value, processuality, urges the stressing of a processual rather than a structural approach to the organization term complex. We again stress the process of "organizing" rather than the structure of the organization. Within organization studies, this shift was already underway when it was given an additional shove by computing. The shift follows from the fact that OS scholars had not been able to identify the ONE BEST organizational structure, despite trying for roughly a hundred years—and most had given up. Our use of the "organizing" element of the complex underlines the new emphasis on activity, rather than on the anatomy of one privileged form, the organization.

Focusing on organizing as a process also brings out synergies with other micro-social processes, including the ways humans arrange their daily activity. Organizing is a general notion, applicable to the range of face-to-face (or in cyberspace, person-to-person) activities, whether newly decided upon or carried out habitually. It is toward just such processual phenomena that our next value, "informating," is inclined. Giving attention to all forms of information is a strong affordance of computing. "Informating" encourages us to examine information closely and see how it is used within various "organizings." We would argue that information sharing is the essence of human organizing. As encouraged by recent scholarship on the similarities between organizations and social movements, close examination brings out the parallels in all forms of human action (Davis et al. 2005). In social movements, as in organizations, we can ask after the kinds of information created, how each is shared, who uses it, and with what authority.

While it is true that different kinds of information have different relevancies, we are unlikely to know which have what relevance a priori, and it is in this sense, and only this sense, that more information is generally better than less. Equally important as the *kind* of information is *with whom it is shared* and which people who get information have *authority to act on it.* It is generally counterproductive for people to have information and not be able to act on it. Automating through computing, rather than informating, is ultimately more about structure than process. In automation, emphasis is placed on marginalizing humans by replacing them with machines and on keeping access to information to a minimum, on structures of control rather than processes of use. When automating, the tendency is to share as little information as possible. In these ways, a processual perspective supports informating uses of computing, while attending to informating encourages attention to process.

Similarly, the kind of organizing we described as at the core of our ninth value, the free orientation in FS, depends upon informating reinforcing a focus on process. Freely available software code greatly encourages the free availability of other kinds of information, plus further use of the information to informate. Free software is about creating and sharing information resources, whereas open source, which allows proprietization, attends first to organizational preservation via ownership. All these organizing values fit well with the service-orientation model of computing organization, whose small scale necessarily encourages attention to the micro-level and to organizing process because there is so little structure. In the service model, information again is key. To work well, actors in the model must have access to as much information as possible. The service model encourages organizing on a small, even individual scale, and it affords organizing that is agile. Small scales discourage complex structures, encouraging instead maximizing the ability of independent agents to come together for particular purposes now, but then to move quickly on to different processes. Dependence on structures, especially on large corporations, is minimized. In this way, corporate commitments to maintaining ridged structures and competitive advantage become a handicap rather than an advantage.

Our final value, participation, ties together the other organizing-level values. When a social formation depends on markets to reproduce itself, ownership is the matter of most concern, especially ownership of profit. Marglin argues that taking control of profit is the most basic thing that managers do, that it exists primarily to insure profit for owners rather than to facilitate the work process (Lippit 1996). The priority of ownership is interrogated when nominal and interval values are encouraged, as opposed to only ratio ones. When values, micro or macro, are nominal and/or ordinal, the pursuit of one can enhance the pursuit of others—when they are compatible. Nominal and ordinal values pursuit reinforces social interactions and affords the building of relationships with others in a strong form of community, as in the process of free software. These organizing values can be seen to fit together as a dynamic set for all person-to-person, micro-social relations, as well as corresponding to the social dynamics we envision at the societal level beyond capital.

CONCLUSION: ON "COMMONNESS" AND THE NEW VALUES

As we will discuss further in our concluding chapter, we write especially for people trying to imagine a future not bounded by markets and the powerful actors who leverage control for their own advantage. Among people thinking about the future, interest in the idea of holding and using resources in common has recently been revived. There is a desire to sustain and build upon the large number of existing commons and also to build new ones. For Americans, the term brings out associations with the shared common, where families in colonial, pre-19th century villages grazed their animals. No longer used for that purpose, some are still referred to as "the common," as in Boston.

Toward the end of her career, Elinor Ostrom argued for seeing the many uses of digital technologies, for example, free software, as being maintained as a common pool resource. An informating strategy similarly supports viewing information as a common good, to be shared as widely as possible. Ostrom was also worked to show that there were alternatives to state control and market control of resources, and access to them. Her third option, the "common pool resource," was something maintained by the group of people who used it. They accessed the resource and maintained it on terms that were not resource depleting, because it was commonly valued. How much of what we are trying to foster in terms of these new values can be achieved through this vehicle of commons?

The idea of fostering nominal and ordinal valuing via commons has great appeal. Ostrom understood that achieving the kind of social relationships that could support common pool resource maintenance was not easy, and that the problems of doing so increased with scale. Central to "commoning" is the creation and maintenance of a robust organizing context. We can imagine a society where many resources are maintained by common pooling, and where new values would be pursued through creating commons for their pursuit. This is not the character of most contemporary social formations. Instead, the market relations that dominate SFR discourage commoning. During any transition to new values, it will be necessary to support commons institutionally until they become robust economic forms. At least for some time, only states will have sufficient power to do this. While the basic aim of the transition to new SFR dynamics will be to reduce ratio valuing and enhance the other types of valuing, it also makes sense to maintain markets that identify popular choices in areas less central to social reproduction. Significant actions by states and markets will likely be necessary for community-governed common pool resources, and other means to pursue nominal and ordinal values, to flourish. Michel Callon writes about "market devices," instrumentalities that have allowed markets to achieve the hegemony they now hold. We argue that we need to achieve "common devices," more vigorous commons institutions, more of them, and covering more aspects of social life. We envision that state and market institutions will continue to be a substantial part of the foreseeable future. Common devises will not be enough on their own. We will need a set of institutions that can support and foster non-ratio values. What these institutions might be, and how they might function, is the focus of the next chapter.

NOTES

1. At the time of writing, computing mediates much of SFR to a very deep degree, so deep that it is difficult to imagine how to end this mediation, if one wished to do so. We think it important to understand that this deep mediation has been achieved by human intervention as much as by demonstration of the functional value of computing. In functionalism, the reason for the existence of a social form is the contribution it makes toward maintaining the social system in equilibrium. Many forms of functionalism take the continuing existence of a practice as a demonstration of the importance of its social function. We think many forms of computing were adopted before functionality could be demonstrated. Consider, for example, the so-called productivity paradox, the fact that for very long stretches of time, it has been impossible to identify a positive impact of computerization of work on productivity statistics. Computerization has come about as much because of specific actions—through the way the funding arrangements of the US National Science Foundation were set up, or the ways in which computing was associated with "being modern"—as by demonstrations of its efficiency and effectiveness.
2. For an example, see Hakken's "Informating in a Demi-Global World" in *Proceedings of the iSchool Conference* (Hakken 2009).
3. Use of the adjective "open," as in the label "open source" has become extremely widespread in computing-related talk, the term having acquired an almost privileged status, which makes at least rhetorical "openness" a necessary quality of any endeavor. The openness of the projects we talk about here are quite strongly analogous to that which Weber is talking about, one where, for example, voluntary participation implies the need for high levels of consensus. See Teli (2010) for discussion of which dynamics change, and which do not, when an open source software project is located within a for-profit corporation.

REFERENCES

Benhabib, Seyla. 1996. *Democracy and Difference: Contesting the Boundaries of the Political*. Princeton University Press.

Bijker, Wiebe E., and John Law. 1994. *Shaping Technology/building Society: Studies in Sociotechnical Change*. Cambridge, MA: MIT Press.

Bijker, Wiebe E., Thomas P. Hughes, Trevor Pinch, and Deborah G. Douglas. 2012. *The Social Construction of Technological Systems: New Directions in the Sociology and History of Technology*. Cambridge, MA: MIT Press.

Blevis, Eli. 2007. "Sustainable Interaction Design: Invention & Disposal, Renewal & Reuse." In *Proceedings of the SIGCHI Conference on Human Factors in Computing Systems*, 503–12. CHI '07. New York, NY: ACM. doi:10.1145/1240624. 1240705.

Bratteteig, Tone, and Ina Wagner. 2014. *Disentangling Participation: Power and Decision-Making in Participatory Design*. Berlin: Springer.

Brodkin, Jon. 2015. "FCC Votes for Net Neutrality, a Ban on Paid Fast Lanes, and Title II." *Ars Technica*. February 26. http://arstechnica.com/business/2015/02/fcc-votes-for-net-neutrality-a-ban-on-paid-fast-lanes-and-title-ii/.

Ciborra, Claudio. 2002. *The Labyrinths of Information : Challenging the Wisdom of Systems: Challenging the Wisdom of Systems*. Oxford University Press.

Coleman, E. Gabriella. 2012. *Coding Freedom: The Ethics and Aesthetics of Hacking*. Princeton: Princeton University Press.

Davis, Gerald F., Doug McAdam, W. Richard Scott, and Mayer N. Zald. 2005. *Social Movements and Organization Theory*. Cambridge University Press.

Ehn, Pelle. 1989. *Work-Oriented Design of Computer Artifacts*. Stockholm, SE: Arbetslivscentrum.

Engels, Friedrich. 1972. *Socialism: Utopian and Scientific*. New York: Intl Pub.

Food and Nutrition in Numbers 2014. 2014. Rome: Food and Agriculture Organization of the United Nations.

Friedman, Thomas L. 2007. *The World Is Flat 3.0: A Brief History of the Twenty-First Century*. Third edition. New York, NY: Picador.

Giddens, Anthony. 2013. *The Constitution of Society: Outline of the Theory of Structuration*. John Wiley & Sons.

Golumbia, David. 2009. *The Cultural Logic of Computation*. Cambridge, MA: Harvard University Press.

Greenwald, Glenn. 2014. *No Place to Hide: Edward Snowden, the NSA, and the U.S. Surveillance State*. New York, NY: Metropolitan Books.

Habermas, Jürgen. 1991. *The Structural Transformation of the Public Sphere: An Inquiry into a Category of Bourgeois Society*. Cambridge, MA: MIT Press.

Hackett, Edward J. 2008. *The Handbook of Science and Technology Studies*. Cambridge, MA: MIT Press.

Hakken, David. 1987. "Reproduction in Complex Social Formations." *Dialectical Anthropology* 12 (2): 193–204. doi:10.1007/BF00263324.

———. 1999. *Cyborgs@Cyberspace?: An Ethnographer Looks to the Future*. New York: Routledge.

———. 2003. *The Knowledge Landscapes of Cyberspace*. New York, NY: Routledge.

———. 2009. "Informating in a Demi-Global World." In *Proceedings of the iSchool Conference*. Chapel Hill.

Hammer, Michael, and James Champy. 2009. *A Reengineering the Corporation: Manifesto for Business Revolution*. New York: Harper Collins.

Harding, Luke. 2014. *The Snowden Files: The Inside Story of the World's Most Wanted Man*. New York: Vintage.

Harvey, David. 2014. *Seventeen Contradictions and the End of Capitalism*. First edition. Oxford: Oxford University Press.

Hernes, Tor, and Sally Maitlis. 2012. *Process, Sensemaking, and Organizing*. Oxford: Oxford University Press.

Hess, Charlotte, and Elinor Ostrom, eds. 2011. *Understanding Knowledge as a Commons: From Theory to Practice*. Cambridge, MA: MIT Press.

Jensen, S., B. Plale, Xiaozhong Liu, Miao Chen, D. Leake, and J. England. 2012. "Generalized Representation and Mapping for Social-Ecological Data: Freeing Data from the Database." In *2012 IEEE 8th International Conference on E-Science (e-Science)*, 1–8. doi:10.1109/eScience.2012.6404486.

Kelty, Christopher M. 2008. *Two Bits: The Cultural Significance of Free Software.* Durham: Duke University Press Books.

Klein, Naomi. 2014. *This Changes Everything: Capitalism vs. The Climate.* New York: Simon & Schuster.

Latour, Bruno. 2005. "Reassembling the Social—An Introduction to Actor-Network-Theory." *Reassembling the Social—An Introduction to Actor-Network-Theory,* edited by Bruno Latour, 316. Foreword by Bruno Latour. Oxford University Press, Sep. 2005. http://adsabs.harvard.edu/abs/2005reso.book.....L.

Lee, Allen, Jonathon Liebenau, and Janice DeGross. 2013. *Information Systems and Qualitative Research: Proceedings of the IFIP TC8 WG 8.2 International Conference on Information Systems and Qualitative Research, 31st May–3rd June 1997, Philadelphia, Pennsylvania, USA.* Berlin: Springer.

Lessig, Lawrence. 2014. *Remix Making Art and Commerce Thrive in the Hybrid Economy.* New York: Penguin.

Lippit, Victor D. 1996. *Radical Political Economy: Explorations in Alternative Economic Analysis.* Armonk, NY: M.E. Sharpe.

Lovelock, J. E. 1983. "Gaia as Seen Through the Atmosphere." In *Biomineralization and Biological Metal Accumulation,* edited by P. Westbroek and E. W. de Jong, 15–25. Netherlands: Springer. http://link.springer.com/chapter/10.1007/978–94–009–7944–4_2.

MacNeil, Iain G., and Justin O'Brien. 2010. *The Future of Financial Regulation.* London, UK: Bloomsbury Publishing.

Marglin, Stephen A. 2008. *The Dismal Science: How Thinking Like an Economist Undermines Community.* First edition. Cambridge, MA: Harvard University Press.

Ostrom, Elinor. 1990. *Governing the Commons: The Evolution of Institutions for Collective Action.* Cambridge University Press.

Pachauri, R. K, and L. Meyer. eds. 2014. "IPCC 2014: Climate Change 2014: Synthesis Report." http://www.ipcc.ch/pdf/assessment-report/ar5/syr/SYR_AR5_FINAL_full.pdf.

Reagle, Joseph Michael. 2010. *Good Faith Collaboration: The Culture of Wikipedia.* Cambridge, MA: MIT Press.

Sandel, Michael J. 2012. *What Money Can't Buy: The Moral Limits of Markets.* New York: Farrar, Straus, and Giroux.

Shannon, Claude Elwood, and Warren Weaver. 1949. *The Mathematical Theory of Communication.* University of Illinois Press.

Simonsen, Jesper, and Toni Robertson, eds. 2012. *Routledge International Handbook of Participatory Design.* First edition. New York: Routledge.

Stevenson, Angus. 2010. *Oxford Dictionary of English.* Oxford University Press.

Tapscott, Don, and Anthony D. Williams. 2010. *Wikinomics: How Mass Collaboration Changes Everything.* Expanded edition. New York: Portfolio.

Taylor, Frederick Winslow. 2004. *Scientific Management.* New York: Routledge.

Teli, Maurizio. 2010. "Collective Ownership in Free/Libre and Open Source Software: The OpenSolaris Case." In *Conference Proceedings of JITP 2010: The Politics of Open Source,* 1:138. http://oss-institute.org/storage/documents/Resources/studies/the-politics-of-open-source.pdf#page=146.

Travica, Bob. 1998. *New Organizational Designs: Information Aspects.* Stamford, CT: Ablex.

Wagner, Ina, Tone Bratteteig, and Dagny Stuedahl, eds. 2010. *Exploring Digital Design: Multi-Disciplinary Design Practices.* Berlin: Springer.

Weber, Max, and Hans Gerth. 1991. *From Max Weber: Essays in Sociology.* New York: Psychology Press.

Weber, Steven. 2005. *The Success of Open Source.* Cambridge, MA: Harvard University Press.

"WebObserver.net—Global | BBC World Service Poll 2010." 2015. *WebObserver. net*. Accessed April 20. http://webobserver.net/2010/12/10/global-bbc-world-service-poll-2010/.

Williams, Bernard Arthur Owen. 1985. *Ethics and the Limits of Philosophy*. Vol. 83, 6. Cambridge, MA: Harvard University Press.

Winner, Langdon. 2010. *The Whale and the Reactor: A Search for Limits in an Age of High Technology*. University of Chicago Press.

Zuboff, Shoshana. 1988. *In the Age of the Smart Machine: The Future of Work and Power*. New York: Basic Books.

———. 2014. "Response to Mathias Döpfner Dark Google." *Frankfurter Allgemeine Zeitung*, April 30. http://www.faz.net/aktuell/feuilleton/debatten/the-digital-debate/shoshanna-zuboff-dark-google-12916679.html.

7 New Institutions to Support New Values

INTRODUCTION

In the previous chapter, we articulated eleven values that could help rebalance the overdependence on ratio values and move us to alleviate the structural crises presently threatening the capacities of our social formations to reproduce themselves. In this chapter, we put forward ways that these values might become socially embedded. The aim is to find a process that could achieve a transformation from one sole ratio value, value, to many values, including nominal and ordinal ones. We will follow a process that sociologists call "institutionalization," or the creating of new institutions. Sociologists generally use the term "institutions" to refer to relatively stable arrangements of people, technologies, and laws, and the social relations and relationships among them. Institutions are complex social forms that tend to reproduce themselves, while simultaneously encouraging people to engage in socially recognized roles and recurrent practices, or instilling governmentality (Burchell, Gordon, and Miller 1991). Engagement with institutions can both sustain and transform them (Miller 2007). Within institutions, the subjectivities of the people taking part in them are constructed and reconstructed. The construction/reconstruction of subjectivities takes place in the relations among individuals, their understandings of roles they are supposed to take, and the practices they carry out, including those that change the institutions. The practices are possible because social arrangements, some of them invisible, allow for the existence of the practices, creating their infrastructure.

PREMISES—ON INSTITUTIONS AND THEIR INTERRELATIONS

In Chapter 2 we drew attention to the dynamic qualities of institutions. While practices may be intentionally oriented toward the reproduction of institutions, their contradictions create the spaces that make social formation reproduction (SFR) change possible. While cultural reproduction serves to replicate as well as extend the concepts through which a people perceives the world, social reproduction involves the social relations and relationships among actual people. Institutions can be seen to be central to both cultural and social reproduction. Unless institutions are changed, there can be little hope of reorienting social formation reproduction to the new values set we suggested in Chapter 6.

While some of the institutions we envision in this chapter already exist in partial form, many do not, and few will continue to play their current role in SFR. We cannot simply create new institutions out of whole cloth; we must engage with the existing institutional order even as it is moving us to the brink of reproductive failure. If we are to foster an orientation that actually moves SFR from ratio valuing alone to include ordinal and nominal valuing, we must have a vision of what will work better. For example, in Chapter 5, we identified the labor form of work relations—that is, work institutions that through markets commodify humans and their ability to do actual work—as a key practice that needs to change. We also identified specific, recent forms of digital technology (DT) use with the potential to transform work away from labor, all of which makes work an important institutional arena for change. In line with our theory of value(s), at the center of our analysis are the institutions that reinforce influence over SFR by and for the working multitudes/class and determine their ability to achieve freedom.

Achieving freedom means institutional forms must contain ideas, visions, or designs for a future SFR. In articulating potential institutions to embody the values we described in Chapter 6, we again recognize that we are engaging in a kind of utopian project. Ours is not the kind of utopian project that tries to predict which institution *will* become central to SFR in the future, nor do we claim that the institutions we describe *should* be the ones to come into being. They are not the Taylorist ONE BEST WAY. We are not engaged in reinventing government on any level. Rather, our intent is to prompt a specific discourse as part of the ongoing debate about how to promote our collective survival *Beyond Capital*. Barring chaos, institutions will have to be developed. Thinking *now* about what they might be, and about what is feasible, is utopian and necessary.

What follows are the ways we imagine a social reordering of values might take place. There are a host of general questions about the institutions inherent in such a project, for example:

- At what level should the new and reoriented existing institutions aim for hegemony—local, national, or global?
- What are the appropriate institutional forms?
- Which important pressure points in SFR should be the first focus for change?

We see no simple answer to the first question, as institutions operate at different levels, and will likely do so in the future. Likewise, with the second question, the answer is complex. For example, constitutional reforms should be part of the state, while other changes such as technological development may be at a "global" level. Others will be from commons—that is, entities that communally care for common pool resources (Ostrom 1990). As markets are a major embodiment of the ratio values/value pursuit that we want to displace, markets would need to be greatly reduced or transformed in their reproductive influence, but some will remain. The pressure points of change are complex, as in all ambitious political and social-distributed actions. This means pressing local social formations as well as putting emphasis on institutions legislatively entitled to intervene. This includes supranational, regional entities, like the European Union, which manages funding lines that can contribute to the fostering embodiment of the nominal and ordinal values we envision.[1]

The main part of this chapter describes potential new instrumentalities that we will call "agencies," one for each of the eleven values we have identified. While we think this strategy makes for clarity and coverage, it is not meant to minimize the need for interorganizational synergy. Effective promotion of the values we are proposing will surely depend upon creating an *overall* reorientation, to be achieved in part through the effective interactions among new institutions and new roles for existing ones. For example, organizations embodying worker empowerment will depend on distributed agency (that is worker groups, unions, as well as communities), while at the same time encouraging collaborative infrastructures. While we describe particular agencies for the pursuit of a particular value, in reality, each institution will work toward multiple values. Each value would be imbricated in many institutions. Indeed, institutions tend to have many foci. For us, the most important thing is that they are effective. This is why we refer to them as "agencies," working bodies that have the value(s) in focus. Their focus derives from having a clear commitment to the task of pursuing a specific value(s), and having the resources (money, personnel, etc.) to accomplish the tasks they are charged with. Agencies will be designed to work together, but not be related hierarchically.

AGENCIES TO INSTITUTIONALIZE THE NEW VALUE SET

Agencies should be thought of as rhetorically illustrative, as pointing to the *possibilities* of structuring institutions rather than detailing how the institutions would actually work. We recognize the drawbacks of this strategy. In actual social change, many of the suggested agencies could have different forms, or they might be replaced by other distributed assemblages (e.g., through constitutional rights, specific targeted reforms, etc.). Nevertheless, our attempt here is to further articulate an important priority, to talk about the *focus of action* rather than focusing on the concrete form of a future institution.

Sustainability Agency

In the context of profound threats, changing our environmental practices would arguably be the basic indicator of a success in marginalizing markets and nourishing the common. The risk of ecological catastrophe is in many ways a function of rampant ratio valuing. The dominance of the reproduction of capital over contemporary SFR compels expanding production irrespective of need, which itself intensifies energy consumption. Hence, efforts to achieve sustainability will only be successful if they displace ratio valuing.

Lawrence Hilty makes distinctions among the direct, indirect, and systemic environmental effects of computing (Hilty 2008). This is a good starting place for thinking about what a *Sustainability Agency* might do. Regarding direct effects related to the technology, such an Agency could act to reduce the ecological impacts of the production of computers, the energy consumption, and contribute to productive efficiency, or "doing more with less." Regarding indirect effects operating at an intermediate scale, the Agency could aim to encourage the optimization of organizing, e.g., by supporting a virtual as opposed to in-real-life meeting, saving transportations costs. In the area of general, society-wide, and systemic effects, the Agency could promote transformations from energy-wasting infrastructures, like individual automobile transportation.

An example of how these systemic effects have worked is the complicity of fields like Human–computer interaction (HCI) with designed obsolescence (Roedl 2015). This is a form of "planned obsolescence," the response to the crisis of insufficient demand that emerged in the capitalism of the 1920s. Obsolescence then combined with advertising efforts to promote increased, often unnecessary, consumption. The field of HCI often contributed to the design of commodities whose period of usefulness is artificially shortened, thereby promoting corporate profits (Roedl 2015). A major part of a Sustainability Agency should be the promotion of counter-design practices that extend rather than reduce the "shelf life" of all useful objects and practices, including digital ones. For example, it could promote procedures that aim for socially robust and enduring computing (Hakken, Teli, and D'Andrea 2010). It could also further the work of those who are thinking about critical design in HCI, and connecting it to critical theory (Bardzell and Bardzell 2015).

There is a significant role for computing in understanding the complexities of climate change. Supporting the development of DT-mediated climate science should be a priority for a Sustainability Agency, including the elaboration of complex ecological models that help project the consequences of current actions into the future. Such models are an important part of identifying practices that could contribute to sustainability, as opposed to those that merely adapt to climate changes. While any model is limited and partial, converging models could be reliable enough to constitute a basis for action. A Sustainability Agency could expand support for DT practices that already help to reduce the impact of computing on environmental conditions.

We agree with Hilty that any re-engineering of the relations between digital technologies and the environment must involve all three kinds of effects: direct, indirect, and systemic. As the systemic effects may be the ones whose reversal could make the most substantial contribution to sustainability, the Agency would direct particular attention to mitigating those first. Since systemic effects are also ones where political dimensions are most obvious, they may stimulate considerable pushback. The Agency would need a program of political intervention to be successful.

Science and Technology Studies offer some suggestions about how the Agency's program might achieve significant social support. Bruno Latour draws attention to "the parliament of things," an assembly that includes scientists, politicians, and decision-making processes, as well as artifacts (Latour 2004). Callon, Lascoumes, and Barthe discuss collective action of people at the local level concerned with environmental issues, one of many social movements emerging as hybrid "parliamentary" forums (Callon, Lascoumes, and Barthe 2009). These are knowledge-producing collectives that question official accounts of techno-science and articulate programs for change that are situated in concrete, lived contexts. The scholars conclude that the hybridization of both science and politics makes both stronger, and both better able to promote the fundamental changes needed. The problem of climate change has gradually been incorporated into more and more political programs, as in the first "People's Climate March" in September 2014.

A Sustainability Agency needs to develop programs to support the emergence of hybrid entities, thereby strengthening decentralization and the emergence of powerful local subjectivities. Its means to do so could include providing grants, promoting new capabilities through training, designing and building new communications media to help programs interact, and so on. In order for all this to matter, this and the other Agencies must have substantial regulatory powers. The forums and other hybrid forms should have actual normative and decision-making power, with binding effects. The need for something like *legislative capacity* is most evident in the ongoing Intergovernmental Panel on Climate Change. They address problems we must deal with, yet they lack the ability to make binding decisions. Such decision-making power need not always imply centralization. If a forum is localized, its binding power should also be decentralized. Local democracy can be time-consuming, but it can also inhibit the rapid generalization of practices that would otherwise greatly compromise sustainability.

New Culture Agency

We discussed in Chapters 4 and 6 how extending the reproduction of culture is crucial to extending SFR. We also described how access to culture is now subjected to a contradictory process. On one hand, there has been an expansion of tools, especially digital technologies useful for modifying cultural products. On the other hand, access to these tools has been regulated and limited through the expansion of intellectual property claims. Further complicating cultural access is the increased use of business models based on subscription or renting instead of ownership. Subscription services like Spotify or Netflix provide access to the products of culture without access to the means to reproduce them—that is, to "mix, rip, and burn," to reassemble things into new cultural entities, or to adapt existing cultural things to new contexts.

Robust forms of and for cultural reproduction need to be fostered, especially in social formations experiencing rapid change. We suggest a *New Culture Agency* to manage these contradictions, which at the start would mean tilting the legal balance against exaggerated copyright and the overextension of patents. Yet, the agency should also have a positive program. For example, the legal contradictions would be lessened if creation claims were lodged collectively rather than individually. Larry Lessig suggests that one way to do this is through open licenses, like Creative Commons (CC). In various writings, he has articulated an intellectual basis for CC (Lessig 1999, 2001, 2004, 2014). The project is oriented toward creating, maintaining, and making it easy to use a set of licenses for cultural products that afford their distribution and circulation while discouraging their proprietarization. According to the project's website, at the time of writing, there are CC affiliates in 70 jurisdictions, and almost 900 million cultural products have been released under a CC license (https://creativecommons.org).

Lessig also argues for the construction of a registry where authors could list works that are available online, another possible Agency project. The proceeds of a small tax on all online sales could be redistributed to authors in proportion to the sale of the work. Proposals for such taxes were mooted in France and Canada in the second half of the 2000s when they were presented as a way to resolve the conflict between authors and consumers over peer-to-peer file sharing. The failure of these proposals was perhaps because of the opposition of key players in the cultural marketplace, the big editorial groups, who feared being "cut out."

Why wasn't there greater support for these ideas? Why weren't authors pushing for this solution? Why was there no broad social debate outside of the corporate world over them? The social practices of cultural production and consumption are complex and involve more than the distribution of revenues. The arts as businesses are increasingly imbricated in the distortion of ratio valuing. The visual arts have seen the advent of huge art fairs that are a marketplace for rich investors who are often simply parking funds in yet another investment. Theaters and filmmakers often argue that online technologies are decreasing their audiences. Meanwhile, the increase in ticket prices to cover loss makes these art forms accessible to a smaller audience. In the US, support for arts education has often been eliminated in tight school budgets or shifted to private providers, if it exists at all. Expanding access to arts education and creative opportunities could fall within the purview of the Agency.

The fate of "open access" in academic publishing sheds light on another series of questions for the New Culture Agency. Open access in academia refers to publishing academic writing in digital forms that are easily and freely available on one or more websites. Any academic can see the difference between the ease with which an open access publication can be obtained in contrast to the difficulties of accessing scholarship through the journals published by big publishers (difficulties often shared with libraries). Further, open access articles often have shorter release times. There are already several existing open access academic journals. Some funding agencies, such as the European Union, are promoting open access to projects they fund. The career structure of academics, in which traditional journals clearly play a big role, remains relevant to possible changes—e.g., in the US, the tenure and promotion process. Even though there are open access journals with high standing, traditional publications often are counted as more important. Very few academics get paid for their writing or work as editors of journals, or for reviewing articles. If the majority of readers access articles digitally, the need for physical printing and distribution is obviated. Several interesting experiments in open access are going on, but closed academic journals and books still get published and sold at a very high cost. The position of the big academic publishers doesn't look weaker, and some, like Springer, may be even stronger. Moreover, traditional proprietary journals now provide authors with the possibility to publish their articles as open access, with the submission of what are called "article processing charges" (APCs). For example, one of us got a proposal for an article processing charge of $3600 for a single article by a well-know journal. Some funding agencies, like the European Union, are considering the APCs eligible for inclusion when funding projects. This is a classic example of an incomplete shift toward open access, with publishers still rewarded for their position, a form of rent. If a shift is taking place, it is not as significant as one might expect. Why is it not happening?

Book publishing in general has seen a change in readership to online providers. Amazon and Google in particular have worked to dominate the online marketplace in different ways. Writers want and need to be read, but the online model short-circuits the editing and oversight that were once afforded to authors, as well as some of the means of disseminating their work. This was both an advantage and disadvantage. Publishers, and increasingly Amazon, hold a grip on who and what is published or distributed. Online publishing presents the possibility of self-publishing and personal dissemination, but this is largely only effective for those who are well known or "eminent." For the rest, the path is relying on search engines and self-promotion.

Mediators of existing publications and online search engines continue to be central to getting authors in touch with potential readers, especially with new ones. The economics and principles of Lessig's approach are only a first step in what might lessen the grip of ratio valuing in the arts and culture. The economics and the principles are right, but the understanding of the existing social relation is too simple, and does not sufficiently address the social goals of singers, academic writers, and movie makers. In addition to *taxes to support the cultural worker* and promoting *open access to cultural products,* the New Culture Agency will also have to find support for design and implement substitutes—whether for Thomson Reuters Web of Science or iTunes or cable TV. These will be needed for *mediating* the supply and demand of cultural products, enabling access for those creating cultural inventions, and mobilizing the attention of new audiences. In addition to fighting restrictions on access to the means of cultural reproduction, an equally important task for the Agency will be to aid in the creation of new works and promote the development of infrastructure for the circulation of intellectual work.

Lobal Agency

In Chapter 6, we introduced the need for a more complex view of the varied scale phenomena typically misidentified as globalization. Michael Hardt and Antonio Negri articulate the range of complexity necessary in regard to shared control by social groups (Hardt and Negri 2009). They move from "a commons" as a localized, institutional arrangement to "the common" as a global political perspective. In articulating the elements of a proper set of scale phenomena, we directed attention particularly to how computing fosters "lobal" phenomena (Hakken 2003) when a large-scale or "global" event has derived from a local solution to a problem of a specific locality. This suggests, paradoxically, that a good way to foster transnational computing solutions is to address local issues, because such initiatives can quickly achieve wider perspectives. "Lobality" has the additional advantage of democratizing the relations among nations, increasing the number of "makers" and lessening the number of mere "takers." Attending to the lobal increases awareness of the situated, both the relational emergence of technologies and discourses as well as of the importance of coordinating the roles that nation state, national capital, and local institutions all play in decision-making.

Rather than creating additional global institutions to address large-scale problems like global climate change, we propose instead a *Lobal Agency.* Its main task would be to support projects that demonstrate the value of starting by addressing problems locally and then projecting solutions to broader, even international issues. For example, this Agency might support Douglas Schuler's proposed World Citizen Parliament, a DT-mediated platform for transnational discussion (Schuler 2013). Maurizio Teli and others have discussed the limitations of such initiatives—in particular, their promotion of deliberative spaces without sufficiently addressing the pre-existing relations of power and the implications for action (Bosio et al. 2014). Still, we identify two important aspects of Schuler's proposal, which has much in common with the "hybrid parliament of things" discussed above. The first is as a demonstration of how the envisioned solutions of various participating groups can be aggregated in terms of shared interests, whether localized in a neighborhood or a town, or geographically distributed. The second is that through research DTs can provide mechanisms for dealing with complexity, e.g., when there is a need for nested decision-making processes.

The phenomena that inspire Schuler include the assemblies that are characteristic of many contemporary social movements, e.g., the Occupy movement. While suggestive, we recognize that decision-making processes have to take into account factors like the reproduction of capital that structurally inhibit many potentially useful perspectives. It would be idealistic to move immediately to create Schuler's Parliament, without first addressing the basic inequalities characteristic of current SFR. The early development of the Internet was shot through with futurist narratives regarding direct decision-making, ideas put paid by the centralizations following the corporate domination of the World Wide Web. Thus, the Lobal Agency might promote initiatives to decentralize DT-mediated discourses by supporting the creation of decentralized arenas for the construction of specific solutions. It could also help connect these discourses, perhaps through the shared interfaces promoted by the Service Agency discussed below. Inspired by existing funding schemes for networking and local initiatives, the Lobal Agency should also fund efforts that articulate at a higher level political demands emerging at the local level.

New Economy Agency

Chapter 5 outlines the problems that often follow from the dominance of ratio valuing. In arguing for re-orienting SFR away from a primarily ratio-value-based system toward one that encompasses ordinal and nominal values, we do not wish to diminish the importance of attending to resource practices. Humans need to produce and consume to survive, so dismissing resource practices makes no sense. Rather, the understanding of value(s) needs to go beyond ratio valuing as the sole measure of economic practice. Like Marglin and Ostrom, we want it to include the organization of production and resource distribution (Marglin 2008; Ostrom 1990). It also needs to envision these processes as working through alternate shared systems aimed at creating a "commonfare." To accomplish such changes, we propose a *New Economy Agency*.

There are many ways such an Agency could work. Rather than trying to list them, we want instead to illustrate what the program could look like by considering what might be done about the issue of money, the prime way ratio valuing is measured. As part of the valuing we critiqued in Chapter 5, we regard money as not necessarily connected with exchange value—the representation of value through prices—as it typically is now. Rather, contemporary digital practices suggest that alternate forms of what we think of as money could be used very differently to promote additional aspects of value. These include promoting small-scale initiatives, strengthening social relations, and more generally reintroducing ordinal and nominal values into economic activities. We foresee that the Agency might aim to meet social goals through promoting the use of "money" in these other ways.

As pointed out by David Harvey, money has three basic functions: first, as a way to store value, i.e., commodity money; second, as a medium of payment and circulation, i.e., coin or paper money; and third, as an expression of the political power of states, i.e., fiat money (Harvey 2014). Harvey focuses mostly on how these three forms of money are potentially in contradiction with each other. It is possible that digitized money could mitigate the negative aspects of the three, but we see the digitalization of paper money as leading to even more complications. One job of the New Economy Agency would be to analyze alternate forms of money. The transformation of paper money into digital representations in bank accounts, finance instruments, etc. makes it possible to create indefinite quantities of money (and thus infinite crises, as described in Chapter 3). However, the emergence of digital currencies, often called crypto-currencies, as they are based on cryptography, are issued and coordinated digitally outside of the current institutional setting backing up money. In the present system, the creation of indefinite quantities of money is connected to the ability of banks to create money through agreed-upon bank-to-bank debt-obligations, a point explored by Mary Mellor (Mellor 2010). The analyses of Harvey, Mellor, and others converge on noticing that the growing possibility to produce money is directly related to the fact that money, as a form of stored value, can be indefinitely accumulated. This is due to its liquid form, i.e., its ability to circulate independently from the social relations where it was initially implicated. Graeber also notes the importance of the liquidity of money in his study of debt (Graeber 2011). When considering how social obligations become quantifiable, Graeber points out that money in its coin and paper forms becomes widespread in periods of violence and when there is a high degree of regulation of strangers. He contrasts coin and paper forms of money to forms that register debts between people known to each other, forms that historically anticipated coin and paper. The older money form, Graeber suggests, depends on the stability and continuity of the social relations in peaceful times.

John Maynard Keynes described how money could regulate international trade through the principle of clearing as opposed to the principle of liquidity (Keynes 2011). The principle of clearing is the basis of a monetary system where money is only a unit of account in a system of balance sheets, something that cannot circulate outside this system. The stress is on what can be done differently via accounting practice forms of money is also part of the European-funded research project D-CENT and basic to the work of Stefano Lucarelli and colleagues (Lucarelli et al. 2014). They argue, "The clearing principle has to do with the establishment of a measure for the exchanges and for the payment of debts which is not in its turn an object of exchange, and with the restoration of a balanced relationship between debtor and creditor" (2014). This capacity to accumulate valuables simultaneously in different ways, or even to accumulate them in one way and not in another, may be what separates digital experiments like Bitcoin from other contemporary money forms. Crypto-currencies can provide space for experimentation, as illustrated by the D-CENT project.[2] However, much remains to be thought through about crypto-currencies. For example, they do not automatically prohibit accumulation—this capacity has to be designed into them.

There are forms of money that discard the commodity form. For example, there is the possibility of *demurrage,* or charging for the detention of assets, where "within the circuit, a percentage of the credits that aren't spent [is] automatically transferred to another account." (Lucarelli et al., 2014, 21). This practice is proposed to prevent the constant accumulation of commodity money. With crypto-currencies, ways of promoting alternative investment might be done more easily, via diverse kinds of digital regulation. Research on holding on to assets points out that possibilities like demurrage can embrace the idea that money loses its value when it is not used (Gesell 1934). In other words, demurrage promotes money circulation instead of accumulation. If we go back to the theory of things of value described in Chapter 5, we can think about circulation and accumulation through the lenses of visibility and invisibility. Circulating money becomes visible in the social relation in which circulation is taking place, while accumulated money is invisible, standing as power for future actions. In this perspective, circulating money strengthens social relations, while accumulated money is a constant threat to their future. As the relation between visibility and invisibility is a complex one, a deeper articulation is needed.

Maurizio Lazzarato discusses additional power connections between what we have described as the invisible (and accumulated) valuables and the visible (and circulating) ones (Lazzarato 2012).[3] When an invisible valuable, money in particular, become visible in the form of a debt, it provides the creditor with substantial influence on the subjectivity of the debtor. The debtor is not only required to make enough money to repay the debt with interest when demanded, but also must conform to the expectations of the creditor, and those expectations may be moral as well as fiscal. When the debt is a collective one, as in state debt, the power of the creditor is exercised on a collectivity. This is another reason for limiting accumulation, as it transforms the character of circulation from a localized relation of ordinal, or nominal, mutual bond into a masked power relation behind a ratio value that unfolds into the future.

In what directions beyond capital should the New Economy Agency experiment? We think a basic principle should be the promotion of money for clearing, to allow accounts to balance each other, instead of for indefinite accumulation, typically by an already privileged few. Such a differentiation could be advanced by adopting new practices such as *demurrage,* where money becomes "old" and loses its value as time goes by, thereby encouraging it to be put quickly back into circulation. This would, for example, address the current problem of "over-saving," letting money lie fallow, rather than investing it. Lucarelli and others suggest other aspects of an alternative perspective on money (Lucarelli et al. 2014). The circulation of money could result in an extra reward of forms of labor that contribute to the common, or the extra could remunerate socially productive activities instead of money-generating ones. Moreover, access to money should not be dependent solely on selling one's capacity to do work. A basic income could be the instrument whereby rewarding labor becomes only one of the ways to access money. The New Economy Agency might well become a way toward redefining how the democratization of what should be rewarded is achieved. It could also provoke a rethinking of central banks as the institutions issuing money, in favor of alternative, participatory, institutional forms for creating money.

Perhaps the New Economy Agency could create a *Distributed Unbank of the Commons*, an institution similar to the project Freecoin promoted by Dyne.org, another of the partners of the D-CENT project ("D-CENT" 2015). Or it could explore ways to expand the "time banks" that have emerged in communities like Ithaca, New York. Nor does "locally" need to refer only to specific places; dispersed social groups could create specific monies to build collective environments. A *Distributed Unbank of the Commons* could support both "placed" and "spaced" localized currencies, allowing different forms of integration within a general infrastructure, using currencies to foster coordination among different working anarchies and institutions. We imagine these institutions as a way to expand understanding of the economic beyond scarcity markets to include the wide varieties of social provisioning. Foremost, we imagine an Agency with a mission to expand economic interactions beyond ratio values, incorporating nominal and ordinal values.

Constructivist Agency

Bruno Latour identifies technologies as one of the main sites where future society is being built (Latour 1990). From his perspective, we could describe DTs as "society made durable." We have discussed the value of promoting an alternative to the technicist design of technology. Such narrow, technical-only perspectives need to be replaced by social constructivist ones if the other institutions we are describing here are to be pursued successfully. A *Constructivist Agency* would encourage more nuanced perspectives on technology creation, ones that acknowledge social construction while still attending to the co-construction of the social and the technical. Such perspectives would create and encourage the design process and digital technologies for cyberspace to emerge.

Giving the Agency a constructivist name would underline its commitment to the kind of analysis that is the hallmark of science, technology, and society

(STS). A constructivist approach to DT use is greatly encouraged in the work of Lucy Suchman (Suchman 1993, 2002a, 2002b). She draws upon feminist theory, in particular, the work of Donna Haraway, to question the role in design of authoritative knowledge (Haraway 1988). In this form, design is an activity that is largely detached from actual work practices. Suchman calls this view "design from nowhere," and argues instead for "design from somewhere" (Suchman 2002a). In her approach, design activities come to include both the local improvisations through which users shape the use of the technology—as through participatory design (PD)—as well as the interventions of the professional designer (Suchman 2002b). Thorough reconfigurations of the actions of users as design would obviate the dichotomy "designer/user."

Another aspect of DT constructivism would be "infrastructuring." This work identifies infrastructures—the "already there" or what has to be dealt with—as particularly relevant to DTs. The concept is borrowed by the design community from a concept in STS in the work of Susan Leigh Star (Neumann and Star 1996; Star 1999; Star and Bowker 2006; Star and Ruhleder 1996). Under the infrastructuring perspectives, software designers transition away from a project-based design activity, often otherwise seen as always starting from scratch (which is encouraged by proprietary law). The newer perspective is to recognize that design needs to be approached as taking place "in the wild" (Dittrich, Eriksén, and Hansson 2002). That is, design should take place in direct connection with (but not in subservience to) the mass of already installed hardware and software applications, and technological working practices (Hanseth and Lundberg 2001). Two inferences from an STS-inspired constructivist view of technology that should frame the work of a Constructivist Agency are that:

- Design comes "from somewhere" as opposed to being "from nowhere," abandoning the idea that designers hold sole knowledge, and questioning the designer/user opposition.
- Many contemporary digital technologies function as infrastructures, which means that DT design must take the production and use contexts of technology seriously, as well as the already-existing technological base.

The utility of a connected participatory infrastructing (PI) perspective becomes especially clear in the design of large-scale entities. Here, design is revealed to be an ensemble of activities, all those making possible, maintaining, and redesigning complex things with digital and non-digital aspects (Pipek and Wulf 2009). The approach stresses the articulation work of all actors involved, leading to DT systems with dynamic characteristics and emergent trajectories. As attention has turned to large-scale infrastructures emerging outside of the workplace—e.g., social media and many other web-based applications—the PI perspective has also been called "public design" (Ehn 2008; Le Dantec and DiSalvo 2013; Teli et al. 2015). This terminology is rooted in other STS approaches. One is that public design is about "matters of concern" to many (Latour 2004), thereby acknowledging that "things" involve gatherings, or "parliaments," where controversies are solved. PI and public design perspectives are also forms of "making things public" (Weibel and Latour 2005), actions that open up space to examine issues that people are concerned about. These scholars regularly acknowledge the influence of Dewey's concepts of "public" and "publics." Publics are groups of people interested in and able to articulate positions on specific issues. DiSalvo and colleagues express particularly clearly what is public in public design (DiSalvo et al. 2014). A society is constituted of many publics and by many publics. Design should support publics as well as contribute to their formation.

The promotion of participatory infrastructuring and public design by the Constuctivist Agency would have to mean acknowledging and appreciating the contestable character of technologies, and rejecting technicist narratives in favor of a frank recognition that technologies have politics (Winner 1980). Second, the Agency would need to demonstrate through well-designed projects how technology design could start with the concrete concerns of people, for example, through participatory design. This means involving users in the definition of the goals of the design project as well as in the interface design. Third, the Agency will need to work against the idea that technology designers possess an all-encompassing vision, affirming the need for a more situated perspective. Promoting PI/public design would necessarily lead to changes in how technological projects are carried out, mostly by replacing the idea that technology designers (and, by extension, other intellectuals in society) have the sole responsibility for design. Sharing of responsibility and power can characterize projects, as will skill sharing. Combining the skills of the main beneficiaries of the design together with the intellectual and communicative skills of the professionals involved can result in better design.

Such a shift would require the Agency to change the way projects are funded, to favor open-ended, socially based projects over those presuming that the answers to research and design questions are already known. Public design and infrastructuring are particularly relevant to the "digital social innovation" approach to DTs. Promoted by the European Union through its research funding, this term encompasses "a type of social and collaborative innovation in which users and communities work together to use digital technologies for knowledge and solutions to a wide range of social needs and at a scale unimaginable before the rise of the Internet" (Bria 2014, 5). If not handled deftly, such complex practices could provide space for the subsuming of collaborative practices into capital reproduction (Morini and Fumagalli 2010). When articulated in terms of public design, digital social innovation should lead to innovation that promotes societal challenges to existing SFR. This means putting the concerns of people at the center and supporting their collective ability to address issues.

At different periods, IT firms have recognized the value of input from interdisciplinary teams in the design process. The study by anthropologists and sociologists of actual use practices (e.g., Kusterer 1978) has been an important step toward designs that are both creative and useful. A Constructivist Agency could draw upon an even wider scope of interdisciplinary work when reimagining technology. Institutionalizing these perspectives will require new incentives, which in turn means two additional institutional changes. The first is to restructure project funding to privilege more open-ended, socially based research and development projects. The second is to modify career reward structures to encourage more interdisciplinary careers.[4]

Democracy Agency

The promise for expanded democracy is at the heart of the imaginary of the Internet. However, increasingly, the Internet is bent to the reproduction of capital. Democracy is central to the pursuit of both our general and our specific values. We share Dewey's vision of democracy, which Erin McKenna has summarized as follows:

> John Dewey's model of democracy requires that we recognize that the unfolding of the future is not determined separate from us, but is intricately connected with us. It requires that we recognize how our participation affects what the future can be. It requires that we recognize that there is no end state at which we must work to arrive, but a multiple of possible future states which we must seek out and try. John Dewey's vision of democracy prepares us to interact with our world and guide it to a better future by immersing us in the method of critical intelligence.
> (McKenna 2001, 83)

It is not surprising, given this idea of democracy, that Dewey spent much of his energy writing about and working for quality public education. One preoccupation of a *Democracy Agency* would need to be addressing the many contradictions of educational practices. In the US the business model threatens to overwhelm schools, undermine the role of educators, and has created an expanded system of debt for college graduates.

The 2013 revelations of surveillance by government agencies eroded the way discourse could be conducted when people are on the Internet. This is often presented as mostly being about privacy, but it is even more about the ability of citizens to speak, think, plan actions, and engage civilly without fear of reprisals—in short, an essential basis of democracy. A reversal of this surveillance trend would be a central task for a Democracy Agency. Moreover, it is not only government surveillance that is at issue: cell phone companies track our moves, sell our location to businesses, and monitor our driving. The Democracy Agency would need to work with citizens to identify when state, corporate, community, and individual actions undermine privacy, speech, and assembly, after which it would need to develop programs to encourage more open and democratic activities.

The Democracy Agency should also support positive democratic affordances of DT, such as the expansion of access to information. There are many possibilities: expanding available information and making it more reliable, encouraging the development of search engines that are built to provide links to better data and not just reinforcing what we might already think, as well as encouraging experiments with expanding online referendum projects. Online collective efforts like Wikipedia and the Stanford Encyclopedia of Philosophy provide suggestive starting points for what might be accomplished. Practices like participatory design both depend upon and afford democracy.

Building on the democratic affordances of DTs and promoting participation depends on moving away from a labor-based society dominated by the mediation of income. Much recent thinking about welfare states highlights the idea of an unconditional basic income. For example, the Basic Income Earth Network (BIEN) advocates an income "unconditionally granted to all on an individual basis, without means test or work requirement" (BIEN website: http://www.basicincome.org/). Services already exist in places like Sweden, where parents are given significant paid leave for childcare, recognizing that caring for children is a basic benefit to society. Rather than creating new bureaucracies to provide more services, BIEN means providing sufficient resources to support effective markets in all areas of need, producing a society functioning both inside and outside of the labor relation. The dissolution of the link between labor and income is increasingly important, as revealed in concepts like "prosumer" and "produser," whose usage is already widespread in the digital domain. This externalizing of production from the labor relation affords and justifies the inclusion of grant income in the future democratic state.

One potential consequence of a basic income for all could be the strengthening of organized work for the public good. Expanded choice in how, when, and if to sell one's labor becomes possible with guaranteed minimum resources for participation in social life. This is a form of redistribution that also affords a rebalance in the labor relation. The Italian economist Fumagalli identifies this as a building block of the welfare state needed in contemporary society, the "*commonfare*" (2015). A combination of income continuity and access to the commons, a commonfare program for Agency promotion might include:

- Shared access to natural resources and public goods, like water, public education, healthcare, a reliable internet, etc., without privatization of their management and distribution;
- Open information about government actions, including control and monitoring of the financial markets as well as giving access to them;

- Reformulating ideas of intellectual property as a way to grant access to a digital commons;
- Expanded understanding of and ways of realizing increasing democratic participation, the creation of more commons, and bottom-up participation in its management.

In short, a commonfare would enlarge peoples' space to choose their life path, eliminating pure economic survival as a concern and also promoting democracy.

Both Dewey and McKenna stress that democracy is a process, not an end state, and what is democratic is a substantive, not formal, property of each social formation. With regard to democracy even more than our other values, moving beyond capital will require a great deal of experimentation, and experimentation approached with humility. To move beyond capital, we must start where we are. To decrease the threats to privacy and therefore democracy that are characteristic of today's "really existing" computing, it will be necessary to reconstruct basic aspects of the digital infrastructure. Such reconstruction will require organized demands for fully working out the opportunities for computing to extend democracy (more about this in Chapter 9). It may well also mean keeping a market in services, to be accessed either through wages or a state-provided basic income.

Process Promotion Agency

We now turn to Agencies that could support more organizational, face-to-face relations and relationships. In Chapter 6, we pointed to the important way processual analyses were replacing structural analysis in the field of organization studies. One implication of moving to greater concern about process rather than structure is a shift in the focus from specific structures (e.g., a specific organization with membership, boundaries, etc.) to organizing initiatives. These may or may not coincide with particular boundaries of organizations. Here, we describe what could be done to institutionalize the processual as a value in organizing. As with our discussion of democracy, we see a possible program for a *Process Promotion Agency* as a means to deinstitutionalize the structure-oriented approach still typical in discourse about organization, as well as to promote approaches stressing process instead.

The Agency would need to address the current power of the legal and historical structures of corporations. Chartered initially by states to serve public purposes, these organizations have come instead to control these very states (see Hardt and Negri 2001). Through the institutionalized hegemony of ratio valuing, they are now bureaucratic giants and the sites of distorted accumulations of capital.[5] Limiting corporate power is an urgent matter because it distorts the relationship between the state and corporations. In the US, such limitation has been made more difficult by the recent US Supreme Court decision declaring corporate personhood. In doing so the Supreme

Court endowed corporations with free speech rights, the right to religious beliefs, and the power to dominate electoral aspects of the public sphere.

An end to the personification of corporate organizations is a prerequisite to promoting the capacity to restructure, and thus to the general processual perspective. The power of corporations needs to be limited, regulated, and then reassessed in light of community needs. Present law requires boards to be answerable to the stockholders, pushing the profit motive (ratio values) ahead of all other considerations. However, such laws could be amended to require corporations to be responsible to their workers as well as to the communities where they reside or where they draw profit. The Agency could be empowered to encourage the prosecution of the executives whose actions put SFR at risk. For example, laws could sanction actions that endanger SFR through environmental degradation or the transfer of corporate value to enrich board members and stockholders at the expense of communities. Treating corporation as made up or "fictive" organizations created by state laws and not "people" is a necessary preliminary step to more general processual valuing. The general goal would be to underline how organizations are social spaces for the development of people and communities rather than entities with a personal "right to hegemony."

A Process Promotion Agency could privilege process by pursuing measures that expand the "restructurability" of existing practices. If organizing is about power, then a processual approach to organization should be democratic, promoting equality in participation, as through limiting the duration and scope of leadership roles. In this way, processual thinking encourages the limitation of formal power. One possible example of processual thinking is in aspects of the Debian Linux distribution, a free software project (Coleman 2012). This project includes a deliberate articulation of a Debian Project culture and formal acculturation of "newbies" as they come into the group. Robustness is promoted through the construction of project tasks as modules, which contain technically separate components that are able to interact easily with each other. Debian remains a hierarchical organization, with a project leader and delegates; however, modularization reduces the scope for those in power to exercise their roles. The project leader is elected once a year by the developers and can be recalled by a majority at any time. There is a written Debian Constitution where the powers of the leader are defined and limited. Many of these powers are oriented toward addressing emergencies and coordinating complex project tasks being carried out by the delegates. The definition of organizational roles through a constitution makes it clear that organizing is understood to be political. Relationships among developers include the capacity to expel a developer, but there is a procedure for appeal.

As in the Debian case, process-based restructuring may, at times, require more rather than less organization, but organization of a type that fosters flexible sociality. Organizing structures typically reinforce self-perpetuation tendencies, but they need not do so. While some free/libre and open-source software (FLOSS) projects carry on for a long time, many end when their objectives are achieved. They are examples of the "new" ad hoc form of organizing afforded by DTs (Travica 1998). We note that even for-profit, limited liability corporations were initially self-limited in time. The construction of railways in the US, for example, was conducted mainly by such time-limited corporate entities.

In addition to promoting restructuring and undermining corporate personhood, the Process Promotion Agency could also encourage other affordances of contemporary DT that privilege process over fixed structures. One example is what Yochai Benkler calls "commons-based peer production" (Benkler 2006), organizational forms more similar to organized anarchy than to structures (Benkler 2013). These peer organizations do not rely upon property or the coercive powers of states. Benkler's examples of successful forms of commons organizing include the Internet Engineering Task Force and Wikipedia as well as FLOSS projects. In particular, Benkler presents Wikipedia as virtually a Weberian "ideal type" of such organizing. Its main traits include: 1) openness through adoption of commons/open licensing; 2) transparency; 3) non-discrimination; 4) discourse and consensus rather than hierarchical control; 5) leadership and facilitation; 6) redundancy of governance pathways; 7) irreverence and resistance. These certainly constitute some worthy processual goals.

The Agency will have to attend to how commons-based peer production forms can still be vulnerable to hierarchy by stealth. Some have deliberately made considered-to-be-necessary new hierarchies visible through labels, such as the "benevolent dictator" of Linux kernel development, while others, such as the corporate structure mimicry of not-for-profit foundations, have surrendered wordlessly. Corporation-based FLOSS projects offer clear examples of the reinstitution of hierarchies. This is the case with the OpenSolaris project of Sun Microsystems (Teli 2010), as well as the web browser Firefox, backed by the Mozilla Corporation. Another matter of concern to the Process Promotion Agency could be the extent to which the forms it creates are extendable to social action domains beyond the digital. Examples of such extensions include banking and finance (with micro-lending and crowdfunding), and the provision of public functions, such as Ushahidi, a mapping tool making digital maps useful in critical situations, like the Haiti earthquake of 2010.

The potential toward hierarchy and the question of extending to other domains make Benkler cautious.[6] He highlights examples of the limit of the processual where it is ultimately overcome by the structural, such as open data. Nevertheless, his major processual contribution is attending to what he calls "working anarchies." These rely on developing consensus regarding viable solutions to problems at hand and rejecting formal authorities. They afford experimenting with alternative forms rather than toward preserving organizational structures. This is why Maha Shaikh and colleagues describe Linux as a "laboratory" (Shaikh, Ciborra, and Cornford 2010). Benkler also favors aggregating people based on voluntarism. Voluntarism is important to explaining how FLOSS projects can produce software that is as good as proprietary software. However, voluntarism cannot be the approach to all of the tasks a social formation wants carried out. Moreover, if voluntarism is conceptualized only at the level of the individual and labor relations are still central to the actual political economy, peer production will not develop (see Hakken and Mate' 2014). The majority of the population depends on labor relations as the way to acquire the means of living, from food to healthcare, from education to leisure. One possible task of the Process Promotion Agency is to create working environments that encourage more of peer production forms, such as those Benkler identifies (Benkler 2006).

Attending to the process aspects of organizations requires changes in their institutionalization.[7] The changes needed to promote the restructuring of existing organizations and the creation of new, process-oriented ones, and thus the agenda of a Process Promotion Agency, includes dismissing the theory of corporate personhood, a paradox that strengthens corporations' influence over SFR. Further, the Agency would need to find ways to put limits on existing corporations, and thus also on the "entitling" of people with power within them. Such changes would allow for more shared decisions and greater democratic control. Making everybody in an organization able to influence its direction depends upon giving workers security in their lives as well as a voice in organizational processes. Equally important would be support for different, more flexible models of organizing.

Informating Agency

In articulating "informating" rather than automating as an organizing value, we have adopted the perspective of Shoshana Zuboff discussed in Chapters 4 and 6. Zuboff focuses on how, through an informating strategy, the information already generated by DTs can improve organizational performance. The improvement is achieved by sharing the information throughout the organization, *and also* empowering everyone to act on what they then know. This means transferring management control, including the payoff from any automating. The application of informating to production also enables the democratic potential, to empower workers instead of subjugating them further to the machine. Zuboff's perspective reflects the work of Norbert Wiener (Wiener 1950) at the origin of modern computing, as well as the stance taken later by participatory design scholarship (e.g., Ehn 1992). All three stress promoting human development through specific DT adoptions.

The *Informating Agency* would connect to DT development affordances and problems, aiming to encourage a change in information sharing practices and associated power relations. As an example of what the Agency might do, consider that it could relate to enterprise resource planning software packages (ERPs) in several ways. These are used by organizations to track resources, their use, and the interrelations among their different parts.

Abstractly, what ERPs do is very simple: they keep track of the production processes. By doing this, they collect information that could be used to inform the processes themselves, but seldom are. Instead, ERPs generally inscribe a rationalistic, top-down management-oriented vision of the way the organization should work, more a tool for automating than for informating (Kallinikos 2004).

However, ERPs are a form into which a new Informating Agency could intervene. One way to make ERPs informate would be to make them distributed—"dERPs"—in two senses. First, in the private/corporate sector, they could provide information as organizational "open data"—that is, as information openly accessible to and therefore questionable by the workers and other stakeholders. Second, dERPs would afford the redefinition of the metrics used to evaluate the quality of production. Distributing all of the information would mean these metrics could be expanded to include creation of knowledge to support the workers, as well as requiring discussion of the criteria for deciding what information to collect. We will explore this further in the following chapter on measures. To support the dispersal of power and decision-making, the Agency could work to turn existing ERPs into dERPs, in contrast to current projects about corporate open data, which tend toward being forms of self-promotion rather than transparency and accountability.[8]

In the public sector, the Informating Agency's role could be about delivering on the full promise of "open data" (OD). There are many weaknesses in current OD narratives, including the fact that these narratives resonate more with informating than automating (and also, in this regard, with "big data"). For example, there is no point in sharing information when decisions to automate have already been made; indeed, sharing the information might cause additional problems. For real OD to work, more information should be made available, but it also needs to be made available to more diverse groups of people in more useable forms. According to the *Open Data Handbook*, a project promoted by the Open Knowledge Foundation, "A piece of data or content is open if anyone is free to use, reuse, and redistribute it—subject only, at most, to the requirement to attribute and/or share-alike" (Open Knowledge Foundation 2015).

Open data initiatives are being pursued in two main social domains, government and science.[9] Focusing on government, we see several efforts to make the data produced by governments in their daily operations more available. Various OD strategies have been enacted by a number of Western countries. Examples include the initiative on Open Government promoted by the US federal government and the Digital Agenda for Europe promoted by the European Commission. In their comparative analysis, Noor Huijboom and Tijs van den Broek identified three main justifications for governmental OD strategies, to: "1) Increase democratic control and political participation . . . 2) Foster service and product innovation . . . 3) Strengthen law enforcement" (Huijboom and van den Broek 2011). They find that the third is seldom central, since the majority of governments justify open data as increasing transparency and democracy and fostering economic growth. However, the approach presumes users who have the skills to use information as it is produced by public administrations. Thus, the orientation is toward those who are already politically knowledgeable or toward entrepreneurial participants. This does not fit with the "5 star model" of open data endorsed by Tim Berners-Lee (Berners-Lee 2006), the "father" of the World Wide Web. Berners-Lee's approach emphasizes people rating the accessibility of data and how well the data is integrated into web use based on ranking. The burden of work is shifted from the data user to the data provider, which structures the information to be as widely useful as possible before it is released.

We are aware that there are critiques of OD, especially in conjunction with big data (e.g., Boyd and Crawford 2012; Johnson 2013). Data does not just come into existence on its own, but is *socially constructed* both in the way it is created and the way it is shared. Acknowledging such construction should shift the focus of institutionalization from the *use* of information alone to its *production* as well. There are examples of organizations manipulating information that is public. Quite notable are data from the Enron scandal and the Greek hidden debt crisis. In both cases, many people involved could see that the information publicly available was fake, i.e., that the data displayed on the balance sheets was misleading or fabricated. The perpetrators were either the people responsible for hiding the real data (e.g., top management or ministers), people who were willing accomplices of those responsible, or people too vulnerable to confront the powerful.

Heretofore, when the more data-powerful have been confronted by the less data-powerful, the latter have succeeded only when supported by forms of collective action (e.g., unions and political parties promoting demonstrations, media attention, riots, etc.) that made up for the relative lack of data power. Whistleblowers—that is, insiders providing information not publicly known—often promote better data power balances and different results. Whistleblowing in the digital domain is connected to the leaking of documents, demonstrated by Wikileaks in 2010 (with the crucial role of Chelsea Manning) and by Edward Snowden's global surveillance disclosures in 2013 to *The Guardian* and Glenn Greenwald (Greenwald 2014). Another case is that of LuxLeaks in Europe, the disclosure of tax agreements between the Grand Duchy of Luxembourg and transnational corporations. Like Manning and Snowden, Antoine Deltour, an identified Lux Leaks whistleblower, faces legal consequences. These cases and the light they cast on fake data illustrate the importance of informating at the societal level, of making information on the functioning of existing institutions—state, corporate, and civil society—generally available, and of using the information to support democratization and restructuring. Without the creation of a general shift toward informating, whistleblowing seldom leads to such structural changes. Without protection, whistleblowers remain at seriously at risk.

Manning is in jail, Snowden is in exile, and Deltour has been charged with theft, violation of trade secrets, and illegal access to databases. Whistleblowers play an essential role in democracy.

These cases identify two important potential roles for the Informating Agency. First, the Agency would need to promote the adoption of stronger procedures, both legal and technological, to protect whistleblowers who provide evidence of wrongdoing. Second, the Agency would need to foster and protect media that are able to protect sources and share information when governments, corporations, or communities fail to be transparent. In parallel, the Agency could explore the institutionalization of a "right to leak," as argued for by The International Consortium of Investigative Journalists, the organization supporting the "Luxleakers" (see "Luxembourg Leaks: Global Companies' Secrets Exposed" 2015). The existence in the US of the Freedom of Information Act has sometimes allowed citizens, watchdog agencies, and journalists to access secret information. All too often, however, organizations have blocked efforts to share information and have hidden materials from the public. The Agency will need to work with groups and citizens to reverse the trend.

For OD to matter, citizens need to be active, but these in turn need platforms for publication as well as the information "opened" to be of good quality. An example is GlobaLeaks, an entity that combines anonymity technologies with ease of use as key components (https://www.globaleaks.org/). The technology affords leaking even in presently closed societies, an institutional outcome in line with the promotion of informating as a value. Such technologies would need to be combined by parallel social initiatives. There have been efforts to articulate a "right to civil disobedience" (e.g., Rawls 1971). Additionally, the Agency would have to work to be sure the data is accurate and representative. Even in an era of true OD, information will not stand on its own. It will still require interpretation, evaluation, and understanding. When agencies like Fox News misrepresent and distort, lie and contort, the Agency will have to find ways of holding accountable those responsible.

Finally, the Informating Agency will need to support net neutrality, the digital infrastructure that does not treat differently the kinds of information that transit on it. This policy position was recently announced by the US FCC (Federal Communications Commission 2015). It includes the so-called FIFO principle, "first in, first out." Both in Europe and in the US, telecoms have regularly tried to change this principle for commercial profit to allow for differential services, e.g., a faster "business class" connection. Ending net neutrality would disadvantage those with less economic power, and it would limit certain communication, reinforcing the power of strong market actors (Zittrain 2008). Disadvantage would also follow if states were to be able to control the speed of encrypted communication as well as the form of encryption. *Citizenfour*, the documentary on global surveillance by Laura Poitras, shows that communication between Edward Snowden and journalists often took place through encrypted channels e.g., the anonymizing software Tor and the cryptographic software GPG (Poitras 2014). The Agency would have an important role in keeping the Internet a public utility.

Digital Freedom Agency

Economists distinguish between investment, a more productive form of capital accumulation, and rent, the less productive form. Investment, they argue, can lead to more jobs, whereas rents are often just taken out of the economy. Critical scholars generally agree that rents, enabled by an intellectual property regime, have been an important vehicle for capital accumulation in the digital domain (see Fuchs 2013; Harvey 2014; Rigi 2014). Institutionalization of our ninth value, "freedom," in a *Digital Freedom Agency*, should discourage the proprietization of conceptual things as a means to gain rent while also encouraging a global intellectual arena to support more investment of resources. These aims are also relevant to increasing access to the means of cultural reproduction.

In Chapter 4, we discussed the distinction between free and open source software. These two ways of promoting similar coding practices are often linked together as FLOSS. Both approaches favor software licensing that allows the reuse, modification, and redistribution of source code. Open source emphasizes the superiority of its practices in comparison to proprietary practices. In free software, the accent is on people' capacity to collaborate and freely use other contributors' codes. It is these latter that the Digital Freedom Agency should promote.

The Free Software Foundation (FSF), for example, promotes a limited set of software licenses. It recognizes that other licenses comply with free software principles, but the FSF mostly supports wide adoption of the GNU GPL, or the GNU General Public License, and growth in the number of free software products. In contrast, the Open Source Initiative (OSI) recognizes a wider number of licenses, and the OS definition encourages the enrollment of corporate actors into the production and distribution of open-source software (Netscape, initially). The practices of OSI have led to "license proliferation." This leads to problems because of the legal incompatibility among licenses, making it harder for software developers to legally combine pieces of code from different projects. Moreover, the proliferation of licenses sometimes means that software again becomes proprietary. In the example of the OpenSolaris project, the code was released in 2005 by Sun Microsystems, Inc. under a new license, the Common Development and Distribution License (CDDL). This was presented as both a free software and an open source license, although in fact it is incompatible with existing free licenses. This limited the applicability of CDDL-licensed software. Some Sun software is integrated into products, like DTrace, a component included in Linux, Apple OS X, and Blackberry's QSX operating systems. In all these cases, technical workarounds are required to avoid licensing incompatibility (De Paoli, Teli, and D'Andrea 2008).

The Digital Freedom Agency would work to minimize the need for such steps. It should be noted that license proliferation is not only a corporate phenomenon. This history of licensing gets in the way of using FLOSS. The Agency would work to end license proliferation and oversee a restricted set of licenses, both simple and more understandable, to reduce the complexity of intellectual property regimes. For example, the Peer Production License, inspired by the principle of "copyfarleft," is explicitly oriented toward preventing organizations trying to commodify work done in commons and it seems a good candidate to be promoted (Vieira and De Filippi 2014).

Because a politics of openness is unable on its own to grant democratic participation and displace ratio values with ordinal ones, more will be required of the Digital Freedom Agency.

What is wanted is the promotion of a free software approach centered on mutual help in development. This would necessitate a restructuring of so-called intellectual property practices in general. Civil law regimes distinguish between two types of authors' rights: moral right and the right of exploitation. Moral right refers to the right of a person to be recognized as the author of something, while right of exploitation refers to the commercial promotion of the something. For example, authors of books retain an eternal right to be recognized as such, while the publisher retains the rights to print and sell copies of the text—to exploit the work. In the domain of Creative Commons, licensing the "Attribution" is virtually mandatory, while the inclusion of other clauses, such as non-commercial and share-alike, depends on the will of the author. A free approach would focus on the value and use of what is being produced rather than exploitation and commercial promotion, which would grant greater continuity to the commons. In the free software world, the continuity of the commons is often promoted through authors ceding rights of use to an organization, such as the Free Software Foundation.[10]

The overall task of the Digital Freedom Agency would be to encourage pursuit of non-ratio values in what is produced, whether it is cultural or economic. It should design and promote mechanisms that address sustainability, the commons, and alternative values. We have started with FLOSS because it is an existing example of how the ultimate goals of computing practices can be rethought. The goal of the Agency, like that of its previously described partner Agencies, should be to keep work processes truly open and focused on rethinking values. Elon Musk has made all patents on his electric car Tesla open because he argues that the primary focus is creating more electric cars to reduce carbon emission. While more cars might not be the best priority, Musk is focused on reducing emission, a necessary goal. Similarly, the Agency could investigate other means to promote non-ratio values, foster experimentation with such means, and work to institutionalize those with the most favorable results. For example, many Western nations grant fiscal privileges and special regulations to support not-for-profit organizations like workers-owned cooperatives. Italian cooperatives are encouraged in this manner, but the amount of profit they can generate is limited and part of the profit is diverted to a national fund devoted to inter-cooperative solidarity. This means many big cooperatives are now acting like corporations and pursuing just value. Is this distortion a consequence of scale? This is an example of the kinds of research question that would be of concern to the Agency.

Service Agency

We have sketched out a collection of Agencies, each pursuing one of the process-oriented, informating, and digital freedom values. Process-orientation might result in production based less on wages and more on the desire to contribute. Informating allows sharing both information and capacities to act on information. Digital freedom involves new avenues for interaction and collaboration. Cumulatively, these value orientations effectively imply reducing the power of the organizational management and the privileging of structure, especially formal. Collectively, these orientations also suggest organizing that is constantly challenged internally, open to scrutiny from the outside, and with significantly dispersed control. These changes should allow the ebullient and affective conduct that have long been discussed in relation to the economy, from Keynes to contemporary critical theory (Pasquinelli 2009).

A *Service Agency* could play an important role in promoting such arrangements, making them easy to set up and an ordinary occurrence. This means moving against all the ways that "bigness" is rewarded when SFR is bent to the reproduction of capital. Structurally "lightweight" organizing is, however, more dependent on voluntary motivation than on the structure characteristic of existing employment organizations. How can production (i.e., accomplishment of tasks) be ensured? Service orientation (SO) is a means of decentralizing computing but still coordinating it. SO in software tries to create ad hoc social relations based on the task at hand. In these transient situations, the brokering of one individual leads to the use by another of a specific piece of software, to produce either data that can be retrieved, or run a process that can be instantiated for a specific third user. Once this has been done, the relations dissolve. In SO computing systems, A relies on service B, service B on service C, and so on. In another instance, B might rely on A, C on B, and so on. These practices typically require very little organizational infrastructure—e.g., there are no employer/employee relations between any As, Bs, and Cs.[11] An economy where these are the typical relations could be better able to avoid the rent-seeking characteristic of monopolistic organizing. It could also protect against vendor dependence, getting locked into an economically doomed but still profitable commodity like Microsoft Windows.

A Service Agency could promote the design of DTs that enable collaborative work, both within and across organizational boundaries. For example, modular design—the organization of processes among distinct units with clear boundaries—can often decentralize control, as coordination becomes based on interconnecting separate actions digitally. Such modularity has been described as key to the development of the Linux kernel, granting both unity and the distribution of work (Narduzzo and Rossi 2004). Modularity not only reduces the need for coordinating communication or what economists call "transactional costs," it also affords easy-to-rely-upon, standardized interfaces between different kinds of work and organization. Modularity affords networking between products and organizations that is fluid as well as open-ended in regard to forms of combination. It can split tasks in ways that are enjoyable on their own, while contemporaneously affording wider participation in production decision-making processes.

Complementing SO with modularity would afford more bottom-up responses to emerging needs while still coping with complex productive efforts. Examples like 3D printing, maker movements, energy grids, etc. show how benefits are not confined to the domain of software or knowledge production: they can extend to domains of material production. The availability of 3D printers that mold plastic or metals suggests space for distributed manufacturing, at least of small runs of components. Maker movements that promote the sharing of technical skills via collaborative projects sometimes make use of such machines. Energy grids can also be opened for commons-oriented management of energy (e.g. the European project CIVIS: http://www.civisproject.eu/). All these modular forms of distributed production tend to favor democratic institutional arrangements.

The possible combinations of decentered service orientation and modularity are many. They provide a general perspective on *how one might produce*, but specific forms of professional practice and political negotiations/struggles determine *how one actually produces*. Actual production also depends on contextual economic relations of power, especially factors aiming to support social change. Forms of organizing governance like working anarchies similarly provide general paths for how to organize the production of a specific piece of good, e.g., to modularize production. However, they require coordination to achieve large-scale production. Ideas of alternative options for achieving coordination come from the history of computing, especially socialist computing. The works of Eden Medina (Medina 2014) and Nick Dyer-Witheford (Dyer-Witheford 2013) point to projects in Allende's Cybersyn in Chile and in the Red Plenty in the Soviet Union. These 1960s projects developed cybernetic mechanisms to coordinate the economy and chart production rather than depending on huge corporations. In both cases, the idea was to provide decision makers with current and reliable information on what was happening in production in order to afford more informed decision-making. Especially in Chile, the collected and analyzed information was redirected to the local productive units—factories, farms, etc. Once these units had a clear idea of the relevant dynamics, they made decisions about production. The underlying concept in both cases was an input–output table, known as the Leontief matrix, named after the Soviet mathematician who first described it. The basic elements of these socialist forms of computing are often part of contemporary corporate business. Google Page Rank is based on input–output tables (see Dyer-Witheford 2013). Technological systems such as the enterprise resource plans run by Walmart are based on similar information collection, aggregation, and communication. They suggest that such technologies can be applied more generally to planning economic interventions, to production, and to distribution.

Yet, how can this be done in a way that is supportive of a utopian social formation oriented to sustainability, broader access to means of cultural reproduction, scale flexibility, and broader understandings of the economic, social constructivism, and democracy? This is a problem where a combination of basic service orientation, modularity, and coordination through general information sharing might offer answers. To promote modularity, a Service Agency could foster the development of a common language of interfaces to support the interaction of local technological systems with a central system similar to Cybersyn under Allende. This would afford the emergence and flourishing of independent, decentralized relations, ones that, thanks to the shared interfaces, could be integrated into a general picture. Such a system would have to be designed to avoid the risk of infrastructuring becoming dominant and controlling.[12] This risk arises whenever technical languages are used to turn social relations into sources of value (as described by van Dijck 2013) rather than as a means to achieve values. A *Service Agency* could guard against this risk by first coordinating with the organizing Agencies—Process Promotion, Informating, and Digital Freedom. Second, educating and empowering a group of citizens to understand the details of how the basic infrastructure works and how to collaborate and coordinate with each other could do much to prevent infrastructure overgrowth.

Participation Agency

The task of a *Participation Agency* would be to create social forms that encouraged wide social involvement in designing the forms of institutionalization called for in this chapter. The Agency will need to sponsor participatory design projects in a wide range of workplace, community, and educational environments, learning from and building upon the Nordic PD tradition. PD involves people not only in interface creation, but also in the definition of the goals of a project, its implementation, revision, and maintenance. In Chapter 6, we identified participation as key to our alternative set of values. In the current capital regime, the worker is a "hand," not paid to think, but to do what she is told to do. The greatest need in a world beyond capital would be for citizens who participated actively in the institutions created to realize a new way of life, while to do so would be embedded in the concept of citizenship. In an important sense, the Participation Agency may well be the most important agency.

This Agency could support and institutionalize several additional programs. One would involve research on the impediments to participation and what can be done to overcome them. Another will be to oversee participation in the programs run by other Agencies and to work with them to increase participation. There would necessarily be an educational component to this Agency, helping people to identify ways to participate and collaborate in problem solving.

CONCLUSIONS

In this chapter, we have engaged in the difficult task of trying to translate the values articulated in Chapter 6 into general ideas of what viable institutions for their pursuit might be created. We acknowledge that in order to undermine ratio valuing and favor ordinal and nominal valuesing *in general*, a profound social transformation is needed. Such a transformation would also require coordinated ways to pursue multiple new values, and well-planned and executed interventions would need to be part of the effort. The Agencies we have described independently here could not be independent from one another in the world beyond capital. They would need to be considered together in their development and political articulation. We suspect that, alone or if part of a limited subset, these Agencies and their instruments would be unable to extend the reproduction of social formations effectively. And we are only proposing what we can imagine now, in a society dominated by ratio values. We anticipate that others will add, amend, and improve upon these ideas.

We have chosen an expository strategy that we acknowledged as simplistic. We identified some notional "Agencies" whose general task would be to pursue a specific value. At times, we may have gotten lost in the details of our imagined Agencies, but we want enough detail to provide for substantive discussion. We also have tried to describe possible programs for each, as well as apt institutional arrangements. At this point, the reader can doubtless see some of the drawbacks of this strategy. It has meant, for example, that we frequently had to name and repeat particular qualities that we hope the Agencies would share. This makes it difficult to stress the interrelations among the Agencies, especially how they are recursive. In the flow of history and change, it is likely that particular organizational forms would need to be privileged over other forms, while at other times, the dynamic would be reversed. We want the Agencies' organization forms to be decentralized but interconnected, and we recognize the contradiction. We think some kind of "working anarchies" will be needed if they are not to end up as bureaucracies, exercising domination over less privileged moments in SFR. We have mostly listed the characteristics that we would like our institutions to have, rather than saying what would give them these characteristics.

Moreover, we have repeatedly stressed how each organization would have to be endowed with the resources and power to accomplish its own tasks.

This is one of several ways in which our institutionalizations require a state, despite our preferences for commons. The reader may notice that we have given little attention to how markets would continue to function in a world in which ratio valuing was "re-balanced," reduced in SFR importance, but still not eliminated. The Agency approach has thus meant not dealing with one of the more difficult Ostrom problems, that of how to achieve a proper balance among states, commons, and markets. Additionally, our "Agency" approach has fostered some infelicitous and awkward language.

We hope our readers see this chapter and the next as a way to formulate some specific suggestions for more general, normative interventions—like the inclusion of new rights in actual constitutional arrangements, or the need to rethink welfare states in terms of "commonfare." For all its drawbacks, we want this approach to show what we mean by "valuesing," talking in ways that do not reduce multiple objectives into some one thing underlying them all. This is among the more insidious rhetorical consequences of the hegemony of the pursuit of value. Concrete imagination is important to the utopian task of thinking seriously about what we might want to happen beyond capital. We recognize that there must be ways of evaluating, revising, correcting, and replacing agencies that miss the mark or fail. As we move beyond capital, there must be ways of revising and correcting what institutions are created, what they do, and what they accomplish. Thus, we turn in the next chapter to the identification and articulation of ways to measure whether the proposed Agencies are successful at promoting the pursuit of the values we have identified.

NOTES

1. Here, we avoid attempting to describe how the institutions we advocate might achieve hegemony, as Engels counseled in *Socialism, Utopian and Scientific* (Engels 1972). We address this question in our concluding chapter.
2. Freecoin is a peer-to-peer currency system, better defined on the project website (http://freecoin.ch/) as "not a currency, but a suite to create P2P currencies." The aim of Freecoin is to foster the emergence of multiple currencies, ones regulated by locally relevant social dynamics.
3. See Lazzarato's work on debtor/creditor relations (Lazzarato 2012). Drawing on Nietzsche, Deleuze, and Guattari, he stresses that debt relations, based on wealth the creditor makes available for the debtor, are power relations.
4. It also depends on confronting how capital reproduction impinges on normal design practices, the understanding of how being something where interdisciplinary teams, including sociologists, anthropologists, etc., can help. To achieve such interdisciplinarity, another institutional move is necessary: *restructuring the career opportunities* of scholars now trapped in strictly disciplinary career paths in academia, while expanding possibilities to do effective interdisciplinary work in organizations (building on the growing interest of social scientists in IT, as described by Melissa Cefkin (Cefkin 2010)). Such restructuring is what will make it more possible for scholars to engage in the Agency's open-ended projects, reinforcing the interdisciplinarity needed to promote a constructivist perspective.

5. Note the rapid emergence of Apple as the largest corporation and most profitable entity in history.
6. This dependence on voluntarism, however, provides an entry point for addressing an under-theorized aspect of Benkler's analysis, its presumption that labor relations will continue to take place mostly within capital accumulation, not outside, in commons-based peer production. He does describe employers who support peer production efforts through hiring employees to work on commons-oriented projects, and he acknowledges the (informating-driven) need to release some control to such workers. Unfortunately, he does not address how continued mediation by markets in labor and being bent to capital accumulation remain as important impediments to peer production.
7. It is not difficult to imagine aspects of this Agency encouraging laws that reduce access to power through inheritance of property, or greater taxation of those with accumulated wealth and property.
8. Nonetheless, forcing corporations to open their data is still an important step toward informating, and the Informating Agency (something like an extended version of the Electronic Frontier Foundation) should have the power to force data openness.
9. In science they are part of the wider movement of "open science", a mixture of rebels and profiteers promoting the Mertonian perspective of "CUDoS" (communism, universalism, disinterestedness, organized skepticism), as the moral traits of scientific communities (Delfanti 2013). A good example of how lack of access to important data inhibits science is the current difficulty researchers have in getting access to the information social networks have about what their users do.
10. The Free Software Foundation is often granted rights to relicense the software through what is called a "Contributor License Agreement." Indeed, it may make sense to promote alienation-by-default. This would reverse the default, author-directed copyright of current practice, promoting instead enduring recognition of the possibility of the continuous reuse of all intellectual work. To this end, the Digital Freedom Agency should also promote inscription of the moral rights into the digital product itself (Gangadharan and D'Andrea 2011).
11. What we here call the "service orientation" has some formal similarity with a noticeable tendency of contemporary organizations to increase control by abrogating the employment relationship and replacing it with sub-contracting; that is, turning employees into formally independent but actually even more dependent "businessmen" (and women). This change is rightly recognized as correlated with an increase in individual and family insecurity. We recognize that the advantages of lightweight organizing for SFR will only be realized if servicers need no longer depend on obtaining contracts for their access to the means of survival. Hence, some form of guaranteed basic income is essential. We discussed this in more detail in a previous part of the chapter.
12. The centralized system would need to be decomposed in modules. The record of contemporary super-computing also suggests some server farming will likely remain necessary. The modules could be managed by independent subgroups, and the local technologies could also be designed modularly, with just the interfaces and the core of the infrastructure needing centralized coordination. The local technologies would provide data to the central monitoring capabilities that in turn would provide information back to the local productive units. Technologies like Blockchain, the building block of Bitcoin that affords one-to-one interaction, might prove to be sources of inspiration by the Agency. The radical decentralization afforded by Blockchain could help guard against the risk of such an infrastructure becoming a new "big brother."

REFERENCES

Bardzell, Jeffrey, and Shaowen Bardzell. 2015. "What Is 'Critical' About Critical Design?." Accessed May 1. http://www.academia.edu/3795919/What_is_Critical_About_Critical_Design.

Benkler, Yochai. 2006. *The Wealth of Networks: How Social Production Transforms Markets and Freedom*. New Haven, CT:: Yale University Press.

———. 2013. "Practical Anarchism Peer Mutualism, Market Power, and the Fallible State." *Politics & Society* 41 (2): 213–51. doi:10.1177/0032329213483108.

Berners-Lee, Tim. 2006. "Linked Data." http://www.w3.org/DesignIssues/Linked-Data.html.

Bosio, Enrico, Tiziana Girardi, Daniela Stefanescu, Vincenzo D'Andrea, and Maurizio Teli. 2014. "Understanding Online Deliberation: The Dis-Alignment between Designers and Users." Paper presented at Internet, Policy, and Politics Conference. Oxford, England.

Boyd, Danah, and Kate Crawford. 2012. "Critical Questions for Big Data." *Information, Communication & Society* 15 (5): 662–79. doi:10.1080/1369118X.2012.678878.

Bria, Francesca. 2014. *Digital Social Innovation. Interim Report*. Brussels, BE: European Union.

Burchell, Graham, Colin Gordon, and Peter Miller, eds. 1991. *The Foucault Effect: Studies in Governmentality*. First edition. Chicago: University of Chicago Press.

Callon, Michel, Pierre Lascoumes, and Yannick Barthe. 2009. *Acting in an Uncertain World*. Boston, MA: MIT Press.

Cefkin, Melissa, ed. 2010. *Ethnography and the Corporate Encounter: Reflections on Research in and of Corporations*. New York, NY: Berghahn Books.

Coleman, E. Gabriella. 2012. *Coding Freedom: The Ethics and Aesthetics of Hacking*. Princeton: Princeton University Press.

"D-CENT." 2015. Accessed May 14. http://dcentproject.eu/.

Delfanti, Alessandro. 2013. *Biohackers: The Politics of Open Science*. London: Pluto Press.

De Paoli, Stefano De, Maurizio Teli, and Vincenzo D'Andrea. 2008. "Free and Open Source Licenses in Community Life: Two Empirical Cases." *First Monday* 13 (10). http://ojs-prod-lib.cc.uic.edu/ojs/index.php/fm/article/view/2064.

DiSalvo, Carl, Jonathan Lukens, Thomas Lodato, Tom Jenkins, and Tanyoung Kim. 2014. "Making Public Things: How HCI Design Can Express Matters of Concern." In *Proceedings of the 32nd Annual ACM Conference on Human Factors in Computing Systems*, 2397–2406. New York: ACM. http://dl.acm.org/citation.cfm?id=2557359.

Dittrich, Yvonne, Sara Eriksén, and Christina Hansson. 2002. "PD in the Wild; Evolving Practices of Design in Use." In *Participatory Design Conference*. http://swepub.kb.se/bib/swepub:oai:bth.se:forskinfoC8D549807517C422C1256BEA0050704B.

Dyer-Witheford, Nick. 2013. "Red Plenty Platforms." *Culture Machine* 13: 1–27.

Ehn, Pelle. 1992. "Scandinavian Design: On Participation and Skill." In *Usability*, edited by Paul S. Adler and Terry A. Winograd, 96–132. Oxford University Press. http://dl.acm.org/citation.cfm?id=146341.

———. 2008. "Participation in Design Things." In *Proceedings of the Tenth Anniversary Conference on Participatory Design 2008*, 92–101. PDC '08. Indianapolis, IN: Indiana University. http://dl.acm.org/citation.cfm?id=1795234.1795248.

Engels, Friedrich. 1972. *Socialism: Utopian and Scientific*. New York: Intl Pub.

Federal Communications Commission. 2015. "Open Internet." March 12. http://www.fcc.gov/openinternet.

Fuchs, Christian. 2013. *Digital Labour and Karl Marx*. New York, NY: Routledge.

Fumagalli, Andrea. 2015. "Commonwealth, Commonfare and the Money of the Common: The Challenge to Fight Life Subsumption." In *Anthology of Dissent*. New York, NY: Peter Lang Verlag.

Gangadharan, G. R., and Vincenzo D'Andrea. 2011. "Service Licensing: Conceptualization, Formalization, and Expression." *Service Oriented Computing and Applications* 5 (1): 37–59. doi:10.1007/s11761-011-0079-6.

Gesell, Silvio. 1934. *The Natural Economic Order 1929/1934*. Translated by Philip Pye. San Antonio: Free-economy Publishing.

Graeber, David. 2011. *Debt—Updated and Expanded: The First 5,000 Years*. Upd Exp edition. Brooklyn: Melville House.

Greenwald, Glenn. 2014. *No Place to Hide: Edward Snowden, the NSA, and the U.S. Surveillance State*. New York, NY: Metropolitan Books.

Hakken, David. 2003. *The Knowledge Landscapes of Cyberspace*. New York, NY: Routledge.

Hakken, David, and Paula Mate'. 2014. "The Culture Problem in Participatory Design." In *Proceedings of the 2014 Participatory Design Conference*. Windhoek, Namibia.

Hakken, David, Maurizio Teli, and Vincenzo D'Andrea. 2010. "Intercalating the Social and the Technical: Socially Robust and Enduring Computing." In *PDC*, 231–34. http://ojs.ruc.dk/index.php/pdc/article/view/1919.

Hanseth, Ole, and Nina Lundberg. 2001. "Designing Work Oriented Infrastructures." *Computer Supported Cooperative Work (CSCW)* 10 (3–4): 347–72. doi:10.1023/A:1012727708439.

Haraway, Donna. 1988. "Situated Knowledges: The Science Question in Feminism and the Privilege of Partial Perspective." *Feminist Studies* 14 (3): 575–99.

Hardt, Michael, and Antonio Negri. 2001. *Empire*. Cambridge, MA: Harvard University Press.

———. 2009. *Empire*. Cambridge, MA: Harvard University Press.

Harvey, David. 2014. *Seventeen Contradictions and the End of Capitalism*. First edition. Oxford ; New York: Oxford University Press.

Hilty, Lorenz M. 2008. *Information Technology and Sustainability: Essays on the Relationship Between ICT and Sustainable Development*. BoD—Books on Demand.

Huijboom, Noor, and Tijs Van den Broek. 2011. "Open Data: An International Comparison of Strategies." *European Journal of ePractice* 12 (1): 1–13.

Johnson, Jeffrey. 2013. "From Open Data to Information Justice." In *Midwest Political Science Association Annual Conference*. http://papers.ssrn.com/sol3/papers.cfm?abstract_id=2241092.

Kallinikos, Jannis. 2004. "Deconstructing Information Packages: Organizational and Behavioural Implications of ERP Systems." *Information Technology & People* 17 (1): 8–30. doi:10.1108/09593840410522152.

Keynes, John Maynard. 2011. *The General Theory of Employment, Interest, and Money*. United States: CreateSpace Independent Publishing Platform.

Kusterer, Kenneth C. 1978. *Know-How on the Job: The Important Working Knowledge of "Unskilled" Workers*. Boulder, CO: Westview Press.

Latour, Bruno. 1990. "Technology Is Society Made Durable." *The Sociological Review* 38 (S1): 103–31.

———. 2004. "Why Has Critique Run Out of Steam? From Matters of Fact to Matters of Concern." *Critical Inquiry* 30 (2): 225–48. doi:10.1086/421123.

Lazzarato, Maurizio. 2012. *The Making of the Indebted Man: An Essay on the Neoliberal Condition*. Translated by Joshua David Jordan. Los Angeles, CA: Semiotext.

Le Dantec, Christopher A., and Carl DiSalvo. 2013. "Infrastructuring and the Formation of Publics in Participatory Design." *Social Studies of Science* 43 (2): 241–64. doi:10.1177/0306312712471581.

Lessig, Lawrence. 1999. *Code and Other Laws of Cyberspace*. New York: Basic Books.

———. 2001. *The Future of Ideas: The Fate of the Commons in a Connected World*. New York, NY: Random House.

———. 2004. *Free Culture: How Big Media Uses Technology and the Law to Lock Down Culture and Control Creativity*. New York, NY: Penguin Press.

———. 2014. *Remix Making Art And Commerce Thrive in the Hybrid Economy*. New York: Penguin.

Lucarelli, Stefano, Marco Sachy, Klara Jaya Brekke, and Francesca Bria. 2014. *Field Research and User Requirements Digital Social Currency Pilots*. D3.4. D-Cent Project.

"Luxembourg Leaks: Global Companies' Secrets Exposed." 2015. *International Consortium of Investigative Journalists*. Accessed May 14. http://www.icij.org/project/luxembourg-leaks.

Marglin, Stephen A. 2008. *The Dismal Science: How Thinking Like an Economist Undermines Community*. First edition. Cambridge, MA: Harvard University Press.

McKenna, Erin. 2001. *The Task of Utopia: A Pragmatist and Feminist Perspective*. Maryland: Rowman & Littlefield.

Medina, Eden. 2014. *Cybernetic Revolutionaries: Technology and Politics in Allende's Chile*. Reprint edizione. Cambridge, MA: MIT Press.

Mellor, Mary. 2010. *The Future of Money: From Financial Crisis to Public Resource*. London: Pluto Press.

Miller, Seumas. 2007. "Social Institutions." http://plato.stanford.edu/archives/fall2012/entries/social-institutions/.

Morini, Cristina, and Andrea Fumagalli. 2010. "Life Put to Work: Towards a Life Theory of Value." *Ephemera: Theory & Politics in Organization* 10 (3/4): 234–52.

Narduzzo, Alessandro, and Alessandro Rossi. 2004. "The Role of Modularity in Free/Open Source Software Development." In *Free/Open Source Software Development*, edited by Stefan Koch, 84–102. Hershey, PA: Idea Group Publishing.

Neumann, Laura J., and Susan Leigh Star. 1996. "Making Infrastructure: The Dream of a Common Language." In *PDC*, 231–40. http://rossy.ruc.dk/ojs/index.php/pdc/article/view/153.

Open Knowledge Foundation. 2015. "Announcing the Open Data Handbook Version 1.0 | Open Knowledge Blog." http://blog.okfn.org/2012/02/22/announcing-the-open-data-handbook-version-1-0/.

Ostrom, Elinor. 1990. *Governing the Commons: The Evolution of Institutions for Collective Action*. Cambridge University Press.

Pasquinelli, Matteo. 2009. *Animal Spirits: A Bestiary of the Commons*. Rotterdam, NL: nai010 Publishers.

Pipek, Volkmar, and Volker Wulf. 2009. "Infrastructuring: Toward an Integrated Perspective on the Design and Use of Information Technology." *Journal of the Association for Information Systems* 10 (5): 1.

Poitras, Laura. 2014. "Citizenfour." Produced in Berlin: Praxis Films, 2014.

Rawls, John. 1971. *A Theory of Justice*. First edition. Cambridge, MA: Belknap Press.

Rigi, Jakob. 2014. "Foundations of a Marxist Theory of the Political Economy of Information: Trade Secrets and Intellectual Property, and the Production of Relative Surplus Value and the Extraction of Rent-Tribute." *tripleC: Communication, Capitalism & Critique. Open Access Journal for a Global Sustainable Information Society* 12 (2): 909–36.

Roedl, David. 2015. "Making Things Last: Obsolescence and Its Resistance by IY Culture." School of informatics and Computing, Indiana University.

Schuler, Douglas. 2013. "Creating the World Citizen Parliament: Seven Challenges for Interaction Designers." *Interactions* 20 (3): 38–47. doi:10.1145/2451856.2451867.

Shaikh, Maha, Claudio Ciborra, and Tony Cornford. 2010. "Hierarchy, Laboratory and Collective: Unveiling Linux as Innovation, Machination and Constitution." *Journal of the Association for Information Systems* 11 (12). http://aisel.aisnet. org/jais/vol11/iss12/4.

Star, Susan Leigh. 1999. "The Ethnography of Infrastructure." *American Behavioral Scientist* 43 (3): 377–91.

Star, Susan Leigh, and Geoffrey C. Bowker. 2006. "How to Infrastructure." In *Handbook of New Media: Social Shaping and Social Consequences of ICTs*, edited by Leah Lievrouw and Sonia Livingstone, 230–45. Thousand Oaks, CA: Sage.

Star, Susan Leigh, and Karen Ruhleder. 1996. "Steps Toward an Ecology of Infrastructure: Design and Access for Large Information Spaces." *Information Systems Research* 7 (1): 111–34.

Suchman, Lucy. 1993. "Working Relations of Technology Production and Use." *Computer Supported Cooperative Work* 2 (1–2): 21–39. doi:10.1007/BF00749282.

———. 2002a. "Located Accountabilities in Technology Production." *Scandinavian Journal of Information Systems* 14 (2): 7.

———. 2002b. "Practice-Based Design of Information Systems: Notes from the Hyper-Developed World." *The Information Society* 18 (2): 139–44. doi:10.1080/ 01972240290075066.

Teli, Maurizio. 2010. "Collective Ownership in Free/Libre and Open Source Software: The OpenSolaris Case." In *Conference Proceedings of JITP 2010: The Politics of Open Source*, 1: 138. http://oss-institute.org/storage/documents/Resources/ studies/the-politics-of-open-source.pdf#page=146.

Teli, Maurizio, Silvia Bordin, Maria Menendez Blanco, Giusi Orabona, and Antonella De Angeli. 2015. "Public Design of Digital Commons in Urban Places: A Case Study." *International Journal of Human-Computer Studies* 81, 17–30.

Travica, Bob. 1998. *New Organizational Designs: Information Aspects*. Stamford, CT: Albex.

Van Dijck, José. 2013. *The Culture of Connectivity: A Critical History of Social Media*. Oxford University Press.

Vieira, Miguel Said, and Primavera De Filippi. 2014. *Between Copyleft and Copyfarleft: Advanced Reciprocity for the Commons*. SSRN Scholarly Paper ID 2468731. Rochester, NY: Social Science Research Network. http://papers.ssrn. com/abstract=2468731.

Weibel, Peter, and Bruno Latour. 2005. *Making Things Public: Atmospheres of Democracy: [exhibition, ZKM, Center for Art and Media Karlsruhe, March 20–October 3, 2005]*. Cambridge, MA: MIT Press.

Wiener, N. 1950. The Human Use of Human Being. Boston, MA: Houghton Mifflin.

Winner, Langdon. 1980. "Do Artifacts Have Politics?" *Daedalus* 109 (1): 121–36.

Zittrain, Jonathan. 2008. *The Future of the Internet—And How to Stop It*. First edition. New Haven, CT: Yale University Press.

8   Measures to Support New Institutions

INTRODUCTION: MEASURING THE SOCIAL CORRELATES OF NEW VALUES AND INSTITUTIONS

Identifying a new value complex is not on its own enough to foster commitment to building a new society. Neither is creating new institutions to incline social formation reproduction (SFR) toward the pursuit of the new complex of values. Nor is it enough to demonstrate that a new complex of institutions *could* support the pursuit of a new value complex. Building successful institutions requires information sufficient to addressing other questions about the new institutions, such as:

- Are they functioning as intended?
- Do the desired social changes match with their design?
- Do they seem to be having the desired consequences?
- Do they increase support for the pursuit of the new values complex?
- Are the new values being pursued effectively?

In order to answer these questions, new information will have to be obtained. In this chapter, we describe some measures and methods that we think will create this information.

Again, we want to be clear about what we *are and are not* trying to do. We *are* trying to project ways to think about the future and how we might know if the values would work once they come into practice. We are not trying to demonstrate that our proposed values *will necessarily* be effective—an impossible task.

To demonstrate that the proposed agencies were working, we would need to have the data necessary to evaluate them. However, the data and information needed to judge their efficacy will be historically contingent, just as the *actual* new value and institution complexes will be. We cannot say that this and only this information, or these and only these data, are the precise ones necessarily indicative of a progressively changing SFR dynamic. Instead, our aim in this chapter is to show the *feasibility* of first, getting the *kinds* of data we would need, second, developing the kinds of measures to generate the kinds of information that we would need to focus on, and third, obtaining metrics analogous to those described here to allow judgment. All of these steps will be needed if SFR is to be truly extended. To make a convincing case that the pursuit of these new value complexes would be worthwhile, we need to be able to show that their efficacy could be measured. This includes being able to specify what data would be relevant, how they could be organized to create the necessary information, and how this would be interpreted (i.e., how knowledge would be created from it). We want to be as clear as we can about the kinds of data and information that could accomplish three aims:

- Lead us to conclude that a particular institution or a particular constellation of new institutional innovations was working well;
- Lead us to the opposite conclusion, indicating the need for change or adjustment;
- Suggest where and how to make interventions and changes.

When using information to make such judgments, one is, in a broad sense, "measuring." Hence, this chapter is about measurement *broadly conceived*. We want to be as specific as we can be about the kinds of data and information that would let us know how effective the new proposed Agencies were, if we had that data at the appropriate future times. Talk about data, information, and knowledge arises in part from basing our intervention program on the digital terrain and the selected practices identified in Chapter 4. We have grounded our program on the recognition that the current SFR is "addicted" to computing, and that computing has a special place in the contemporary cultural imaginary. We will argue that in this cultural imaginary, change is also largely associated with "use of computers." To succeed, an intervention program will need to engage the support of active computer users, both professional and non-professional, since others will look to their expertise in terms of the project's feasibility. To engage computing supporters, we need to use their language, including data, information, and knowledge.

What do we mean by talking about measurement *"broadly conceived"*? Our general goal is to undermine the exclusive emphasis on ratio values while also reorienting SFR toward nominal and ordinal values. The reader might object that "measurement" implies numbers and since only ratio values provide numbers, our project is impossible. A typical justification for market mediation, for example, is the claim that only markets can provide the forms and volume of necessary numerical information for a social formation to be properly "steered" (Habermas 1975). But do markets provide enough information to evaluate whether a particular value is being realized, or how well it is being realized? Do markets identify if an institution is being supportive of the values it is supposed to afford? We agree with the criticism of markets that stresses the narrowness of the information typically provided by them, as well as the many kinds of fetishistic pseudo-concreteness characteristic of market-based numbers.

Our notion of "broadly conceived measurement" turns on differentiating numbers from metrics, which contain things that numbers do not. Consider, for example, the answer to a question like, "Have you had enough to eat?" The question implies a simple judgment—is your hunger satisfied, or not? The answer is a measurement, a metric, but it is not a number. While markets do produce numbers, they tend to be of the "how many people bought blue soap powder rather than green" variety. Such numbers generally fail to give the information that allows for the specification of the values whose reproduction is extended by a practice, the degree of their value realization or institutional supportiveness. New, different, broader metrics to help draw valid inferences from information are needed, which means different as opposed to merely more information.

In this chapter, we identify metrics appropriate to our task, whether or not they provide numbers, and explain how it should be possible to gather and use what they show us. We start by discussing metric practices that are generally useful, the kinds that help make our goal less daunting. We then turn to a critique of existing popular market-oriented measures. Our argument here is that the information normally generated by markets allows inferences about only a narrow range of issues. We need broader sources of information. Based on these considerations, we suggest sets of metrics relevant to each of our values and associated institutions. If sufficient information relevant to these metrics was gathered, it could provide a basis for deciding whether or not SFR was evolving and changing. The aim again is to demonstrate the feasibility of developing metric sets that would enable both specific and general conclusions about efficacy. Finally, we summarize these metric suggestions by articulating the general principles for adequate measures on which they are based, as well as discussing why their articulation is important in gaining support for our interventions project. We conclude by addressing the extent to which measuring "commonness" will typically be an element of the new metrics.

SOME PHENOMENA THAT MAKE OUR TASK LESS DAUNTING

We recognize that the task taken on in this chapter is large, even overwhelming. To foster activities oriented toward the pursuit of nominal and ordinal values, actions that foster turning relations into relationships, we also need to undercut the social emphasis on ratio valuing. For example, adopting the new values regime will involve changes in what are thought of as economic. It will also reduce emphasis on what is currently recognized as economic. As in the last chapter, we first offer ideas oriented toward the macro-level of social formation, and then the micro-level of organizing, to clarify what we have in mind.

The Pro-Change Rather than Pro-Status Quo Associations with Computing

Computing is popularly associated with broad, basically positive, social change. This is a contradictory but on-balance an important characteristic of popular views. While there may or may not be positive change, such associations have the effect of undermining presumptions of the "we've always done it this way" sort. They also undercut the naïve conservatism that denies change in social formation reproduction. The perception that "things are already changing" provides space to foster change in other ways.

General perceptions can also be mobilized against efforts like ours when mediated primarily through market/ratio framings, for example, the claim that "free" (i.e., not-interfered-with) markets are the best mechanism for separating good developments from bad ones, the idea that states inevitably are captured by certain social groups, and so on. Such premises are central to debates over the long-term, empirical implications of computing. Whether computing is on balance is a good or a bad thing, or whether the positive change presumptions are justified, is not our question. The association of computing with positive change adds credibility to our project of building change on selected computing practices. We focus on only "selected" practices since computing *in general* is subject to current forms of SFR, and hence many computing practices have social correlates (e.g., loss of sociality, threats to privacy) that would not provide a basis for the positive change we envision.

This situation suggests a number of metrics to pay attention to, including:

- The extent to which the new institutions succeed in expanding the scope of the practices to be reinforced;
- The extent to which negative phenomena associated with computing are discouraged;
- A general index of the speed of movement toward new SFR dynamics.

In what follows, we suggest several such metrics for each of our values.

Evaluation Research

Evaluation research (ER) is another factor whose existence helps our case. Sometimes treated by scholars as a trivial field of applied research, we think ER is actually quite important. Contemporary ER arose from an interest in seeing if social programs—like those included in the US "War on Poverty," for example, the Head Start education program—were attaining their goals. ER accepted that such questions could not be answered by simply relying on information generated by markets, even when supplemented by information generated via bureaucratic accounting. Rather, determining the social value of social programs was the very thing deemed most important. Its value had to be determined through activities enabling judgment on whether program goals had been accomplished. While powerful efforts have been made to reduce evaluation to numbers—indeed, the "demand for numbers" in arenas like educational research has reached fetishistic proportions—the basic ER process has proven somewhat resistant to such reductionism.

Two interventions into ER help explain why it continues to attend to nominal and ordinal values, and thus why it provides conceptual tools that are useful in clarifying our tasks in this chapter. One is an intervention by Michael Scriven, generally acknowledged in the US to be a mid-twentieth-century evaluation expert. Scriven critiqued the standard evaluation approaches as being too tied to initial program aims (Scriven 1991). While acknowledging that it was important to know if a program was doing what it was supposed to do, he made a case that many interventions had unintended consequences, and that these, for good or ill, could outweigh the intended ones. He therefore argued for "goal free" evaluation, for attending to *all* of the correlates of an intervention, not just the intended ones. This insight makes it possible to put judgments about program performance in their appropriately broader social contexts.

Scriven's "goal free" rhetoric, while arresting, is an overstatement. In fact, his approach called for evaluation that is not "goal bound." The important consequence of his intervention was an increased breadth of ER vision. Instead of a narrow focus on goal-derived "evaluative criteria," ER could attend to all the potential correlates of the intervention. Moreover, in practice, Scriven's approach meant involving members of the institution that was the locus of the intervention in identifying the list of potential correlates/criteria. These individuals would be most alive to any unintended but still significant consequences. This participatory approach, as in participatory design (Simonsen and Robertson 2012) and participatory action research (Whyte 1990), is essential to creating good metrics.

Another ER intervention worth attending to, this time specifically in educational evaluation, is that of Benjamin Bloom and colleagues (Bloom, Hastings, and Madaus 1971). They differentiate between two kinds of evaluations. One is "in process" evaluation to support immediate course corrections, the kind through which teachers attempt to help students become more reflective and self-critical about how they are pursuing an educational task. It is an intervention aimed at helping the student maximize learning accomplishments, in process or what Bloom called "formative" evaluation, and it should generally be less judgmental and more encouraging. The second, final or "summative" evaluation, occurs at a different time, i.e., after the intervention is completed. It is also more oriented to external criteria and aims at final judgments. When Bloom's distinction between the formative and the summative is combined with Scriven's non-goal-bounded approach, the result is closer to what we want: encouragement for the pursuit of explicit values, overall specification of what has and has not been accomplished, and identification of what else has happened that is important, even if it was unintended. These are the aims for the metrics described in the remainder of the chapter.

Leontief Input–Output Matrices

Evaluation research is useful as a possible model of the kind of measuring we would like to foster at the specific organizational or "micro"-level. When thinking about the more macro phenomena characteristic of social formations, we find it helpful to think about what we have in mind as a giant Leontief input–output matrix. Wassily Leontief was a Soviet economist who was interested in helping to develop an economic practice that could be used by Soviet planners (Leontief 1986). He conceived of an economy as composed of a number of sectors, each of whose outputs could be thought of as inputs for other sectors. In a balanced economy, the output of all sectors exactly equaled the input needed by all sectors. Therefore, overall, what was produced equaled what was needed. While inputs and outputs can be expressed in value terms, this need not be so. Inputs and outputs can often be measured in physical terms, such as the numbers of units, mass, etc. It is important to try to identify the conditions of production where the sum of outputs equals the sum of needed inputs as much as possible.

Many economists have chosen to approach economies in input–output terms. Leontief inspired what came to be known as the cost–benefit analysis (CBA), for example (Bergh 2002). However, a major limitation of CBA follows from the typical decision to attend only to those dimensions of cost or benefit that are measurable in value terms; in practice, this means attending only to market-generated data. In contrast to CBA, we think of the elements of our broader "economy" as a sub-set of a "hyper-" Leontief matrix, one that attends to nominal and interval values as well as ratio ones. Such a hyper-matrix would serve a fundamental purpose, namely, to conceive of human activity in a single framework, one that is oriented toward the pursuit of values of all kinds, not giving attention solely, as does current SFR, to ratio valuing/markets.

Viewing social formations as such hyper-input–output matrices could have additional benefits. For example, it communicates the interdependences of the pursuit of multiple values. What is attained pursuing output relevant to one value is relevant as input to the pursuit of others. A second benefit is the notion of measuring the degree of "balance" between inputs and outputs in a social formation. The notion of a moving balance fits with a program of gradual de-emphasis on ratio valuings and an increase of nominal and ordinal valuings, reflecting nicely the idea of social formation reproduction. "Balance" in the Leontief sense is similar to the notion of "balance" in an eco-niche, as something that can be striven for but is rarely actually reached. This is because of frequent changes, either in the elements of the system or changes in their context.

In ecology, context factors include factors partly influenced by human activity, like climate change (World Wildife Fund 2015). In social ecology, contexts include deliberate interventions, as in fostering the pursuit of some values while inhibiting the pursuit of others. Each of the institutions described as Agencies in Chapter 7 would need to be fostered; some could be fostered together in more integrated approaches, but all interventions would be subject to the consequences of the institutions' interdependencies. A literal construction of a hyper-Leontief matrix would surely help us anticipate the interactive consequences of interventions. Here, we abjure this task, partly because it is far beyond this book's scope, but also because the effort makes sense only in relation to actual interventions into SFR based on a real, new value complex. The idea of such a matrix, when connected to the change presumptions of computing, and combined with the evaluation ideas of Scriven and Bloom, encourages us to pay attention to connections among values indicators and to unexpected, unanticipated correlations, as well as to distinguish between those potential correlations still "in process" and those that are more stable.

CRITIQUES OF EXISTING (MOSTLY MARKET-ORIENTED) METRICS; SOME MIGHT STILL BE USABLE

It might be tempting to begin developing such a macro-Leontief matrix using existing market data. We need to spell out some of the consequences of using such information to establish the efficacy of new value and institutional complexes. Much of the available information is generated from markets, which generally means it only allows for inferences about ratio values. Our main point about using this information is a variation on the old saw about searching for lost keys under the streetlight. If values were a set of keys, we would not search for them under a "streetlight" (the illuminations offered by markets) just because this is where the light is brightest (the information is richest). Rather, we need to find ways to bring light to, or create information about, the areas where we suspect we may have lost them. If we are insightful, we might still be able to make some use of the existing streetlights.

PROBLEMS WITH SOME CURRENT METRICS

One factor that helps when daunted by our measurement tasks is to remember the inadequacy of existing measurements. Consider the question reportedly raised by Queen Elizabeth II of Great Britain, about why no one anticipated the social crisis set off in 2007 by the financial markets. We recognize that a few people *did* anticipate the crisis, both contrarian investors and institutional economists. So the queen's question really should be: Why wasn't more attention given to economic measures indicating that the chances of a severe crisis were important, and not trivial? The answer is that these warnings were drowned out by celebrations of the "Great Moderation." Most of those whose opinions were considered worthy enough to be attended to were convinced that danger of any potential crisis had been solved, so they weren't interested in measuring its chances. What were they looking at?

The Dow—The Dow Jones Industrial Average is one example of a metric that is given great prominence by mainstream economics but actually does not measure what it is presumed to measure. It is generally presumed that the Dow measures total market value by measuring the total value of an eponymous group of "normal" stocks or shares of limited liability corporations. This metric is the most-often-reported indicator of market activity, and comparisons over time are reported as if they are indicators of market vitality or morbidity. While corporations are clearly not, in common sense terms, a life form, they sometimes do "die" (go bankrupt) or their values fall drastically. Periodically, the stock of such dead, or sick, or stagnating corporations are removed from the Dow Jones and replaced by others that are "performing better." Hence, tracking of the numerical movement of the Dow Average over time is not really an index of comparative market performance. It is regularly skewed on the upside, and it is remarkable that there is no effort known to us to "discount" or account statistically for this skewing when reporting the Dow Average. In reality, the Dow is a comparison of apples with oranges (or one set of apples with another set of fewer of these apples and some oranges). Imagine the derision that would be heaped on a sports statistic that allowed a team to eliminate poor performances from its record!

Productivity—Another even more important example of a widely used but deeply flawed market metric is "productivity." This is taken to be as a measure of economic output in relation to economic input. If it were, an increase in this statistic would be a measure of how many more widgets a typical worker made in comparison to her previous output. Increases in productivity numbers are often attributed to the use of new technology.

Measuring productivity makes common sense. Presumably, we all have "productive" days, ones when our efforts seem to be fruitful, versus days when we accomplish almost nothing. However, there are reasons to be cautious about what statistics, such as those labeled "the rate of productivity increase," actually measure, as well as how they are used. Productivity numbers play an important ideological role in justifying current SFR. The idea that the social product "pie" normally gets bigger in relation to people's social input efforts is important to market enthusiasts. Productivity increase is used to "explain" how there can be an increase in overall social well-being without any redistribution of wealth from the wealthy to those not so blessed. If productivity is improving, then theoretically, all are benefiting—except this ignores how the benefits are distributed. If all were benefiting, there would be no need to strive to influence SFR dynamics, particularly given the risks associated with social change. Thomas Piketty's *Capital in the 21st Century* critiques in detail the idea that the expansion of the worker-benefiting pie is normal rather than a result of unusual conditions (Piketty 2014).

There is no direct measure of change in the capacity to make commodities. Sometimes, productivity data are created post facto out of statistics that compare reported commodity output with the reported input of the time workers expended, presuming constant effort. In many instances, the measure of productivity is based on a different fiction. For example, the service sector is now far and away the largest gross sector of "developed" economies. In the US, it hovers around 80% of the economy. Producing more in services than in manufacturing or agriculture is taken to be significant indicator that an economy is "developed." However, the output of services is notoriously difficult to measure. One could count, for example, the number of clients or customers served, but this says nothing about the quality of service. What if the service worker (say, a social worker) had simply had her allotted number of cases doubled? Measuring service output relative to quality is so hard that many economists just take salary as a proxy for productivity. Those paid more are said to be proportionally more productive than those paid less. As pay is often demonstrably related to workers' collective power vis-à-vis employers, to take income as a measure of an individual's productivity rather than of power is patently false. To then add salaries up and call it a measure of general productivity is equally flawed. Recently, in several developed nations, state-sector employers have unilaterally cut the pay of public employees, actions then correlated with "a decline" in productivity! Whatever productivity statistics might indicate, there is reason to be cautious about using them.

Productivity Paradox—One of the most interesting examples of the nexus of computing and the economy is the so-called "productivity paradox" (Harris 1994). From roughly the early 1970s to around 1995, US investment in computing went up regularly, when productivity statistics stagnated or declined. As the economist Kenneth Arrow was said to have quipped, one could see the productivity benefits of IT everywhere but in the statistics! After puzzling over this paradox, Alan Greenspan was greatly relieved when around 1995, productivity rose. However, the rise was short-lived, disappearing in the first decade of the 21st century. The debate over this paradox raged among economists (Harris 1994), but we think it a false problem, likely an epiphenomenon of the fact that productivity statistics don't actually measure productivity. There was absence of evidence that computing led to greater productivity, but it had little impact on decisions to buy and implement them. There was widespread belief that they would at some future date increase productivity, evidence notwithstanding.

Gross Domestic Product—To talk realistically about productivity, we would need actual measures of the social product as well as social inputs.[1] David Pilling of the *Financial Times* recently reported on all the problems with another often-quoted statistic that claims to do so, the national gross domestic product, or GDP (Pilling 2014). His examination of the statistic was occasioned by a recent 5% rise in the British GDP, which was not a consequence of more stuff being made, but by a decision to include prostitution and the illegal drug trade in the GDP (from which they had previously been barred). There are established standards for calculating GDP, so it is not the absence of standards that Pilling concentrates on, nor the way they are adhered to by one or another nation. Rather, Pilling is concerned that the statistics about things counted or not counted are often fictive (including the service-sector productivity measures mentioned above). The foundational problems with this metric, given its almost reverential treatment in public discourse, are so legion that it raises other questions. Why are such poor statistics given so much attention? What do they actually measure, as opposed to what they are claimed to measure? What is the source of the bad faith that leads to these particular statistical forms of, in Marx's memorable phrase, the "fetishism of commodities?"

These problems with existing metrics mean they have less utility for our measuring needs. They complicate our task by making it necessary to invent new metrics. We might articulate better ways to measure than the metrics we have critiqued, but our primary need is to measure other things, the ones on which we have focused. This critique makes the case that the metrics typically used in dominant conceptions of the economic are inadequate. We still think it possible, by being clear about what we want to know, to reach a better standard—and the bar is set low!

CURRENT METRICS OF POSSIBLY GREATER USE, IF DONE CRITICALLY

Baseline Social Satisfaction Data—There are other kinds of information being generated that we could use. Among the information we need are ones that set baselines about, for example, general levels of satisfaction or dissatisfaction regarding peoples' influence over the conditions of their own lives. General social surveys generated by the National Opinion Research Center in the US offer some information along these lines, especially when it is possible to track attitude changes over time (Sterrett et al. 2015). At the same time, we must not confuse people's sense of their influence with their actual influence. As ethnographers, we need to listen to the "natives," but we also need to be aware that, on occasion, they are wrong. That is, we need to find ways to supplement self-reports on baseline satisfaction metrics.

Accounting—Accounting claims to measure the performance of organizations. Standard accounting practices are almost completely oriented toward profit or loss in private sector organizations. These are, of course, the market metrics that we are trying to get away from. Even in regard to what in the US are called not-for-profits and in the rest of the world are called NGOs, the accounting orientation is toward surplus, which is thought of as being something like profit.

However, there are some accountants who recognize the limitations of current accounting practices. Hannele Mäkelä is a Finnish accountant critical of the utility of the existing standard, narrow accountancy tools. She suggests instead using the tools developed for dealing with what in Europe are called "social enterprises," organizations such as cooperatives that operate to fulfill social rather than capital reproduction purposes (Mäkelä 2015). European nations have different formal terms and legal requirements to qualify as such an entity. From this work, it will be possible to identify several alternative accounting techniques that move toward the kinds of nominal and ratio metrics in which we are interested.[2]

Big Data—At the time of writing, "big data" (BD) is garnering a great deal of attention. The information referred to with this term is generally "born digital"; it is generated as a matter of course in typical acts of computing (Brust 2015). In terms of the data-information-knowledge-wisdom continuum, it would be more accurate to speak of "big information," since it already has a context—that is, it has generally been deliberately collected by specified actions. Thus, the label "big data" diverts attention away from the manipulations to which it has already been subjected. Most data are already "cooked" to some extent, but this is particularly true of BD. Additionally, it is not clear how much information is enough to count as "big." BD excludes the kinds of information we have talked about in our discussions of informating, for example, "real-time" information about an existing process, unless the information is accumulated over long periods of time.

The existence of BD follows from the fact that every user logs on, then chooses information sources and perhaps downloads selections of the information available at a given site, etc. Similarly, to send a text message or place a phone call, a cell phone has to connect to a cell tower; its location is established, the intended recipient of the message identified and located, a communication channel created, and so on. Big data counts things that can be counted and also sorted into various piles designed into the artifacts and technology actor networks of which they are a part. The piles can then be manipulated, as well as represented by various types of visualizations. A typical representation is to show them as digraphs or networks, in which each unit acting, no matter how many times, is represented as a node, and any existing connections, no matter how many, are represented as one connection.

Much BD would seem to be relevant to value/ratio valuing. An advertiser can be more selective about which potential customers to reach, what commodities to offer, etc. (van Dijck 2013). However, the relevance of such information to our kinds of questions is not at all clear. For example, what new social relationships do people wish to establish? What ordinal or nominal values shape their choices? We don't want just to know that a network connection of some sort exists. We want to know about the *character* and the *quality* of that connection, but these are precisely the kinds of information that network maps abstract away.

As ethnographers, we have additional reasons for being skeptical about claims that big data or big information can help us address basic questions about digital technology- (DT-) related changes in human sociality or the reproduction of social formations. Big data enthusiasts are likely to ignore any baseline factual matters, such as the social background of users of Facebook or Twitter. These users are a select group (richer, more connected, more Global North, more female, etc.) and so are not a representative sample of all humanity. Inferences drawn from the online behavior of such users to humans in general are of questionable value. There is also reason to think that behavior online is often different from that offline. This also makes BD's utility suspect for generalizing about anything other than the specific online behaviors from which it is taken. BD procedures, like "data mining," are problematic in other ways. Information ("data") is "mined" when a data set derived from some online behavior is searched for any existing correlations among its elements. Some correlations are identified as "interesting," and these possibly checked to see if they are "real" or artifacts of previous manipulation. Despite careful attention, we have yet to hear a justification for such empiricist procedures. They abandon the careful experimental procedures for doing science, such as hypothesis formation and testing. The representativeness of correlations established by "data mining"-born digital information needs to be established, not merely asserted.[3]

Data generated online—"born digital"—faces the problem of rapid changes in and between online platforms, thus increasing problems in interpretation. Short-term patterns can be mistaken for long-term patterns. A data set could reflect an early interest, or initial resistance, or any number of reactions that could vary over time. Fifteen years ago, social scientists were enthusiastic about the possibility of collecting data from large surveys. Digital technology made it inexpensive to send surveys to large samples of respondents, obviating stamp licking, mailing, and transcribing. Researchers projected that the technology would obviate concerns about scale; since even if only a small portion of the intended audience responds, there would still be a large number *in toto*—e.g., the law of large numbers (Bainbridge 1999; Wellman et al. 2001). However, willingness to fill out surveys online fell precipitously, the number of completed questionnaires falling rapidly toward zero, perhaps in response to the rapid rise in survey requests.

When information is demonstrably derived, in a representative manner, from data about long-term, normed activities, we can see its likely usefulness. When it is only recently born digitally, there is reason for skepticism. When used carefully and derived from practices demonstrably normalized but also with substantial design affordances, as in gaming, we are more hopeful (Gross, Hakken, and True 2012). The utility of even this information for understanding human behavior may remain limited, because there is little space to reflect the actual value commitments of users.

For all these reasons, in what follows, we say little about the relevance of the existing data, focusing instead on thinking about new types of information and associated new metrics that will need to be developed. To examine all existing information in regard to each needed metric is an exercise that would quickly become its own book. Instead, our aim is to establish the feasibility of measuring the performance of institutions with regard to a new set of values—again, not because this is *the* right value set. Equally to purpose is underlining how the measurement task is as important as identifying the value set and the process of institution building. We first address the measures relevant to our general social formation-level values and institutions, and then move on to the person-to-person, organizational ones.

SOME NEW MACRO-LEVEL APPROACHES TO INFORMATION AND METRICS

Sustainability

Sustainability is a value at the center of our book. Given our assessment that current forms of SFR are not sustainable in the long run, we need a social formation with new reproductive dynamics. Discussions of sustainability in previous chapters highlighted three dimensions of the connection to computing. Most important is the "contribution" of digital artifacts and practices to the ecological destabilization of SFR, e.g., computing artifacts are reliant on difficult-to-mine rare metals and there is wasteful planned obsolescence in artifacts like laptops and cell phones, as well as extensive "creative destruction" associated with them (Roedl 2015). The second dimension is the contrasting positive influence of computing if it were to become a model of socially sustainable practices, as in socially robust and enduring computing (Hakken, Teli, and D'Andrea 2010). The third is the specific role of computing in the development of better understandings of complex, environmentally relevant phenomena, like global climate change (Hilty 2008).

It is difficult to conceive of future SFR as no longer highly mediated digitally, let alone a successful campaign to get rid of computing. Computing will be implicated in any serious effort at sustainability; thus, something like the institutions described in Chapter 7 will be needed to maximize its positive contributions to sustainability and minimize its negative ones. From the perspective of measurement, this means creating:

- Better, more specific measures of the continuing contribution of computing to understanding and combating climate change;
- The means to measure how much computing contributes to understanding the challenges to sustainability and the rate of growth of such contributions;

- Metrics that trace the rate of adoption of social practices that are more generally robust and enduring, rather than highlighting those where digital mediation plays a role;
- Ways of evaluating the success of campaigns to promote artifact designs that minimize dependence on difficult-to-obtain materials, as well as replacing market-centered incentives to afford the proliferation of models and design for its own sake.

Efforts to Increase and Broaden Access to the Means of Cultural Reproduction

In Chapter 4, we relied on Lawrence Lessig's account of the general importance of cultural reproduction to SFR to identify the place of the new forms of and participants in cultural reproduction afforded by computing (Lessig 2014). Lessig made four basic points:

- Some "hackers" and "rippers and burners" were expanding the means of cultural reproduction.
- Rigid laws on digital property risked undermining such expansion;
- Without substantial means to extend cultural reproduction, SFR was at risk.
- Steps to expand the ambit of forms of computing that "remix" cultural heritage are generally needed.

For Lessig, the most important part of the list is in the realm of the legal, both to reduce the penalties for trafficking in cultural materials and to encourage more use of computing in the arena of the cultural. In Chapter 7, we discussed how a New Culture Agency could carry out such interventions.

One advantage of the way Lessig raises this issue is that it contains implicit metrics. These include two key elements: first, the notion that one can measure in some sense the extent and forms of cultural innovation and, second, the presumption of a measureable rate of the cultural innovation necessary to sufficiently support the reproduction of any particular social formation. Given our grave doubts regarding the sustainability of current SFR, our measuring problem is somewhat different from that implicit in Lessig's account. Rather than trying to articulate what level of cultural innovation is necessary to sustain current SFR, we want metrics that are relevant to the attainment of the kind of alternative social formation we envision.

At a minimum, with regard to the means of cultural reproduction, we need to be able to measure:

- The existing and the possible forms of innovation in cultural reproduction and their influence, including the "negative" innovation of things such as those that would reduce the scope and importance of "digital property";

- The forms and rate development of additional ways to compute that could extend cultural reproduction further;
- A general theory of, and the amount of, "ripping, mixing, and burning" by cultural forms that foster the rise of new SFR dynamics over the existing ones;
- Whether the amount and forms of innovation and extended cultural reproduction are sufficient to meet the minimum standards suggested by the general theory.

Phenomena Associated with Changes in the Scale of Human Activity

One of David Harvey's most important contributions to the comparative study of social formation reproduction has been his emphasis on its spatial aspects (Harvey 2007). Where capital accumulation takes place is as important as when. Another is his demonstration of how market institutions tend to increase attention to value in general and undercut attention to use values. In so doing, he makes clear the tendency of markets to focus attention on the generalizable (e.g., the "globalizable") rather than on the lower-scale, specific aspects of SFR.

In critiquing globalization discourses in Chapter 4, we commented on how globalization talk tends on the one hand to assume rather than attend to globalism as a maximum level state or condition. This talk focuses mostly on the most macro-level phenomena, such as what is relevant to social formation as wholes rather than specific organizing *within* them. Like Harvey, we critique the implicit assumption within globalization discourses that change is unidirectional, a dynamic that only affords movement toward the global level, even though it is empirically difficult to find such phenomena. While the scale of social practices may on balance be increasing rather than decreasing, their reproduction is a long way from taking place only on the global level. Hence, the specific geographic ambit of a social practice remains an important characteristic with special relevance to SFR, including its relevance to the micro-level of organization.

These considerations seem to have conflicting implications for our project. On the one hand, we acknowledge that one general affordance of computing is to "decouple space from place" (Wellman 2001). That is, digital mediation has a general tendency to foster the movement of sociality from being centered on the face-to-face toward "cyberspace," the realm of what we call "virtual" social interactions and relationships that are not geographically located. On the other hand, the forms of sociality afforded by nominal and ordinal values tend to depend on "grounding" in specific places and times. To avoid attempting to recouple space and place, or to make multiple-value

SFR more virtual, we look for a "both/and" strategy. What we want to encourage are forms of computing that do reinforce face-to-face-contact activities, such as activities that in the past have been productive of participation or the construction of commons. At the same time, we also wish to foster computing's capacity to create new kinds of social relating that transcend locale, as in large social movements. This is, of course, why we create institutions that aim to afford lobal phenomena.

Consequently, we have multiple measurement challenges with regard to the scale of multi-values SFR, including the need for measures of:

- Each of the multiple scales at which current SFR dynamics are manifest and the proportions of all SFR that each level involves;
- The social correlates of efforts to foster lobality, including evaluative ones;
- Changes in scale dynamics as the institutions described in Chapter 7 are implemented;
- Identification and analysis of the place, space, and time implications of vestigial, "old" dynamics and their relation to the rise of new ones;
- Specific attention to the scale and time correlates of particular computing practices.

Broader Understandings of "The Economic"

As argued previously, an important mechanism through which ratio perspectives have come to dominate values and valuation has been the equation of the economic with scarcity-related market practices. This is a conceptual shift that led to the economic being perceived as distinct from and causally prior to other aspects of human life, such as the construction of social relations and relationships. Advocacy of this narrow perspective has in recent years been the province of academic neo-classical economics and neo-liberal policy, as critiqued by Marglin and Tsing (Marglin 2008; Tsing 2005). In the previous chapter, we discussed several institutional innovations that could combat such views, providing instead broad support for an expansion of nominal and ordinal valuing and a curtailing of ratio valuing in economics and public policy. A goal of such institutions must be a broadening of the sense of the economic to include all these valuing processes, as well as the reinstitutionalization of a broad conception of the social—what Bruno Latour calls *Reassembling the Social* (Latour 2005). Under a broad conception, "the economic" can be understood as a focus on *all* the social means humans use to support their physical subsistence and reproduction, or "work" in the anthropological sense (Hakken 1987). Such an alternative economic discourse would aim to end attending only to responses to scarcity, replacing it with noticing all forms of meeting material needs. Economic attention to mystical phenomena like financialization, rather than being of greatest concern, would then tend toward critiques of how they interfere with providing subsistence and how they can therefore be discouraged.

To measure the success of such a program, data could be usefully gathered on:

- The forms and the extent of use of alternative forms of money when tied to distinct valuesing activities;
- The relative growth in subsistence activities being mediated by nominal and interval, as opposed to ratio valuing; that is, the extent to which market mediation is marginalized in favor of more direct social mediation, as through commons;
- The extent to which market monopolization and other forms of rent seeking, like financialization, remain influential over or are marginalized in relation to SFR;
- The comparative change in discourse, e.g., the relative frequency of indicative language, like "the economic" or "the economy" in the neoliberal as opposed to the broader "work" sense.

A Social Constructivist, Rather than a Technicist, Perspective on Technology

While the technologies in use can be analyzed abstractly and from several different perspectives, they remain complex actor network unities whose initial elements are frequently reformulated in practice. Understanding them to be social *re*constructions in more or less constant reproduction undermines the current tendency to think of them as distinct technical artifacts or commodities (see Hakken, Teli, and D'Andrea 2010). This perspective increases the recognition of the number of points where one might intervene to influence the social construction of technological processes, as well as broadening awareness of the forms of possible intervention. Institutionalizing a social constructivist position would substantially increase the general scope of efforts to change the fundamental dynamics of SFR.

For example, educational institutions would be a central focus of further social constructivist work. The process is manifested in the slow but increasing attention given to subjects like social informatics, human-computer interaction, participatory design, critical design, and human-robot interaction in computing education. Equally important are the various mechanisms through which broad cross- and trans-disciplinary perspectives, ones that include attention to social sciences, the arts, and humanities, are represented in formal and informal curricula, as well as into the specialist training offered by professional associations. Social media of various types, both didactic ones like Wikipedia, and more bi-directional communicative ones like blogs and listservs, can also be important.

To measure the effectiveness of such interventions, it will be necessary to collect data on:

- The extent to which communication and sophistication of analysis with the social constructivist perspective is integrated in new institutions;

- The extent to which critiques of technicism are integrated into the education programs of such institutions;
- To what degree actual computing practices, such as system design, development, and maintenance, reflect social constructivist, as opposed to technicist, perspectives.

Democracy

The potential for change argued so far depends upon a general increase in the extent of substantive, as opposed to formal, democracy in society. Measures of democratic participation have often been confined to the question of the percentage of eligible voters participating in elections. Other statistics that broaden the understanding of democratic participation need to be added. Employment statistics can identify the ability of people to engage in civic participation or work in several ways, for example, differential pay by gender or race for the same work, provisions for sick leave and childcare, or the percentage of different populations either employed in an area or in leadership positions. All of these measures contributed to our general understanding of both levels of participation in elections or work, as well as affordances to participation in the workplace. However, rarely are they acted upon to redress the problems they raise. In the area of voting, there is expanding evidence of the corrosive effects of money in politics, especially recently in countries like the US, which has long claimed democratic leadership. It is no accident that Larry Lessig has turned his efforts from fighting the copyright wars toward finding ways to reduce the effect of money and the resulting corruption in US politics.

Elections are only one indicator of democratic participation in society, and the values we propose are interconnected to expanded participation. For example, the value of informating implies the gathering and sharing of information from all areas of the proposed values. This is centrally important to the ability to expand participation that is based on information.

To figure out if substantive democracy promotion is working, we will need measures of:

- New analysis of the forms of democratic action and how much there is of each;
- The ways each newly reinstitutionalized value contributes to increased democracy and to what extent;
- If and to what extent the relevance of ratio valuings like money decreases in the processes of electing officials and the legislative and judicial processes;
- How much talk occurs about ways to expand democratic participation, and how the talk gets translated into action;
- The degree of transparency in both practices and planning, and how that transparency allows for further citizen input—this is part of what is integral to informating;

- How participative alternative licensing schemes, commons-based production, or other new activities are developed and encouraged.

SOME NEW, MICRO-LEVEL METRICS WITH WHICH TO EVALUATE NEW VALUES AND INSTITUTIONS THAT WOULD ALSO BETTER ENABLE ONE TO REACH NEEDED EFFICACY

The following are examples of the kinds of metrics relevant to each of the organizing, more micro-computing-based values we identified in Chapter 6 as worth pursuing and developing.

Promotion of Processual Perspectives

Our concern here is to reflect changes in thinking about organizations that have developed as alternatives to Taylorist theories of hierarchy and control. We want to indicate changes that mark a shift from trying to design and implement the best organizational structure toward trying to foster the strongest organizing practices. Among the goals of the Process Promotion Agency would be increasing the capacity of organizations for self-restructuring and the use of DT's affordances for new types, such as ad hoc organization and new types of commons. Another part of its program would be to undermine the legal doctrine of corporate personhood that has served as an important enabler of the ability of corporations to block process innovation as well as pursue rents.

Additionally, the Processual Agency would address issues like:

- Increasing organizational restructuring and identifying the interests and concerns from which it develops, what social groups are most interested, and where there are successful examples;
- Identifying the types of interventions that seem most successful at fostering new commons and new forms of participation, and how successful they are;
- Examining and promoting legislation, litigation, and popular organizing that are most successful at undermining the doctrine of corporate personhood, and the social correlates that follow from these actions;
- Identifying events that are perceived to be successful moments in the development of processual perspectives;
- Researching other social processes where there are correlated, successful, process-oriented interventions, and if there was an expectation of success that was not realized, why;
- Identifying and promoting the ecology of organizing efforts where process initiatives fit.

Informating

Informating is about gathering as much DT information as possible about organizational efforts and their contexts, spreading that information as widely as possible in the organization, and creating conditions where those getting information have the authority to act on it. The importance of the information used to informate being of high quality is worth focusing on for a moment. Let us presume for a moment that a social organizing process has resulted in the institutionalization of a social consensus behind the pursuit of values like those discussed in Chapter 6. Information about the extent of organizing success regarding each of the values would be needed. Thus, "quality" is not just some abstract notion of "good" data vs. "bad" data that inheres in the data themselves. The important quality dimension would be the extent to which the organizing generated gathered information about each of the agreed-upon values. The information about organizing that attended to many or all the values would be more useful than if only one or two values were being attended to. Informating is of central importance to the general process of transforming society and to organizing. Much about the quality of any information about general informating can be gained at the person-to-person level.

These considerations translate directly into four kinds of organization-level informating metrics about:

- How much data and information, of what kinds, and with what level of accuracy and granularity a particular organizing effort creates;
- The number, kinds, and quality of mechanisms available to those involved in the organizing to turn data into information and the information into knowledge;
- The ways data and information are shared both within and outside the organization, including the number, kinds, and quality of the means to communicate such data;
- The number, kinds, quality, and breadth of availability of the means to act on data. The extent of hierarchy in the organizing could be an inverse proxy for the means to act, while change away from hierarchy and toward organizing "flatness" could provide a direct proxy.

It is relatively easy to imagine "meta" metrics that might provide good summaries of each of these types of metrics, and we would want such metrics. For example, a priority would be to develop an index that summarizes the information being produced: how much information, how many kinds, both old and new, and what importance in organizing the information evokes.[4]

The Free Approach to Digital Openness

Of the many practices promoted as "open" in the contemporary world, we focused on those that developed around the non-proprietary, "open source code" model of software development. In this initiative, the basic or "source" elements of computer code are made freely accessible, and this access generally improves the quality of both the specific code itself and also the general quality of the code, all the while lessening the time needed to create it because of modularity. Removing the process from the profit motive is a form of openness that can increase both the number of people attending to the code and its reuse instead of "reinventing the wheel." Openness in this sense directly contradicts framing code as "intellectual property," where ownership is used to extract monopoly rents. In Chapter 7, we addressed the possibility of extending this model in order to open work processes and focus thinking away from ratio valuing. Openness in both the specific computing and in broader valuation would need to be supported by changes in laws that make it more difficult to invent and secure so-called intellectual property.

To the relevant indexes discussed above, we would add the collection and analysis of information regarding this value:

- The extent of the adoption of alternative licensing schemes like the GNU General Public License for the release of code, and of Creative Commons for other conceptual activities;
- The extent of experimenting with various open forms of organizing additional to the informating, processual, and service-oriented forms discussed here;
- The changes in the law intended to enable free open sourcing and to discourage privatization of information and knowledge. Further, whether the changes in law discourage privatization for market leverage, and generally the extent to which what is supposed to be enabled is enabled and what is meant to be discouraged is discouraged.

The Service Approach

We have used the term "service orientation" to characterize organizing that is radically reduced in both scale and structure, at the same time that the flexibility of the overall ecology of organization increases. In service-oriented social formations, individuals, families, and small groups of collaborators are the units through which values are pursued. The values would be pursued in multiple, often-changing relations and relationships. Service-oriented social processes manifest less hierarchy in social interaction, and they reduce the "path-dependent" dynamics of geographical fixity stressed by David Harvey (Harvey 2007). Changing legal structures to discourage rather than encourage the growth of organizing scale is one path to pursuing a service orientation, as larger scale is what is currently rewarded, even at the cost of functionality. A general shift in social sustenance away from the job and toward civic involvement will also contribute to the service approach. Finally, creation of institutions that directly foster a service orientation would be a priority.

Examples of information to evaluate change toward a service orientation would include:

- The general patterns of change in organizing practice, starting from a baseline census that includes (but then goes beyond) market-oriented organizing, as well as indexes for average size, degree of hierarchy, rigidity of structure, and the basis or organizing;
- The extent to which organizing changes toward becoming increasingly based on individuals, families, friends, and collaborators, as well as the degree of role flexibility;
- The extent to which organization becomes "virtual," not tied to a particular place or places, so more geographically flexible;
- The extent of the expansion of laws supportive of service orientation as opposed to ones that afford incorporated structures;
- The extent of shifting social sustenance to an active citizen model and away from a capacity-to-work model;
- The success of institutions created to foster service orientation, the number of service-oriented ecologies supported, and the kinds of these ecologies and their relative strength vis-à-vis market ecologies.

Participatory Rather than Exclusionary Design

This organizing-related value and the need to measure its correlates follows directly from what is required to informate—organizing structurations that share information as widely as possible as well as extend authority to people to act on its implications. The literature on participatory design (PD) in information systems development (Simonsen and Robertson 2012) demonstrates three notions now increasingly taken for granted:

- Information systems developed with substantive user participation actually work better and foster more user support than those developed in other ways.
- Participation is a general characteristic of all phases of robust and enduring information system development, which even in passive forms is essential to system utility.
- The success of social media platforms as the financial and activity centers of current computing depends greatly on fostering a "participatory culture" (e.g., starting with Facebook, Twitter, and now many other forms, including crowdsourcing and social economy). The culture of these platforms is sometimes similar to that fostered via PD, and this culture can be improved and encouraged via PD-type practices.

A useful and productive way to create robust information systems is to involve those who will be using the system and to have them participate in their creation and maintenance (Bratteteig and Wagner 2014). We have broadened the field by indicating where such participation would be essential to changing SFR dynamics. Thus, we would need to be able to measure:

- The information on the extent of informating and dispersal of authority;
- The information on organizing scale and size discussed in the next section;
- The frequency, forms, and nature of PD-type activities in organizations;
- The creation and extent of use of new, more participatory media and other social forms.

CONCLUSIONS: A GENERAL BASIS FOR FINDING ADEQUATE MEASURES

We have aimed to identify the *kinds* of metrics that would be needed in an intervention project like ours, as well as to suggest *how viable* they would be. We have not argued that the metrics identified here are the ones such a project would require, or the best ones, or a comprehensive list of what might be needed. We only say that the creation of metrics is possible and necessary, although many would be difficult to get right immediately.

We want to conclude this chapter on measuring by identifying what can be said in general about how metrics might, can, and could be specified. These metrics are not a matter of general reasoning of an abstract positivist sort. They need to be grounded in specifics, derived from metric search projects whose presumptions are clearly articulated. Our search projects are framed in terms of a number of premises:

- First, we are convinced that the long-term reproduction of current social arrangements is at great risk, and so there is a pressing need to identify alternatives to them that could be more viable.
- Second, we believe that workable alternatives can be articulated in terms of new values.
- Third, where possible, the alternatives should not be invented out of "whole cloth," but instead be implicit in existing social processes with presence in SFR.
- Fourth, some of the ways people compute now could contribute to an viable set of values that points toward alternatives.
- Fifth, the values implicit in such computing practices can be articulated as a new set of values, even though many of them reframe values or are the result of promising practices.
- Sixth, to persuade others to pursue an alternative value set, we want to be able to flesh out an institutional basis of acting on the alternative values.
- Finally, it is also necessary to describe the kinds of metrics that would allow us to evaluate the progress of and limitations of the institutions as they work.

The kind of metrics chosen must reflect the nature of the values themselves. We have argued for a close connection between the vulnerability of current SFR and the hegemony of ratio-type market valuing that dominates it. We need to find ways to undercut ratio valuing and reaffirm nominal and ordinal valuations to create a viable SFR. The metrics appropriate to our project combine numerical counting metrics as well as many that are nonnumerical. The metrics we present here are not merely topics where any range of "information" nuggets can be assembled. Instead, we have tried to articulate metrics with clear connections to the relevant values.

Important to this project is seeing the connections; many of the metrics related to one value are also relevant to others. Likewise, the micro- and macro-values constitute sets, where the members are internally interrelated to each other, as are the larger sets as well. Rather than making each Agency responsible for developing its own metrics, we would propose an overarching *Measurement Agency*. This Agency would be responsible for creating and implementing the metrics discussed here. It is the interrelations among the values, institutions, and metrics that make us optimistic about being able to create an institution set up to pursue a clearer articulation of goals; one that can gather the information necessary to making the judgments based on the information drawn from the metrics. This Agency could be responsible for new measuring "streetlights," ones set up in the areas where the keys are most likely to be found.

Why Articulating Such Metrics Is Important

Whenever those engaged in a practice presume that more information is better information, fetishism ensues. Additional bits of information are so likely to be significant that they justify waiting for "more information." This is one computing practice that we definitely do *not* see as foreshadowing a new SFR dynamic. The presumption of the radical equality of every bit of information on which such fetishism is based easily leads to the avoidance of making decisions, effecting changes, or making commitments. This fetish is one of the characteristics that often creates public mistrust of "experts," as described by Anthony Giddens (Giddens 1991).

We want to acknowledge that our pessimism about the long-term fate of social formations radically wedded to the ratio valuing of markets may not be justified. Capitalism might survive in a more humane form than now seems plausible. This too would require thinking ahead. Rather than waiting until we have irrefutable proof for our view of capitalism's future, we find it preferable to think ahead by preparing to act beyond capital and sharing our best scholarly contribution with the project of changing the dynamics of SFR. At various times in the past, humans have risked a great deal in efforts to change "the way things are" toward a more desirable "way they might be." Each of us every day makes choices informed at least in part by the belief that our choices may, in at least a small way, make things better for a relevant collective or future generations, not just for ourselves. Persuading people to coordinate their actions, to intervene together in hopes of changing basic parameters of our lives, should be easier when we can honestly present the change as an extension (while also a redirection) of the way things are going. On its own, however, this is not enough. We also need to consider the plausibility of institutions that could support the redirections toward new value complexes. Measurement is central to our project, both to see if the new direction works, and also to change direction when things aren't working.[5] Without reliable measures, our means for reaching such judgments are greatly impaired. Particularly for the computing professionals and practitioners we want to convince to join us if we are to succeed, we need to argue that our plan will be capable of monitoring itself.

Metrics and Commons

To what extent can the metrics we outline here be summarized in "commons" terms? One way commons are relevant is that it will not be enough simply to share a commitment to measuring in the abstract. Our metrics are unlikely to have general utility unless they are measures "held in common" because they tell us what we need to know. Further, in addition to common (shared) metrics, implicit in many of our metrics are some quite "commons" notions. A commitment to informating rather than automating, for example, is a commitment to the creation of common data, information, and knowledge bases—to public transparency—as well as to a common right of all to act on what is shared with them. The confidence to act depends upon a sense of being committed to a common project and to the understanding that when we act, we act in common.

Shared metrics and shared commitment to use them constitute an essential element to carrying out our project. At the same time, access to the information that will be needed to apply these metrics will depend for some time on the ability of states to demand it. Market data will also continue to be of use. In sum, our project with regard to metrics could substantially expand the degree of commonality, but it will not make all measurement into a common. In our final chapter, we turn to the questions of what a transition to an alternative SFR dynamic might be like and the conditions under which it might happen.

NOTES

1. Having a real measure of productivity would mean having a common way where all inputs and outputs could be expressed. For roughly its first 100 years, until late in the 19th century, political economy accepted this as the value of labor, or the worth of the actual effort expended by the average worker. Since the neo-classical revolution in economics, the emphasis has been placed instead on the average value of capital.

2. We note that these social enterprises are very different from the pseudo-social entities recently dubbed the "sharing economy," e.g., Uber and Airbnb. In their current configuration, these entities are more about bending social relations/relationships to the reproduction of capital than creating a less market-oriented economy.
3. One can conceptualize ways, such as methodological triangulation, in which the blindness of big data could be lessened. Its results could be combined with those of other research methods, like ethnography. However, such rapprochements depend upon BD users seeking out and joining informed dialogues with those for whom data-based social theorizing is common. This dialogue is discouraged by many typical BD tropes, such as the idea that only the methods of those analyzing BD are truly scientific. See Chapter 4 for a more extensive critique of BD.
4. This index might be supplemented by another designed to reflect the importance to transforming SFR of the organizational context. Some existing organizations (e.g., the continuous flow type featured by Robert Blauner (1964)) already produce a great deal of good-quality information.
5. We do not see it as necessary to eliminate market-based ratio valuing, but to circumscribe it enough to allow the flowering of nominal and ordinal valuing. We hope for an experimental approach toward deciding where it makes sense to circumscribe markets, as well as which values, institutions, and measures to pursue in place of what was not circumscribed before. We anticipate that people can determine when it is time to change or abandon one experiment in favor of another.

REFERENCES

Bainbridge, William Sims. 1999. "Cyberspace: Sociology's Natural Domain." *Contemporary Sociology* 28 (6): 664–67. doi:10.2307/2655538.

Bergh, Jeroen C. J. M. Van den. 2002. *Handbook of Environmental and Resource Economics*. Cheltenham, UK: Edward Elgar Publishing.

Blauner, Robert. 1964. *Alienation and Freedom: The Factory Worker and His Industry*. Chicago: University of Chicago Press.

Bloom, Benjamin S., John Thomas Hastings, and George F. Madaus. 1971. *Handbook on Formative and Summative Evaluation of Student Learning*. New York: McGraw-Hill.

Bratteteig, Tone, and Ina Wagner. 2014. *Disentangling Participation: Power and Decision-Making in Participatory Design*. Berlin: Springer.

Brust, Andrew. 2015. "Top 10 Categories for Big Data Sources and Mining Technologies." *ZDNet*. http://www.zdnet.com/article/top-10-categories-for-big-data-sources-and-mining-technologies/.

Giddens, Anthony. 1991. *Modernity and Self-Identity: Self and Society in the Late Modern Age*. First edition. Stanford, CA: Stanford University Press.

Gross, S., D. Hakken, and N. True. 2012. "Studying Social Relations in MMOG Play: An Illustration of Using Ethnography to Frame #x201C;Big Data #x201D;" In *17th International Conference on Computer Games (CGAMES)*, 167–74. doi:10.1109/CGames.2012.6314571.

Habermas, Juergen. 1975. *Legitimation Crisis*. Translated by Thomas Mccarthy. Boston: Beacon Press.

Hakken, David. 1987. "Reproduction in Complex Social Formations." *Dialectical Anthropology* 12 (2): 193–204. doi:10.1007/BF00263324.

Hakken, David, Maurizio Teli, and Vincenzo D'Andrea. 2010. "Intercalating the Social and the Technical: Socially Robust and Enduring Computing." In *PDC*, 231–34. http://ojs.ruc.dk/index.php/pdc/article/view/1919.

Harris, Douglas. 1994. *Organizational Linkages: Understanding the Productivity Paradox*. National Academy Press. http://www.nap.edu/openbook.php?record_id=2135&page=13.

Harvey, David. 2007. *The Limits to Capital*. Updated edition. London: Verso.

Hilty, Lorenz M. 2008. *Information Technology and Sustainability: Essays on the Relationship Between ICT and Sustainable Development*. BoD—Books on Demand.

Latour, Bruno. 2005. *Reassembling the Social: An Introduction to Actor-Network-Theory*. Oxford: Oxford University Press.

Leontief, Wassily W. 1986. *Input-Output Economics*. Oxford University Press.

Lessig, Lawrence. 2014. *Remix Making Art and Commerce Thrive in the Hybrid Economy*. New York: Penguin.

Mäkelä, Hannele. 2015. "Accounting, Corporate Social Responsibility and Politics." Accessed May 8. http://lta.hse.fi/2013/2/lta_2013_02_d4.pdf.

Marglin, Stephen A. 2008. *The Dismal Science: How Thinking Like an Economist Undermines Community*. First edition. Cambridge, MA: Harvard University Press.

Piketty, Thomas. 2014. *Capital in the Twenty-First Century*. 3rd edition. Cambridge, MA: Belknap Press.

Pilling, David. 2014. "Has GDP Outgrown Its Use?" *Financial Times*, July 4. http://www.ft.com/intl/cms/s/2/dd2ec158-023d-11e4-ab5b-00144feab7de.html.

Roedl, David. 2015. "Making Things Last: Obsolescence and Its Resistance by IY Culture." School of informatics and Computing, Indiana University.

Scriven, Michael. 1991. *Evaluation Thesaurus*. Fourth edition. Newbury Park, CA: SAGE Publications.

Simonsen, Jesper, and Toni Robertson, eds. 2012. *Routledge International Handbook of Participatory Design*. First edition. New York: Routledge.

Sterrett, D., J. K Benz, T. W. Smith, E. Alvarez, D. Malato, and T. N. Tompson. 2015. "General Social Survey: Chronicling Changes in American Society." http://www.apnorc.org/projects/Pages/general-social-survey-chronicling-changes-in-american-society.aspx.

Tsing, Anna Lowenhaupt. 2005. *Friction: An Ethnography of Global Connection*. Princeton, NJ: Princeton University Press.

van den Bergh, Jeroen C. J. M. 2002. *Handbook of Environmental and Resource Economics*. Cheltenham, UK: Edward Elgar Publishing.

Van Dijck, José. 2013. *The Culture of Connectivity: A Critical History of Social Media*. Oxford University Press.

Wellman, Barry. 2001. "Physical Place and Cyberplace: The Rise of Personalized Networking." *International Journal of Urban and Regional Research* 25 (2): 227–52. doi:10.1111/1468-2427.00309.

Wellman, Barry, Anabel Quan Haase, James Witte, and Keith Hampton. 2001. "Does the Internet Increase, Decrease, or Supplement Social Capital? Social Networks, Participation, and Community Commitment." *American Behavioral Scientist* 45 (3): 436–55. doi:10.1177/00027640121957286.

Whyte, William Foote. 1990. *Participatory Action Research*. Newbury Park, CA: SAGE Publications.

World Wildife Fund. 2015. "Ecological Balance." http://wwf.panda.org/about_our_earth/teacher_resources/webfieldtrips/ecological_balance/.

9 Conclusion

INTRODUCTION AND SUMMARY

We want to begin by summarizing our arguments for talking about what is to happen "beyond capital," our effort to outline a system that could provide satisfying lives for the many. Then we address the problem of transition, how we might move from where we are now toward extended social formation reproduction (SFR) dynamics that displace those currently mediated by capital reproduction. Finally we consider the implications of our analysis for computing professionals and all others who think of themselves as "computing people," a group that is crucial to our project.

Our introductory chapter described a growing awareness of crises in capital reproduction, a broad recognition that societies attempting to keep their current social dynamics will become less able to provide a satisfying life in the future. The dynamics of current social formations are bent primarily to the reproduction of capital and point toward growing social inequality, the collapse of the environment, and increasingly sharp social crises. These concerns are what drive us to consider what dynamics might arise if SFR was no longer bent primarily toward capital reproduction. In Chapter 2, we described several theoretical tools that could help this project, such as those enabling a focus on SFR.

We began Chapter 3 by analyzing the role of computing in the world crisis that began in 2007 and 2008. Our analysis also points toward the complex potentials for transforming SFR correlated with computing. We go on to critique several forms of analysis that misrepresent the relationship between computing and social change, identifying three general mistakes:

- First, overstating the way that digital technologies (DTs) change things or "transform" SFR;
- Second, oversimplifying the relationships between computing and social change;
- Third, misidentifying or misunderstanding specific computing-related social changes or socially related computing changes.

In Chapter 4, we set out to investigate what happens when alternatives to value and its pursuit are put forth. We present a set of selected computing practices where alternative values are implicit, ones with the potential to transform and extend SFR. We justify our focus on the use of digital technologies to find the suggested alternatives, such as the important role DT use has attained in mediating general SFR practices. The way computing has captured much of the cultural imaginary, becoming generally perceived as the most important cause of social change, is both an effect and a cause of DT's important roles. We also address why we will not focus in detail on examining capitalism's problems. Many writers have already done so and we anticipate that others will continue the task.

The theoretical argument underlying our alternative analysis is presented in Chapter 5. We identify the hegemonic position of ratio valuing in current SFR. Over-reliance on value, located in markets and currency relationships, distorts the valuation system, relegating to near-obscurity other nominal and ordinal values. From a broad anthropological (ethnological) perspective, this narrow valuing focus is unusual; indeed, overly narrow valuing has been characteristic of past ways of life that had difficulty surviving. We argued that abandoning attention to nominal and ordinal values is problematic and needs to be reversed, that a broadening in valuation is what will extend the capacity for SFR survival.

Accomplishing this broadening means adjusting cultural reproduction, in particular, the concepts of "values" and "the valuable." We see a possibility to foster a wide-ranging discourse to identify new, additional, and revised values that will echo among a large number of people, networks, and organizations. To convince potential participants that this discourse will be useful, in Chapter 6, we make explicit the values implicit in the suggested computing practices we identified in Chapter 4. We argue that at least one possible set of alternative practices oriented toward a new values set might be the basis for an intervention to change SFR dynamics. We make no claim that this is the only a set of such practices, nor even the best set, but we argue that such an alternative set is plausible.

After articulating these values in Chapter 6, we illustrate how the values could be institutionalized in Chapter 7, provisionally setting forward some institutional frames for suggestive practices, offering several ways this might be accomplished for each value. In Chapter 8, we propose a set of measures that might plausibly be used to see if the institutions we have identified can be successful or not. These last three chapters together are an attempt to make our project sufficiently concrete for the reader to judge if it is worth joining with us.

THE TRANSITION PROBLEM

We have tried to avoid creating the impression that we view the values implicit in the selected computing practices as leading inevitably to the transformation of SFR or to a new SFR dynamic. Rather, the displacement of current SFR dynamics will likely only happen as a consequence of powerful interventions by people who want change and are largely in agreement about what that change should look like. Nor do we see the particular set of new/refocused values that we presented as being the only, or even the most predictable, set for building alternative values. The actual values, institutions, and measures that turn out to be central to the alternative dynamics will arise in the process, change, and struggle to free SFR from being dominated by the reproduction of capital. To presume that all we need to do is identify the values, institutions, and measures, and do so via analysis rather than through actual social practice, is to commit the kind of intellectual hubris that Friedrich Engels soundly critiqued in *Socialism, Utopian and Scientific* (Engels 1880).

Nonetheless, we want to contribute to such interventions. We have written this book because we wish to encourage those open to participating in the conversation about formulating a program of change to do so. We hope to engage as many as possible to participate in a discourse on alternatives that move us toward a viable future. We are particularly concerned with getting the participation of those who work with digital technologies, as their work is implicated both in how values get realized now and in the pure-value practices embedded in many present computing practices. Moreover, as DTs are increasingly imbricated in more and more forms of cultural and social reproduction, we each become "computer people," if not computer professionals. Realizing our part in computerizing SFR is a necessary step for each of us as we join the project to influence the values embedded in computing.

Success in fostering a rich discourse on alternative futures among computing people is a first step, but it will not be enough. There must be other complementary efforts to change SFR dynamics. These efforts can intervene directly in social practice, i.e., social movements to achieve other institutionalizations and discover other ways to construct alternative values and alternative futures. Our identification of computing-based alternative values makes explicit what we see from where we are, as computing researchers. Our perspective needs to be combined with others.

What kinds of social movements might achieve a transformation of SFR dynamics? The recent social and economic crisis spawned more than the occasional demonstration. The Occupy movement surprised many political pundits. It was more widespread, lasted longer than anticipated, and continues to emerge, as it did in Hong Kong in 2014. Like many others who took some part in that effort, we found disappointing its disinclination to focus on alternative programs. In particular in the US, people resisted stating "demands" or furthering discussion in other ways about "what is to be done." This disinclination contributed to the movement's inability to grow beyond a specific tactic, the "liberation" of particular occupied places. Once the places were retaken by the state, the movement dissipated.

We think this problem arose in part because of the absence in Occupy of a discourse about the future that was sufficiently dense to afford the formation of specific demands or extended strategies. The failure of social movements to bring about deep change can make imagining an alternative future more difficult, but this need not be the case. The lasting effects of involvement in social action are likely to include the development of a shared culture, identification of some practical and political strategies, and shared evaluations of collective experience. The next step is to integrate these effects into an existing, broad discussion of where to go and the various options for getting there (Hardt and Negri 2012).

Our contribution can be read as an external, scholarship-based discussion of potential valuation practices that could be reappropriated by activists in contemporary social movements. We say "external" because we have not focused on an analysis of Occupy, nor any other social movement located in a particular place. Some readers may find this disappointing and be tempted to dismiss our ideas because of this. However, we want to take our analysis one step further. We want to address the plausibility of the transformation we advocate by envisioning how the kind of redirection of social formation reproduction we have in mind *might* actually be how it comes about. While we certainly do not think that such a transformation is primarily a matter of design, we do think it important to describe the kinds of collaborative practices that could bring it into being.

EXISTING ALTERNATIVE THINKING THAT IS CRITICALLY RESPONSIVE TO UNFOLDING EVENTS

To be successful, the kind of interventions we foreshadow in this book will clearly depend on developing collective responses to some quite important questions, such as:

- How do we understand the dynamics of current social formation reproduction?
- How can one assess the potential influence of a values change on such dynamics?
- How might we identify potential sources of power to change the current dynamics?
- What are the concepts around which such power might be organized?

We believe that a sufficient number of people can become motivated to participate in the talk and action necessary to such endeavors. Several factors already provide bases for anticipating their participation in talk about alternative future. We think this process has already begun.

MANY ARE ALREADY THINKING CRITICALLY, INCLUDING ABOUT ALTERNATIVES

Our research reveals that a number of people are already engaged in talk about alternative futures. One cannot live in many parts of the world without being confronted by the prod for alternative thinking that surrounds climate change or global warming. Books, from Rachel Carson's *Silent Spring* (Carson 2002), written in the early 1960s, to Naomi Klein's recent work, *This Changes Everything* (Klein 2014), are widely read and commented on. Many organizations, groups, and, in some countries, political parties are putting forward alternative practices and taking action against pollution. The people already engaged in current social movements, whether they are institutionalized like Greenpeace or more autonomous like San Precario, are making and encouraging change, as are the remnants of older movements like trade unions and cooperatives ("Precaria" 2015).

Some academics, journalists, and other social commentators whose jobs allow or have required them to do so are imagining alternative futures directly. Among them are Elinor Ostrom (Ostrom 1990), Amartya Sen (Sen 2014), and Paul Collier (Collier and Dollar 2002). Others are warning of further financial or social crises, or are trying to articulate what to do to prepare for the capital crises of the future. Those who have recognized the role of computing in the crisis are among those who see a large gap between the practices that seem to have contributed to the crisis—the creation and sale of arcane financial instruments, the encouragement of multiple "morally hazardous" activities, like the sale of doubtful instruments by those who negotiated them, the reliance through such instruments on ever greater amounts of debt to keep the economy afloat—and the measures taken since to discourage them. The notional value of the collateralized *debt* obligations that were at the heart of the last crisis is now exceeded by collateralized *loan* obligations being created at the center of financialization. In the US, the relatively modest reforms of banking contained in the Dodd–Frank legislation, such as the application of the Volcker Rule to some banking institutions, have already been blunted by Republican control of the US Senate. This reflects the explicit desire of the Wall Street institutions that switched support away from the Democrats. As the opportunities to make super profits from formal banking were lessened by regulation, there was a switch to more risky investment, such as those offered by "shadow banking" institutions like hedge funds and private equity firms that remain largely unregulated. Before the 2007 crisis, many *Financial Times* (FT) writers, acting as the main voices of contemporary capitalism, tended to offer ever more elaborate explanations for the Great Moderation. As we write, the tendency of FT writers is to identify the particular risky practices that will set off the next financial crisis—e.g., Satyajit Das's "Eerie Economic Parallels with 1997–98 Have the Making of a New Crisis" (Das 2015).

A major consequence of the financial crisis and the Great Recession has been to de-legitimate the celebratory "end of risk" happy talk that preceded it. At the same time, it has re-legitimated general discussion of both that particular crisis and also of those likely to follow, including the one that might prove terminal for the capitalist system. Awareness of the need for this discussion is heightened by the continuing anemic economic performances of the world's largest economies and the continuing absence of recovery indicators that are as rosy as those of the past. Fears of apparently unending crises, like those in Greece or the continued lack of growth in southern European countries, have replaced visions of the end of risk.

In addition to more analyses like these, social groups are becoming more open to discussion of alternatives. Some are forced to do so. For example, recent university graduates have difficulty finding jobs other than precarious ones and are clearly concerned about the future. In the US, students take on more education debt in the hope that additional degrees will keep them from sinking economically. The cost of this debt to students, some government funded, some privately funded, all with higher-than-the-current-rate interest rates is preventing many young people from prospering even if they have employment (Denhart 2013). At the same time, the federal government continues to provide tax exemptions to large corporations, farm subsidies, and exemptions to those still able to own their own home. In Europe, the rates of under- and unemployment among the young remain high, their lives contrasting greatly to those who have had jobs for a long time. What kinds of future prospects exist for social formations that burden their "best and brightest" youth with long-term, high, unforgivable debt and/or very low access to meaningful work? Recent funding programs, as well as the emergence of collaborative practices like co-working or crowdfunding efforts to create new commons, encourage thinking more about the alternative imaginaries.

Young ex-students are not alone. Thomas Piketty's description of increasing inequality as the normal state for capitalism is only one of many analyses that open to question the legitimacy of the long-term, near-monopoly, over-valuing of ratio practices. Globalization and technological change are increasingly recognized as exacerbating economic stress rather than providing relief. In many countries, the proportion of the number of those eligible who bothered to vote is increasing. The large turnout of voters in the Scottish referendum led to comments that voters participated when they were given real issues to decide. Meanwhile, many voters are choosing marginal parties of the right and left. At the center of politics is the question: what are the alternatives to the economic stagnation that is making the vast majority of the world's population more miserable?

MANY WITHIN COMPUTING QUESTION ITS DIRECTION AND EXPLORE ALTERNATIVES

Computing professionals (CPs) may be the best positioned to benefit from the mediation of social reproduction by computing. Yet CPs are often concerned with the long-term implications of this change. Entities like Google morph from trying to be ethical paragons who "do no evil" into the targets of litigation over questionable practices, as well as the prototype of thinly veiled dystopian critiques, like Dave Eggers's *The Circle* (Eggers 2014). The future hype or boosterism so common to previous "compu-speak" continues, but it is more limited, often to television and web advertising. Lest it ring increasingly hollow, growing doubts about the future foster an ironic pose even in these media. Skeptical, sometimes cynical, thinking reaches deeply into the consciousness of future computer people, including the ranks of computer science and informatics majors. (The former now constitute the largest undergraduate major at Stanford University, while the latter are effectively the second largest at Indiana University in Blooming-ton.) While still confident in their ability to find employment, they wonder if they want to contribute to a world where "there is no such thing as pri-vacy." Should they instead fight to keep privacy? What, in the long run, is the point of computerization, if the result is more control for the few and less for the many?

Such questions arise directly in the attempts of computing students to plan a career. They see a computing industry engaged in numerous "rear-guard" actions to preserve its dominance in the face of new challenges, one recent manifestation in the move to "the cloud." They recognize that, while some actions may extend the reign of proprietary software a bit longer, in the long run, free approaches undercut the prospects of an independent income from software development. As a cloud-based rental model replaces the outright-purchase model of software, the opportunities to profit from designed obsolescence are reduced in favor of constant income from rent. When software is being rented, new code is incorporated immediately, rather than held back by the requirement that users "upgrade," but there is less room for innovations from outside the corporations. And users are tied to those corporations. Organizations now see computing as part of their main "line" of function, no longer as an ancillary support, which reduces the number of "pure" computer jobs. Increasingly, students need to combine their DT training with knowledge of a supplementary "application area," like health or marketing, or social media. This expands their intellectual per-spective, but may mean incurring more student loan debt. Economically, the return for such extra education may actually be falling, like their expected career trajectories, as each new conquest of another social arena takes more time and offers less appealing rewards (Turkle 2011).

At the same time, their career of choice finds itself increasingly on the front lines of public concern. Issues include "net neutrality," or the deeply imbricated relationship of the computing industry to the national security state, or the way in which people's sense of their own identity is increasingly mediated by the big data patterns perceived in their acts of consumption. Computing professions continue to be predominantly male, without space for the inclusion of those who might effectively expand and redirect its pri-orities. Some students and young professionals want to identify alternatives to the "getting rich" motivation for a career choice, an increasing narrative among the social and community informatics students we encounter.

The concerns of university students merge with those of existing social groups, organizations, and movements, already building parts of alternatives. Fear of career failure not only prompts attention to current problems in the field, it also fosters talk about what alternatives there might be, encouraging concern for creative alternatives. This can make young CPs, like others who are frustrated, more responsive to the insistent talk about social policies that are alternative to the apparently endless "austerity" of the European nations. In Southern Europe, there are large votes and potentially pluralities for parties favoring radical alternatives, even if they are split between left (Syriza and Podemos above all) and right (Golden Dawn, Lega Nord).

Flourishing buying clubs, cooperatives, and other social entities adopting "commons" rather than "for profit" forms are involved in large numbers in the practical creation of alternatives to markets and ratio valuing. Throughout the Global North, one can see, in aspects of a broad "maker" movement[1] stimulated by the rise of "openness," the desire to reduce the degree of dependence on the corporate/market system. First raised through the development of free and/or open source software, a broader "openness" movement has nourished many of the suggestive digital practices we have discussed at length. This movement promotes initiatives like "open government," the push toward increased accountability of organizations through "transparency" and "corporate social responsibility," and "open access" when publishing publicly supported research.

A myriad of organizations and social movements actively build alternatives and attract attention. Some we have already discussed include Creative Commons and the Free Software Foundation. Associations of existing organizations, like the Italian Coalition for Civil Rights and Freedoms, expand the impact of engaged individuals and organizations rethinking their role. Bottom-up social movement initiatives, such as the Italian "San Precario," or the Associations for Consulting in the Advanced Tertiary Sector are restructuring the way that fostering a dialectical relationship between precarious workers and traditional trade unionism defends labor. Freelancers' or artists' organizations like SmartEU provide services to people and organize the public actions of a growing number of highly educated, precarious workers, who have been labeled the new "Fifth Estate" by Italian sociologists Allegri and Ciccarelli (Allegri and Ciccarelli 2013).

Sometimes, even states get involved in encouraging SFR alternatives. The P2P Foundation supporting peer-to-peer alternatives is an example of research and activism joined together, as shown by the FLOK Society project in Ecuador (P2P Foundation 2015). Through supporting the initiatives of research institutes like the National Institute of Advanced Studies, the state of Ecuador promotes transition from a national economy dependent on foreign capital and oil extraction to a more commons-based one, where collective knowledge becomes a main training resource and global development a goal. An international research team has identified some additional adjustments that could create the conditions for a successful transition away from markets. Although the project was only recently completed and its effects have yet to be evaluated, its very existence indexes the willingness to pursue alternative thinking.

In the domain of digital technologies, a plethora of organizations and professionals now deal with "digital social innovation." They encourage the design of genuine alternatives and engage in actual projects of transformation. Nations in the Global North, but also in the South, include many people and organizations engaged in the theoretical articulation and practical elaboration of alternatives. We hope that this book engages with them and also contributes to their thinking. The conversation about what happens beyond capital will provoke new actors and build alliances among participants and with concerned computing people, alliances that leverage technology to encourage alternatives.

THE BELIEF THAT CHANGE IS AFFORDED OVER STABILITY

A final factor affording talk about directed change is less a particular set of practices and more a general mindset. There is an increasingly shared presumption that change, as opposed to stability, is the default social condition. As conservative social movements become more reactionary, they advocate for an illusory past. Almost no politicians advocate for the classical conservative position of defending things as they are. While we are still far from globality, people tend to be more aware of the rest of the world, in part because of the media and technology. Computers and mobile phones are one reason, but longer lives and more education, along with extensive trading patterns, contribute to the awareness. To the extent that computing has "decoupled space from place," people living today are able to be in touch with social formations that are different from their own. Perhaps more importantly, they see these different social formations *changing over time*, and they apply the awareness of change to their own social formations. Even the fifty years of misguided "computers change everything" rhetoric has added to this sense that change, not stability, is the afforded state.

Because the basic social posture is no longer concern about *whether* change will take place, but is instead about *what* change, there is room for comparing the advantages and disadvantages of different change possibilities. Once the desired changes as well as undesirable changes are identified, the next logical issue is to consider how to intervene. How do we foster desirable change and discourage destructive change? This question is increasingly prevalent among computing people, who are accustomed to change but often more discerning about whether the new way is an improvement or just different.

BROADENING AND GENERALIZING EXISTING ALTERNATIVE DISCOURSES

Thinking about alternatives, questioning the direction of computing, looking for alternatives, and a general belief in change are just some of the reasons we believe that well-framed talk about alternative futures is important to beginning a conversation that questions the current modes of capital reproduction. Of course, this requires clarity about what "well-framed" means. Our critique of the dominant value system and the limitations of ratio valuing is one step in this framing. We have joined others in arguing that more and deeper crises can be expected, and, like them, see little reason to expect that social formations based on the reproduction of capital will solve the problems humanely or prevent more crises. It is clear that a discussion of the future needs to focus on how to escape from dependence on the reproduction of capital and attend instead to alternative SFR dynamics. Some framing of discourses on alternatives will likely be done under duress, as crises make the need for doing something different more obvious. However, those wishing to go beyond capital, like all who would intervene collectively, can't just wait for "the contradictions to heighten" via crisis. Contradiction and crisis often result in bad alternatives being selected under duress: we need to imagine good ones. What should those of us committed to fostering alternative discourses do?

ALTERNATIVE 1: BRINGING TOGETHER EXISTING ALTERNATIVE DISCOURSES AND THEIR VENUES, BOTH FACE-TO-FACE AND DIGITALLY

One obvious starting point is to bringing together the thinking, questioning, and suggested alternatives discussed above. We also suggest others try sketching out alternative institutions, as we did in Chapter 7, and we encourage collaboration among the many looking for alternatives. Digital technologies provide ready instruments for this. The humble listserv, for example, remains a useful tool to bring together discussions of and audiences for alternative talk. Consider, for example, the "Liberation Technology," "Institute for Distributed Communication," and "Community Informatics Researchers" lists, all examples of how discourses on alternatives are already being integrated. Listserv computing has generally escaped the fate of social media by not being harnessed by corporations, as captives of capital bent to its reproduction. Nor are listservs straightjacketed into the "one-to-many" communicative dynamic of the blog. Blogging, as it focuses on primarily expressing an individual point of view, can even divert attention from building shared perceptions. Also of note are the numerous efforts, such as "diaspora," to create digital communications platforms that are alternatives to market-oriented social media like Facebook and Twitter (Sena 2012).

Local meetings and conferences remain important places for the discussion of what is wrong with current dynamics and alternative conceptions, and what is to be done about them, as well as with what aim in mind. The various "digital labor" and "social forum" conferences, the latter at regional, national, and international levels, are examples. Often, these events assemble both scholars and activists, and those categories turn out to be more relative than absolute. In Trento, Italy, the annual Festival of Economics brings together eminent Italian and international speakers to address a broad range of issues relevant to economic futures. In 2014, a collection of local commons- and community-based organizations put together an alternative festival where people addressed similar issues to those we have raised here. This is an example of actions taking place that repurposed the time and space of existing events. The same alternative festival in other moments or places would not have been as visible as this one was, or as able to point out as directly the limitations of discourse in the mainstream festival.

Part of our decision to write this book, place it with this publisher, and produce it in this form is our understanding that academics occupy an important place in framing broad societal discourses. This means they can play an important part in gathering, broadening, and generalizing the discussion of interventions to change the dynamics of SFR. Academic competition is one of several dynamics that encourage teachers to consider alternative framings of intellectual issues as well as alternative programs for pursuing social objectives. Like the work of all professions, academic teaching and research are experiencing digital mediation, often with discomforting results. We have noted the attempts of university administrations to computerize in a manner that decreases the control of academics over their labor. Control over work is even more serious for the high number of precariously positioned (adjunct) professors and researchers, who have less control over teaching, higher workloads, and little chance of stable employment. Academic work is one arena where it makes sense to informate, perhaps by applying the distributed enterprise resource planning software packages discussed in Chapter 7 as a means to strengthen the position of existing academics, adjunct professors, and precarious researchers.

The need of academics to do research may mean continued attention to the changing world and new alternatives. For those of us now employed in academic computing (such as Hakken, with a stable position, and Andrews and Teli, precarious researchers), each new development, from the "social computing" of a few years ago to the "big data/data science" preoccupations of the present, pushes the relationship of computing with social change more to the center of attention. Even the increasing attention to pre-professional issues implied by the development of informatics and academic IT initiatives increases attention to what exists in the world, what problems need to be addressed, and what alternatives are worth considering.

At present, we do not see academic computing as a hotbed of thinking about alternative forms of SFR. Still, in their typical course, academic fields provide starting places for the thinking and criticism we wish to foster. Consider, for example, the arena of teaching in computing ethics. In his work in this area, Hakken has found fruitful ways for bringing together students' concerns about their professional careers with their ideas about broader issues regarding the future. They shared with him a concern about how the absence of a shared ethical sensibility among computing professionals is a central reason for a general absence of acting collectively. A denser sense of computing ethics depends upon the development of a shared discourse and shared standards, matters themselves requiring disciplined investigation of alternative futures. Thinking about such futures, while growing out of professional concerns, raises broader questions can be extended to include all the reproductive processes already or soon to be mediated digitally.

Thinking ethically is central to becoming a computing professional and making computing into a profession, while ethical thought about computing leads quickly to articulation of broader views about "how we should live." The generality of these discourses leads us to an optimistic view of a potentially strong voice for computing professionals in conceptualizing alternative futures. This should also be the case for those in the many other fields experiencing computerization, in that they can also bring their experiences into more general public discussion of computing.

ALTERNATIVE 2: REVIVE SOCIAL MOVEMENTS IN COMPUTING

In the past, social movements have been an essential part of successful interventions in SFR. Our experience convinces us that academics and intellectuals, both in computing and more generally, can play an important part in the changing SFR. We think this is true in spite of the widespread anti-intellectualism prevalent in the US. Such efforts are based on the idea that improving professional environments and acting on broader social issues are complimentary. We have all done academic organizing in the fields where we were trained—anthropology, sociology, and literature—as well as among academics more generally—both New Left organizations and professional organizations—and specifically in computing. This last involved work in or support for organizations like Computer Professionals for Social Responsibility (CPSR) and Computers for Social Change; public interest entities like the Creative Commons; overtly political free/libre and open-source software initiatives; support of organizations like the Electronic Frontier Foundation, and numerous initiatives that can be grouped under a "community informatics" banner, like Access to Knowledge and community technology centers.

We have highlighted the important role we see for particular computing practices as inspirations for the interventions we advocate. We see the
attention paid to computing and those who compute as an important public
focus. This attention is indicative of the large extent to which computing
has captured cultural imaginaries, as illustrated by how applications of
DTs now dominate much of what in the past was more generically treated
as "development." But the reason we highlight computing is also, in part,
structural. In order to digitally mediate a new social arena, we must take
a broadly holistic or "systemic" view of existing social dynamics and their
contexts, ranging from the small network of friends to the global system
for accessing capital. Many important public issues now turn on how the
correlations between computing and social change are conceptualized and
acted upon. The character of computing is integrally related to the dynamics of SFR.

This section is headed "reviving" rather than "initiating" or "continuing"
computing-related social movements. We say reviving because there are
important previous social movements in computing and we want to highlight their relative absence now. We are not suggesting that they be recreated
as they were, but that the reasons for their initial existence continue, and
the need for their work still exists. The experience of Computing Professionals for Social Responsibility is illustrative of where organizing in the
computing space is at the moment. In the early 1980s, CPSR came into
existence to coordinate the interventions of various computer professionals
who opposed the "Star Wars" missile defense system advocated for by US
President Ronald Reagan. This opposition was based partly on technical
arguments, such as the impossibility of creating a complex computer program of up to a million lines that somehow, even though it was never tested
under "real world" conditions, would be bug-free (as it would have to be if
it were to be a meaningful deterrent). The early CPSR members understood
that technical arguments alone would not stop Star Wars; the opposition
would also have to be politically effective. They tried to turn the network
of individual activists into a national (and eventually international) organization. As suggested by their name, they took as their model the various
profession-based organizations that had arisen in other fields, such as Physi-
cians for Social Responsibility, rather than the more general, sectarian, New
Left political formations of the past.

CPSR had importance in the world of computing, as, for example, a
co-sponsor of several early participatory design and other conferences (e.g.,
Directions and Implications of Advanced Computing). However, by 2010,
CPSR was no longer functioning for several reasons. There were contradictions in its organizational model, in that it tried to build local "chapter" presences in specific locations, even though it had begun as a national
network of individuals. Chapters were also built around diverse aims and
initiatives, from The Computer Museum in Boston to sub-units of academic
computer science departments. The disparity and lack of contact often

resulted in detached efforts. Equally significant was that CPSR failed to formulate a specific set of shared objectives, and thus became reactive rather than proactive. Without coherent objectives, it was difficult to organize a meaningful, shared action agenda. The problems with CPSR also reveal contradictions more characteristic of academic organizing in what are now called the STEM (science, technology, engineering, and math) fields. Identity dynamics turn on technical or scientific issues that are framed obscurely, even denying the relevance of social or overtly political matters.

The CPSR experience suggests that there are many reasons why organizing in the computing space is difficult. In writing this book, we want to use it as a means to identify others who share our general project. We hope to find like-minded activists in academic contexts like STS Italia, the Indiana University STS group, and the Participatory Design, Digital Labor, and International Society for Information Studies Conferences—indeed, among all those who see a change in values and valuing as central to the redefinition of our SFR.

ALTERNATIVE 3: INFRASTRUCTURE AN INTERNATIONAL MOVEMENT, COMMONS, AND ECONOMIC ALLIANCE

While our analysis of values leads us to give conceptual priority to projects of values reorientation, this does not imply that the conceptual will happen first. Numerous efforts to build institutions based on nominal and ordinal rather than ratio values are already underway. We understand that action comes from context. We can imagine in particular that those sharing a commitment to creating commons will increasingly collaborate as they move forward. This may well be the way for projects to formulate alternative valuations, build institutions, and measure their correlates moving forward. Examples like the Global Commons Trust point in interesting directions (Quilligan 2009).

We can imagine such alternative commons and commons-supporting efforts gradually turning into an actual alternative economy, one that provides a strong context for things like locavore food, social economy, credit unions, worker cooperatives and ownership, and local state initiatives. Having a substantial presence is probably necessary before non-market forms are able to replace corporate market forms. This process will likely take time, as well as a series of increasingly deep crises in financial and corporate market institutions. Nevertheless, examples of such trials are present, like the Cooperativa Integral Catalana in Spain, which is already promoting new forms of cooperation and experimenting with alternatives.

A network of connections based on local initiatives could intersect with existing social movements to support the discussion of alternative social dynamics in computing academic and professional practices. We envision such a network as fostering deeper thinking about a values-transforming agenda as well as making increasingly more complex interventions into public debates over computing policy and professionalism. Basing such efforts at least partly in academia makes sense because academics in a number of fields are engaged in articulating "futuring" agendas.

Whether it makes more sense to conceive of this computing movement as being composed of individuals or as a coalition of existing networks and organizations remains to be seen. We do see achieving substantial organizational momentum as important, although we are sensitive to the many new organizing forms, actions, and even social relations made more possible by the spread of computing. It remains to be seen whether it is useful to put energy into infrastructures or to respond spontaneously to emerging possibilities.

IMPLICATIONS FOR THE ROLES OF COMPUTER PEOPLE AND PROFESSIONALS

We conclude by returning to the special place in these interventions for people in two roles: computing professionals and computing people. Contemporary computing professionals and computing people can and should play a central role, preferably in alliance with those who are already engaging in building alternatives. In the former group, we put those who, like our students in Indiana and in Trentino, are preparing for careers where they will exercise considerable influence over what computing gets done, and how it is carried out. In our experience, many of them go into computing fields with the expectation of rewards in terms of salary and good conditions of work. When they do get jobs, as most do at least for now, they often find these expectations are only partially fulfilled. One reason is a general decline in the conditions of workers, including professional workers, as reproduction gets tied ever more closely to capital in neo-liberal, globalizing social formations. A particular irony is that computer professionals are often responsible for implementing the very computer systems that deskill professionals, something that becomes more obvious as efforts like participatory design become more challenged in academic research and practices.

Moreover, computer professionals have not been very successful in organizing to defend a professional interest. They lack the control over access to the field achieved by other professions, such as doctors and lawyers. While the professional organization that some of them join, the Association for Computing Machinery (ACM), does have a code of ethics, its provisions are somewhat contradictory. For example, they call on computing professionals to maintain allegiance both to a code of professional conduct and to the interest of their employers, without addressing what to do when these conflict. Further, the ACM has no means of sanctioning those who violate its code, not even a minimum means to publicize violations. In essence, anyone can call themselves a computer professional, and nothing professional can stop them from engaging in activities that others find fundamentally destructive.

There is clearly a need for a rich discussion of computing ethics, social responsibilities, and what computing professionals might or might not do as part of a campaign to create a broader social movement. Yet computing professionals face an additional problem in creating a profession, which is blurring the line between them and more general computing people. Computing increasingly takes place in boundary-crossing networks rather than in bounded organizations. It used to be relatively easy to distinguish between the professionals responsible for running systems and those using them. As computing pervades most if not all aspects of both labor and leisure, distinguishing between systems operators and users becomes less significant to the imbrication of the individual in the practice. Most workers, especially professionals, are expected to develop proficiency with computing in their field, while those with the primary responsibility for systems must be more and more familiar with their area of application. Yet this blurring might in the long run be to the advantage of the beyond capital project, by creating a group of people who are able to understand a larger range of questions, and relate to complex aspects of machines and social groups together. As computer professionals look more like computer people, computer people will need to better understand the perspective of computer professionals.

They are both needed in the struggle to go beyond capital.

NOTE

1. The response to the maker movement has been large and varied. In many instances, it has been turned into a for-profit effort.

REFERENCES

Allegri, Giuseppe, and Roberto Ciccarelli. 2013. *Il Quinto Stato. Perché il lavoro indipendente è il nostro futuro. Precari, autonomi, free lance per una nuova società*. Milan: Ponte alle Grazie.
Carson, Rachel. 2002. *Silent Spring*. Boston, MA: Houghton Mifflin Harcourt.
Collier, Paul, and David Dollar. 2002. *Globalization, Growth, and Poverty: Building an Inclusive World Economy*. Washington, DC: World Bank Publications.
Das, Satyajit. 2015. "Do Eerie Parallels Presage New Crisis?" *Financial Times*, February 14, 22.
Denhart, Chris. 2013. "How The $1.2 Trillion College Debt Crisis Is Crippling Students, Parents And The Economy." *Forbes*. August 7. http://www.forbes.com/sites/specialfeatures/2013/08/07/how-the-college-debt-is-crippling-students-parents-and-the-economy/.
Eggers, Dave. 2014. *The Circle*. New York: Vintage Books.
Engels, Frederick. 1880. *Socialism: Utopian and Scientific*. https://www.marxists.org/archive/marx/works/1880/soc-utop/index.htm.
Hardt, Michæl, and Antonio Negri. 2012. *Declaration*. New York? Argo-Navis.

Klein, Naomi. 2014. *This Changes Everything: Capitalism vs. The Climate*. New York: Simon & Schuster.

Ostrom, Elinor. 1990. *Governing the Commons: The Evolution of Institutions for Collective Action*. Cambridge University Press.

P2P Foundation. 2015. *Commons Transition: Policy Proposals for an Open Knowledge Commons Society*. Amsterdam, NL: P2P Foundation.

"Precaria." 2015. *Precaria*. Accessed May 15. http://www.precaria.org.

Quilligan, James Bernard. 2009. "People Sharing Resources Toward a New Multilateralism of the Global Commons." *Kosmos* Fall/Winter 2009, 36–41.

Sen, A. K. 2014. *Collective Choice and Social Welfare*. Amsterdam, NL: Elsevier.

Sena, James A. 2012. "The PC Evolution and Diaspora." *CrossTalk* (March/April): 23.

Turkle, Sherry. 2011. *Alone Together: Why We Expect More from Technology and Less from Each Other*. New York: Basic Books.

Index